RENNY DARLING'S

Happy Holidays & Great Celebrations

A Culinary Treasure

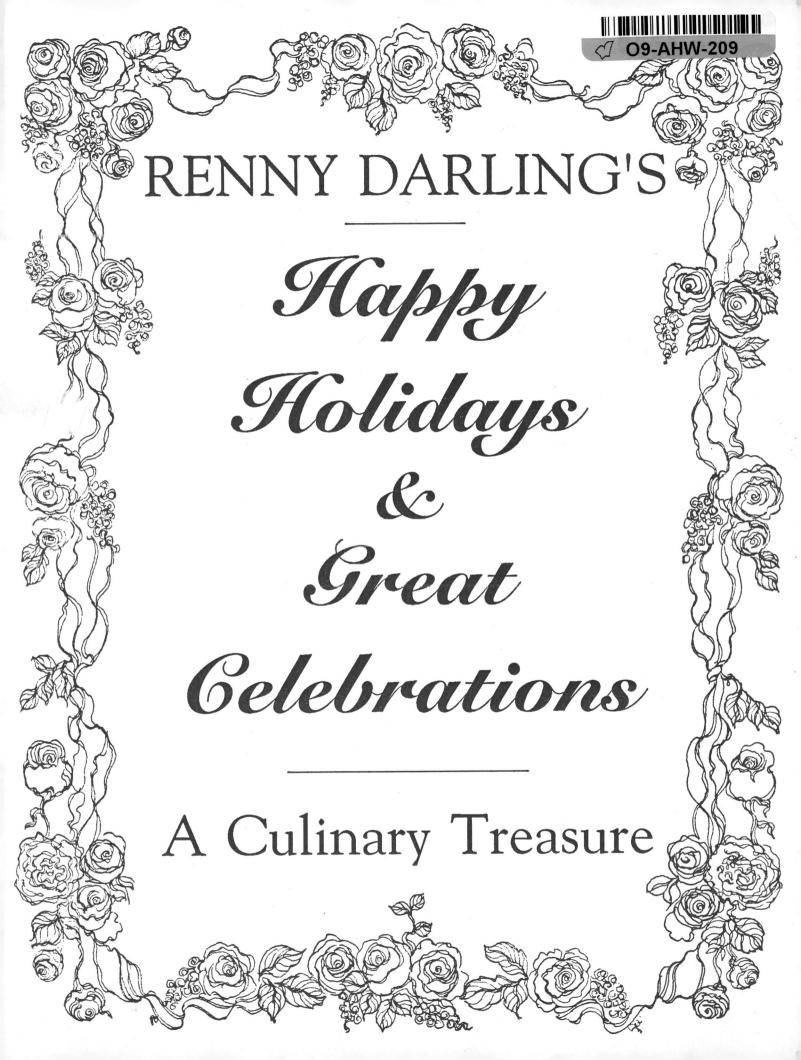

Simply Delicious Cookbooks
by Renny Darling

The Joy of Eating
The Love of Eating
The Joy of Entertaining
The Joy of Eating French Food
Great Beginnings & Happy Endings
With Love from Darling's Kitchen
Easiest & Best Coffee Cakes & Quick Breads
Entertaining! Fast & Fancy
Cooking Great! Looking Great! Feeling Great!
The Moderation Diet
The New Joy of Eating
Happy Holidays & Great Celebrations
Vegetarian Fast & Fancy

Cover art and borders by the distinguished artist
Christina Ladas

First Edition

Copyright © 1994 by Renny Darling

Published by Royal House Publishing Co., Inc.
433 No. Camden Drive, Suite 400
P.O. Box 5027 - Beverly Hills, CA 90210

Printed in the United States of America
Library of Congress Catalog Card Number: 94-66319
ISBN: 0-930440-34-X

The Contents

Great Celebrations

The Introduction

Celebrating holidays and special occasions with family and friends is one of the true joys of life. Sitting around a table, sharing love and friendship, is the stuff memories are made of. And in addition to all this, the memories of delicious food adds to the joys of the remembering.

Holidays and Celebrations are truly a time for giving thanks...for birthdays, anniversaries, homecoming. It is a time for families and friends to join together. It is a time where love and friendship abound. And these are the times that enrich our lives and elevate our spirits. There is nothing I love more than sharing Holidays and Celebrations with family and friends.

The menus that follow were planned to be versatile. They range from the very formal New Year's Black-Tie Dinner to the most informal After-Taxes Dinner. There are menus for every meal of the day, including breakfast, brunch, lunch, tea, dinner and even a midnight supper.

"Happy Holidays..." begins with the year's finale, the grand feasts of the festive Holiday Season, Thanksgiving, Christmas and the New Year. This is a time of pure magic, pure fantasy for so many of us. The menus and recipes range from the traditional, to the classic, to new and inspired dishes. The dinner and brunch menus would serve well at any time.

The major Holidays follow, with the exception of an After-Taxes Party, which was added for the sheer fun of it. The Queen of Hearts Champagne Breakfast for Mother's Day (with Dad close by) is within the capabilities of the most inexperienced cook. There are many breakfast choices that follow that would require a little more experience. And for Dear Ol' Dad, our Man of All Seasons, a very special Italian dinner. And finally, Happy Birthday America has enough recipes to create a dozen backyard banquets.

"Great Celebrations..." reflects American taste and knowledge of the great cuisines. Americans are very familiar with international dishes, and, I do believe, there are more knowledgeable cooks in our nation today than you will find anywhere else in the world.

"Great Celebrations..." reflects a sampling of menus of some of the great cuisines. A Chinese New Year Banquet, "East of the Sun & West of the Moon", Mardi Gras in New Orleans...Cinco de Mayo...Columbus Day. From Mexican, Basque, French, Russian to Greek, Italian, Indian, and American, of course. For the ladies, a Ladies of the Club Luncheon, a Sedate & Proper Victorian Tea, a Noisy and Boisterous Kaffee Klatch At the end of this section you will find 16 mini-menus, that are delicious and entertaining. Of course, any of these menus are appropriate for any celebration, birthday, anniversary, graduation, or simply "Let's Get Together."

It is my hope that you will derive a large measure of pleasure from my book. And it is also my hope that its subtitle "A Culinary Treasure" will fulfill its promise to you. I wish you all...good times with love and friendship.

Renny Darling

A few words before you begin...

- Always READ A RECIPE over very carefully. Then, ASSEMBLE ALL YOUR INGREDIENTS before you start preparation.

- Always PREHEAT YOUR OVEN.

- COOKING TIMES are always approximate due to slight variations in oven temperatures, the kind of pan you are using, etc. Look for the description in the recipe to guide you, such as..."until a cake tester, inserted in center, comes out clean..." or "until top is lightly browned..."

- The number of SERVINGS is also approximate, depending on the number of courses and accompaniments.

- TO AVOID BREAKAGE, small delicate baked goods are much easier to cool on brown paper or parchment paper, rather than on a rack. These papers are inexpensive and can be purchased in rolls.

- Do not dilute BROTHS even if they are labeled "double strength".

- Unless noted otherwise, when BUTTER is called for, it is sweet or unsalted. When a recipe calls for "butter, softened", it is butter that is still slightly chilled but soft and pliable. "Butter, at room temperature" refers to butter that is soft, but not to the point where it is oily.

- The flavor of NUTS is greatly enhanced by toasting. Toast nuts in a single layer in a 350° oven for 8 minutes, or until just beginning to take on color. Do not overtoast or nuts will become bitter. Store nuts in the freezer for longer shelf life.

- When a recipe calls for "ORANGE ZEST" OR "LEMON ZEST" it refers only to the orange or yellow part of the peel. When "grated orange" or "grated lemon" is called for, this refers to grating the whole fruit. Of course, use thin-skinned oranges or lemons. If the skins are very thick, you will have to grate the zest and the fruit separately.

- LEMON JUICE is always freshly squeezed.

- Good OLIVE OIL, like wine, has a beautiful bouquet. I have tried many olive oils that were "cold pressed" "first pressed" "pure extra virgin", etc. that were less than satisfactory. You are going to have to experiment to find one with a wonderful fragrance and good flavor. Keep olive oil in the refrigerator for longer shelf life. It will firm up a little, but there is always some that remains liquid. In any case, it softens in seconds.

- Always sift POWDERED SUGAR to remove unsightly lumps.

- RICE is always long-grain, unless otherwise noted.

- TO SEED TOMATOES, cut tomatoes in half and squeeze out the seeds. Or, use a small spoon and scoop out the seeds.

- As a general rule, "fresh" is better than "frozen", and "frozen" is better than "canned". Fresh herbs are better, but dried herbs are more readily available. Make certain dried herbs are fresh, as they lose their potency after 6 months.

Part One

Happy
Holidays

Celebrating Holidays are my favorite times of the year. It is a time when children come home from school, families get together, friends visit and share good times. It is a time when we pause for a moment and give thanks for all good things. And central to all holidays and celebrations is the pleasure and joy of sharing good food.

The recipes throughout have been designed to be elegant enough to serve when you are entertaining in style, and yet, easy enough to prepare at any time for family and friends. Recipes that are finicky or temperamental will simply not be found here.

This section starts with the time between Thanksgiving and the New Year when the air is charged with magic and electricity and we put on a little more of a "show" than we do at other times of the year. The menus share tradition and inventiveness and will make you feel like a "star". For, what is a "show" without a little round of applause and a few cries of "bravo".

Thanksgiving is a very special holiday, celebrated all across America. It is a time when classic and traditional foods abound. And it is reflected here with an enriching of our best loved dishes. The dishes in the Thanksgiving Sampler are coordinated so that you may pick and choose your favorite dishes and create dozens of menus, all in the great tradition.

The Christmas menus, with the many options, will also furnish dozens of memorable Christmas dinners. Brunch is a favorite way to entertain during the Holiday Season and the Christmas and New Year Brunch presented here will also offer numerous choices. These are excellent brunches to consider at any time of year.

For Valentine's Day a light supper in the late evening with champagne and the ultimate romantic accompaniments, caviar and smoked salmon. The menu is a little extravagant, very indulgent, but easy to prepare.

Easter, Passover, Rosh Hashanah are sacred religious holidays and again traditional dishes have been given an extra touch of deliciousness.

Mother's Day Breakfast is a trove of wonderful breakfast choices. The Cheese Blintze Casserole is one of the best. And for Father, on his day, a treasure of family favorites.

And the Fourth of July, a celebration of America's birthday, with dozens of traditional and best loved dishes. All of these dishes translate well for any backyard banquet.

A Classic Thanksgiving Holiday Sampler

Holiday Mulled Apple Cider
Holiday Mulled Wine

Fresh Vegetable Platter with Imperial Emerald Dill Sauce

Puree of Honey Carrot Soup with Apples & Cinnamon

Breads
The Best Banana & Cranberry Bread
The Best Apple & Orange Pumpkin Bread
Spiced Pumpkin Orange Muffins
Date & Pecan Pumpkin Bread

Turkey & Stuffings
Traditional Thanksgiving Turkey with
Old-Fashioned Bread Stuffing or
Old-Fashioned Soda Cracker Stuffing
Raisin Cornbread Stuffing with Apricots
Chestnut Pudding with Carrots & Raisins

Sweet Potatoes
Classic Brown Sugar Glazed Sweet Potatoes
Candied Sweet Potatoes with Orange & Cinnamon
Orange-Glazed Sweet Potatoes
Sweet Potato Pudding with Raisins & Pecans

Cranberry Mold or Relish
Cranberry Tangerine Mold   or
Cranberry Sauce with Orange & Apricots
Cranberry Sauce with Apples & Apricots

Vegetables
Peas & Onions French-Style
Glazed Baby Carrots with Parsley
Brussels Sprouts with Mushrooms, Shallots & Garlic

Desserts
Spiced Pumpkin Cheesecake with Brown Sugar Creme Fraiche
Holiday Praline Pumpkin Pie with Cognac Creme Fraiche
Thanksgiving Apple & Cranberry Pie in a Butter Cookie Crust
Thanksgiving Southern Pecan Pie
Chocolate Chip Cookie Pie

Easiest & Best Family Egg Nog

Holiday Mulled Apple Cider

This can be prepared 1 day earlier and stored in the refrigerator. Reheat over low heat at barely a simmer. Avoid using an aluminum pan. Enamel pans are best.

- 2 quarts apple cider
- 1/2 cup light brown sugar
- 2 cinnamon sticks
  peel of 1 orange and 1 lemon
- 12 whole cloves
- 6 whole allspice
  orange slices and lemon slices studded with whole cloves

In a 4-quart non-aluminum saucepan, place all the ingredients. Bring mixture to a boil, lower heat and simmer for 10 minutes. Strain into mugs and serve with a cinnamon stick as a stirrer. Yields 8 cups or 12 servings.

Holiday Mulled Wine

I like mulled wine with the flavor of apple. Cranberry juice can be substituted for the apple cider.

- 1 quart apple cider
- 1 bottle (750 ml) burgundy or port
- 1/2 cup light brown sugar
- 2 cinnamon sticks
  peel of 1 orange and 1 lemon
- 12 whole cloves
- 6 whole allspice
  orange slices and lemon slices studded with whole cloves

In a 4-quart non-aluminum saucepan, place all the ingredients. Bring mixture to a boil, lower heat and simmer for 10 minutes. Strain into mugs and serve with a cinnamon stick as a stirrer. Yields 8 cups or 16 servings.

Easiest & Best Family Egg Nog

This can be sparkled with the addition of Cognac and Kahlua liqueur, but this recipe is for the kids.

- 2 quarts prepared egg nog
- 1 quart egg nog ice cream, scooped into balls

In a small punch bowl, place the egg nog and ice cream and ladle into small serving glasses. Serves 8.

Fresh Vegetable Platter with Imperial Emerald Dill Sauce

If you need to have a small introduction to dinner, this is a rather light one to consider. Sauce can be prepared 1 day earlier and stored in the refrigerator.

Imperial Emerald Dill Sauce:

1	package (10 ounces) frozen chopped spinach, defrosted
3	sprigs parsley, stems removed, use only the leaves
2	green onions, use the green tops and the white bulbs
1/2	cup mayonnaise
3/4	cup low-fat sour cream
3	tablespoons lemon juice
1/2	teaspoon dried dill weed
	salt to taste

On a large platter, on a bed of lettuce, arrange an abundance of sliced red and yellow peppers, carrots, celery, cucumbers, zucchini, mushrooms, cherry tomatoes, jicama, etc. in any combination you desire. Slice the vegetables straight, on the diagonal, into circles, sticks, curls, etc. Decorate platter attractively with a few whole vegetables, such as yellow or red peppers, whole zucchini, etc. Place the Imperial Emerald Dill Sauce close by for dipping.

To Make Sauce:
Place spinach in strainer and press out the excess liquid. You should have about 3/4 cup spinach. Set aside. Place remaining ingredients in a food processor and blend at high speed until almost smooth. Stir in spinach. Place mixture in a bowl, cover and refrigerate until ready to use. Yields about 2 1/4 cups.

Puree of Honey Carrot Soup with Apples & Cinnamon

This is one of the nicest soups to start a holiday feast. It is festive and interesting with a promise of good things to come.

1	pound fresh baby carrots
2	apples, peeled, cored and sliced
2	onions, chopped
6	shallots, chopped
2	cloves garlic, chopped
6	cups chicken broth
1	tablespoon honey
	salt to taste
1	cup half and half
12	teaspoons low-fat sour cream
12	sprinkles cinnamon

In a covered Dutch oven casserole, simmer together first group of ingredients for 30 to 40 minutes or until vegetables are soft. With a slotted spoon, transfer the vegetables to a food processor and blend until the mixture is pureed. Return vegetables to the pot with the broth and stir in the half and half. Heat through, but don't allow to boil. Serve with a teaspoon of sour cream and a sprinkle of cinnamon. Serves 12.

Spiced Pumpkin Orange Muffins

1	egg, beaten
1/3	cup oil
1	cup sour cream
2/3	cup sugar
3	tablespoons grated orange (1/2 medium orange)
1	cup canned pumpkin puree
2	cups flour
1	tablespoon baking powder
3	teaspoons pumpkin pie spice

In the large bowl of an electric mixer, beat together all the ingredients until just blended. Do not overbeat. Divide batter between 12 paper-lined muffin cups and bake in a 400° oven for 20 minutes. Allow to cool in pan for 15 minutes, then remove from pan and continue cooling on a rack. Yields 12 muffins.

The Best Banana & Cranberry Bread

This is one of my favorite breads. It is a poetry of flavors and textures. It has a great "crumb" and can be cut into the thinnest slices. To insure success, do not puree the bananas. Mash them coarsely with a fork and then stir them in. If the bananas are pureed, it will take forever to bake the breads and results will be less than satisfactory.

1/3	cup sour cream
1 1/4	teaspoons baking soda
1/2	cup butter
1 1/4	cups sugar
2	eggs
1	teaspoon vanilla
1 3/4	cups flour
2	medium bananas, coarsely mashed (about 1 cup)
1	cup frozen cranberries
1	cup chopped walnuts

Stir together sour cream and baking soda and set aside. Beat butter and sugar until light and fluffy. Beat in eggs, one at a time, beating well after each addition. Beat in vanilla and sour cream mixture until blended. Stir in the remaining ingredients just until blended. Do not overmix.

Divide batter between 4 greased mini-loaf pans (6x3x2-inches) and bake at 350° for 45 minutes, or until a cake tester, inserted in center, comes out clean. Allow to cool in pans for 15 minutes, and then remove from pans and continue cooling on a rack. Yields 4 mini-loaves.

The Best Apple & Orange Pumpkin Bread

This bread is truly a little treasure. The flavors of apple and orange and spices make this pumpkin bread deeply fragrant and totally irresistible. It is one of our favorite Thanksgiving breads. These freeze beautifully, wrapped in double thicknesses of plastic wrap and then foil. Remove wrappers to defrost.

2	cups sugar
2	eggs
1	cup canned pumpkin puree
1/2	cup oil

1/2	orange, grated (about 3 tablespoons fruit, juice and peel.) Remove any large pieces of membrane.
1	apple, peeled, cored and grated

2 1/2	cups flour
1 1/2	teaspoons baking soda
2	teaspoons pumpkin pie spice
1	teaspoon cinnamon
1/2	cup yellow raisins
1/2	cup chopped walnuts

Beat together first 4 ingredients until blended. Stir in the orange and apple until blended. Stir in the remaining ingredients until blended. Do not overmix.

Divide batter between 4 greased and lightly floured mini-loaf pans (6x3x2-inches), place pans on a cookie sheet and bake at 325° for 45 to 50 minutes, or until a cake tester, inserted in center, comes out clean.

Allow to cool in pans for 15 minutes and then, remove from pans and continue cooling on a rack. Yields 4 mini-loaves.

Date & Pecan Pumpkin Bread

This is a little variation of my Apple & Orange Pumpkin Bread. While it only varies slightly, it does have a totally different taste and character. Thought you would like to have it as an alternative. These freeze beautifully, wrapped in double thicknesses of plastic wrap and then foil. Remove wrappers to defrost.

- 2 cups light brown sugar
- 2 eggs
- 1 cup canned pumpkin puree
- 1/2 cup butter, softened
- 1 teaspoon vanilla

- 2 1/2 cups flour
- 2 teaspoons baking powder
- 2 teaspoons pumpkin pie spice
- 1 teaspoon cinnamon
- 1 cup pitted dates, chopped
- 1 cup pecans, chopped

Beat together first 5 ingredients until blended. Stir in the remaining ingredients until blended. Do not overmix.

Divide batter between 4 greased and lightly floured mini-loaf pans (6x3x2-inches), place pans on a cookie sheet and bake at 325° for 45 to 50 minutes, or until a cake tester, inserted in center, comes out clean.

Allow to cool in pans for 15 minutes and then, remove from pans and continue cooling on a rack. Yields 4 mini-loaves.

Traditional Thanksgiving Turkey with Old-Fashioned Bread Stuffing

1   turkey (about 15 to 18 pounds), thoroughly cleaned
     and patted dry

Baste turkey, inside and out, with Basting Mixture. Pack Old-Fashioned Bread Stuffing loosely into the neck and body of turkey. Pull neck skin over to the back and skewer it down. Skewer body opening with poultry pins. Lace string around pins, back and forth. At the last turn, bring the string under the legs and tie them together. Baste turkey again.

Place turkey on a rack in roasting pan, tent loosely with foil and baste often with Basting Mixture and juices in the pan. Continue baking and basting until turkey is done. (If special directions for roasting appear on the wrapper, follow them. If not, use the approximate roasting chart below.) Remove skewers and set turkey on a platter. Let it rest for 20 minutes, so that it will be easier to carve. Remove any fat from the gravy. Gravy is delicious and does not need to be thickened.

Basting Mixture:
- 1   cup melted butter
- 1/2 teaspoon salt
- 2   teaspoons onion powder
- 2   teaspoons garlic powder
- 2   tablespoons paprika

In a saucepan, heat together all the ingredients until blended. Use a 2-inch brush for basting turkey.

Roasting Chart

Under 12 pounds	325°	25 minutes per pound
Over 12 pounds	325°	20 minutes per pound

Roasting times are approximate. If you use a meat thermometer, insert it in the center of the inside thigh muscle. It should register 185° when turkey is cooked. You can test for doneness by moving the drumstick up and down. If it gives easily, turkey is done.

Old-Fashioned Bread Stuffing

This is enough stuffing to fill an 18-pound turkey. I prefer baking the stuffing separately to avoid any problem of contamination. However, a stuffed turkey does look beautiful, so use good care in handling.

1/2	cup butter
3	large onions, chopped
1	cup chopped celery
1/2	pound mushrooms, thinly sliced
2	eggs, beaten
1/4	cup chopped parsley leaves
2	teaspoons poultry seasoning
1/2	cup melted butter
	salt and pepper to taste
2	packages (8 ounces, each) herb-seasoned stuffing mix
2	cans (10 1/2 ounces, each) chicken broth

Saute onions and celery in butter until onions are soft. Add mushrooms and saute until mushrooms are tender. Place mixture in a large bowl and stir in the next 7 ingredients. Stir in only enough chicken broth to hold stuffing together. This can be used to stuff the turkey or it can be baked separately.

To Bake Separately:
Place stuffing mixture in a 12-inch round baking pan, sprinkle with 1/3 cup chicken broth and heat for 30 minutes.

IMPORTANT:
1. Do not stuff turkey far in advance of roasting. Stuff shortly before roasting.
2. Remove stuffing before storing leftover turkey.
3. Improper handling of stuffing can lead to growth of harmful bacteria. So please take care to stuff turkey shortly before roasting and remove stuffing from turkey before storing.

Old-Fashioned Soda Cracker Stuffing with Onions, Carrots & Mushrooms

This is another marvellous stuffing filled with flavor and goodness. This stuffing can be prepared exactly the same, substituting bread cubes for the soda crackers. The combination of vegetables, garlic and herbs is truly wonderful. Stuffing can be baked separately in a 10x3-inch round baking pan. Bake for 40 to 45 minutes, or until top is lightly browned.

9	cups coarsely crushed soda crackers (about 12 ounces)
1/2	cup melted butter

3	onions, chopped
2	stalks celery, minced
2	carrots, grated
4	shallots, minced
6	cloves garlic, minced
1/2	pound mushrooms, sliced
1/2	cup melted butter

2	teaspoons ground poultry seasoning (or more to taste)
2	tablespoons minced parsley leaves
	salt and pepper to taste

2	eggs, beaten
3	cans (10 1/2 ounces, each) chicken broth. (Use only as much as needed to hold stuffing together.)

In a large bowl, place crackers and melted butter and toss lightly until crackers are evenly coated.

In a skillet, saute together the next 7 ingredients until vegetables are soft and most of the liquid rendered is evaporated. Stir in the seasonings and parsley and cook and stir for another 2 minutes. Place vegetable mixture into the large bowl with the crackers and toss lightly until blended.

Stir in the eggs. Now, add only enough broth to hold the stuffing together. Stuffing should not be mushy or dry. This will fill a 15 to 18 pound turkey.

Note: -*When stirring ingredients, I have asked you to* **toss lightly** *to blend. The idea is to keep some texture to the crackers and not to allow them to turn into mush.*

Raisin Cornbread Stuffing with Apricots

This delicious stuffing, much like a fluffy pudding, is a grand accompaniment to roast ham, chicken or turkey. Dried fruits can be varied...figs, currants, dates can be substituted.

1/2	cup chopped dried apricots
1/2	cup yellow raisins
2	apples, peeled, cored and grated
1/2	cup sugar
2	teaspoons pumpkin pie spice
	pinch of ground nutmeg and ground cloves
2	tablespoons butter

1	package (8 ounces) corn bread stuffing mix
2	eggs, beaten
1 1/2	cups apple juice
1/2	cup chopped pecans

In a skillet, saute together first group of ingredients until apples are tender and apricots are softened, about 12 to 15 minutes. Place mixture in a large bowl and stir in the remaining ingredients until blended. Place pudding in a 10-inch round porcelain baker and bake at 350° for 30 minutes, or until top is beginning to crisp. Serves 12.

Chestnut Pudding with Carrots & Raisins

This recipe can also double as a stuffing for roast capon or Cornish hens. I prefer to bake this separately and serve it in a silver pie plate.

1	onion, chopped
2	medium carrots, grated
4	tablespoons butter

1	can (15 1/2 ounces) chestnuts, drained and coarsely chopped
1/2	cup chopped apricots
1/4	cup yellow raisins
1	package (8 ounces) herb-seasoned stuffing mix
2	eggs, beaten
	salt and pepper to taste

1	cup chicken broth, as needed

In a skillet, saute together first 3 ingredients until onions are soft. In a large bowl, place onion mixture and remaining ingredients, adding enough broth to make a moist pudding. Place mixture into a greased 10-inch deep-dish pie plate and bake in a 350° oven for 30 minutes or until pudding is set. Serves 6.

Classic Brown Sugar Glazed Sweet Potatoes

Potatoes can be prepared 1 day earlier and stored in the refrigerator. Bring to room temperature before heating. This is the classic recipe...the simplest and easily one of the best. But there are a few alternatives, which are found at the bottom of the page.

    3   pounds sweet potatoes or yams, scrubbed clean
         pinch of salt

    1/2 cup brown sugar
    1/3 cup melted butter

         sifted brown sugar

In a large stock pot, cook potatoes in simmering water until potatoes are almost tender, about 20 minutes. Allow potatoes to cool; peel and cut them into 1/2-inch slices. Place potatoes in one layer in a 9x13-inch non-stick baking pan, and sprinkle with a little salt (optional). Stir together butter and sugar and brush evenly over the potatoes. Bake at 350° for 25 minutes, or until potatoes are tender, spooning a little of the butter and brown sugar on the tops every now and again. Serves 6.

Additions:

Orange-Flavored:
Grated Orange is a very nice addition. Add 2 tablespoons of finely grated orange peel to the butter and brown sugar mixture.

Apricot-Flavored:
Add 1/2 cup finely chopped apricots and 1/4 cup apricot nectar to the butter and brown sugar mixture.

Walnut or Pecan Topping:
Sprinkle top with 1/4 cup chopped pecans or walnuts.

Cinnamon-Flavored:
Add 1/4 teaspoon ground cinnamon to the butter and brown sugar mixture.

Sweet Potato Pudding with Raisins & Pecans

This lovely little casserole can be prepared in advance and heated before serving. Our family likes raisins but they can be substituted with dried apricots.. If you use a porcelain baker, then you can bake and serve from the same dish, which is helpful when you have numerous courses.

6 large sweet potatoes

1/3 cup butter, softened
1/3 cup cream
1/3 cup brown sugar
1 egg, beaten
1 teaspoon cinnamon
salt to taste

1/2 cup yellow raisins

1/2 cup coarsely chopped pecans
1/4 cup brown sugar

Cook potatoes in simmering water until soft. Plunge potatoes into cold water and then, peel them. In a large bowl, mash potatoes with the next 6 ingredients until blended. Stir in the raisins.

Place mixture into a greased 9x13-inch porcelain baker and sprinkle top with pecans and brown sugar. Press pecans lightly into the potatoes. Bake at 350° for 35 minutes or until piping hot. Yields 12 servings.

Candied Sweet Potatoes with Orange & Cinnamon

These are especially nice during a hefty holiday dinner, as they contain no butter, are sweetened with orange juice and are candied at the end with a light sprinkle of brown sugar. It is not very traditional but very delicious. The entire dish can be prepared in advance, but the crusty sugar may soften a little.

> 2   cups orange juice
> 1   teaspoon vanilla
> 6   large sweet potatoes or yams, peeled and cut into 1/4-inch thick
>   slices. Sprinkle with a little salt.

> 1/2   cup dark brown sugar
> 1/2   teaspoon cinnamon

In a 12x16-inch baking pan, place orange juice and vanilla. Place potato slices in pan, overlapping slightly. Cover pan tightly with foil and bake at 350° for 30 minutes. Remove foil and continue baking for 15 or 20 minutes or until potatoes are tender.

Stir together brown sugar and cinnamon and place in a strainer. Strain the sugar mixture evenly over the potatoes. Broil potatoes for 1 minute, or until sugar is melted...but not burnt. Serves 12.

Cranberry Sauce with Apples & Apricots

If you are looking for a recipe for cranberry sauce, that has a little more than just cranberries, this is a good one to consider. It is an exceedingly tasty relish and a lovely accompaniment to turkey. This is a fruity and tart relish and not very sweet. You may wish to add a little sugar.

> 2   medium apples, peeled, cored and grated
> 1   cup dried apricots, coarsely chopped
> 1   cup orange juice
> 1/2   cup sugar
>
> 1   package (12 ounces) fresh or frozen cranberries

In a covered saucepan, simmer together first group of ingredients for about 30 minutes or until apples are soft. Stir in the cranberries, and continue to simmer for 10 to 12 minutes, or until cranberries have popped but are not mushy.

Brussels Sprouts with Mushrooms, Shallots & Garlic

- 2   packages (10 ounces, each) frozen Brussels sprouts
- 1/2   cup chicken broth
- 1/4   teaspoon dill weed

- 1/4   pound mushrooms, thinly sliced
- 3   shallots, finely minced
- 3   cloves garlic, minced
- 2   tablespoons butter

- 2   tablespoons chopped chives
        salt and pepper to taste

In a saucepan, simmer Brussels sprouts in chicken broth and dill until they are tender, and drain.

In a skillet, saute together mushrooms, shallots and garlic in butter until mushrooms are tender and most of the liquid rendered is evaporated. Add sprouts, chives and seasonings and heat through. Serves 6.

Orange-Glazed Sweet Potatoes

This is a variation of my favorite apple recipe. It is especially nice because it does not contain butter and the orange juice and cinnamon add a great flavor. This can be prepared in advance and heated before serving.

- 6   large sweet potatoes, peeled and cut into 1/4-inch slices.
        pinch of salt.
- 2 1/2   cups orange juice
- 1   tablespoon grated orange zest (orange part of the peel)
- 1   teaspoon vanilla

- 1/4   cup cinnamon sugar

In a 9x13-inch baking pan, place sweet potatoes in overlapping slices. Sprinkle with a pinch of salt. Stir together orange juice, orange peel and vanilla and pour over the potatoes. Cover pan tightly with foil and bake at 350° for 30 minutes. Remove foil and continue baking until potatoes are tender, about 15 minutes. Mash potatoes (add a little orange juice, if necessary) and place in a 12x3-inch round baking pan.

Sprinkle cinnamon sugar over the top and broil potatoes for 1 minute or until sugar is melted and top is lightly browned. Careful not to burn. Serves 12.

Cranberry Tangerine Mold

This is a great mold to serve around Thanksgiving. It is almost a relish, filled as it is, with all manner of good things. A thin-skinned orange can be substituted for the tangerine with equally excellent results.

1   package, (6 ounces), black cherry gelatin
2   cups boiling water

1   cup canned Whole Berry Cranberry Sauce (8 ounces)
1   small tangerine, finely grated. Use fruit, peel and juice (about 4 tablespoons). Remove any large pieces of membrane.
1   can crushed pineapple (1 pound 4 ounces). Do not drain.
1/2   cup chopped walnuts

Combine gelatin and boiling water. Stir until gelatin is dissolved. Add the cranberry sauce and stir until the sauce is melted and the berries float loosely. Add remaining ingredients and stir to mix well. Pour mixture into a 2-quart mold and refrigerate until firm.

Unmold by placing mold in warm water for a few seconds until it is loosened and inverting it on a serving platter. Decorate mold with tangerine slices around the rim and some pretty green leaves. Serves 12.

Cranberry Sauce with Orange & Apricots

1   small orange, grated (about 4 tablespoons fruit, juice and peel).
      Remove any large pieces of membrane.
3/4   cup orange juice
1/2   cup chopped dried apricots
1/2   cup sugar

1   pound fresh or frozen cranberries, picked over for foreign particles

In a saucepan, simmer together first 4 ingredients until orange peel is softened, about 20 minutes. Add the cranberries and continue simmering for 10 minutes, or until cranberries begin to pop.

Peas & Onions French-Style

2 packages (10 ounces, each) frozen petit peas
1/3 cup chopped green onions
2 tablespoons butter
1 cup finely shredded Boston lettuce
1/4 cup rich chicken broth
1 tablespoon chopped parsley leaves
1 tablespoon lemon juice
salt and pepper to taste

In a saucepan,, simmer together all the ingredients for about 5 minutes, or until peas are tender. Serves 8.

Glazed Baby Carrots with Parsley

This very simple vegetable dish is really just right when it accompanies a monumental feast. There was a time that baby carrots could only be found frozen. Now they are sold fresh in every supermarket. They are tender, sweet and delicious when glazed. Carrots can be prepared earlier in the day, stored in the refrigerator and heated before serving.

1 pound fresh baby carrots

2 tablespoons butter
1 tablespoon sugar
2 tablespoons chopped parsley leaves
salt to taste

In a saucepan, cook carrots in simmering water until tender, about 8 minutes. Drain carrots thoroughly. In a large skillet, place remaining ingredients. Add the carrots, and cook and stir for 5 minutes, or until carrots are glazed and butter and sugar are syrupy. Serves 6.

Holiday Praline Pumpkin Pie with Cognac Creme Fraiche

Looks like a lot of steps, but this is really an easy pie to prepare. Using the prepared crust, simplifies preparation. However, if you prefer to make a great cookie crust, try Butter Cookie Crust on the recipe that follows.

> 1   9-inch frozen deep-dish pie shell, baked in a 400° oven
>   for 8 minutes, or until crust is just beginning to color

Pumpkin Filling:

1	can (1 pound) pureed pumpkin
3	eggs
1 1/2	cups half and half
3/4	cup sugar
1/4	cup brown sugar
3	teaspoons pumpkin pie spice

Place pie plate on a cookie sheet. Beat together the filling ingredients until blended and pour into prepared pie shell. Bake at 375° for 45 minutes. Sprinkle top with Praline Pecan Topping and continue baking for about 10 minutes, or until a knife, inserted 1-inch off center, comes out clean. Serve with a spoonful of Cognac Creme Fraiche. Serves 8 to 10.

Praline Pecan Topping:

1/2	cup chopped pecans
1/3	cup brown sugar
1	tablespoon melted butter

Stir together all the ingredients until blended.

Cognac Creme Fraiche:

1/2	cup half and half
1/2	cup low-fat sour cream
1	tablespoon sugar
1	teaspoon Cognac (see Note)

In a glass jar, stir together all the ingredients until blended. Allow to stand at room temperature for 2 hours or until thickened, cover jar and refrigerate.

Note: -If you prefer to omit the Cognac, then substitute 1 tablespoon of sifted brown sugar for the sugar.

Thanksgiving Apple & Cranberry Pie in a Butter Cookie Crust

Apples and cranberries are wonderful together. My favorite pan, of course, is a 10-inch heart-shaped pan. A 10-inch springform pan or tart pan with a removable bottom works well, also. The crust is marvelously flaky. It is a soft dough and can easily be pressed into the pan, avoiding the need to refrigerate and then roll out the pastry.

Butter Cookie Crust:

1	cup butter (2 sticks)
2	cups flour
1/2	cup sugar
1	egg
2	tablespoons water
1	teaspoon cinnamon sugar

In a food processor, blend butter, flour and sugar until butter particles are the size of small peas. (Do not overprocess or the flakiness will be lost.) Lightly beat together the egg and water until blended. Add to the butter mixture and pulsate 4 or 5 times, or just until dough clumps together (adding a few drops of water, if necessary.) Place dough on floured wax paper and shape into a disc.

Pat 2/3 of the dough onto the bottom and up the sides of a greased 10-inch heart-shaped pan with a removable bottom. Bake in a 375° oven for 20 minutes, or until crust is lightly browned. Place Apple & Cranberry Filling evenly over the crust. Divide remaining dough into three parts. With floured hands, pat each part into a 5-inch circle and place on top of pie. Sprinkle top with 1 teaspoon cinnamon sugar. Continue baking for about 30 minutes, or until top is golden brown. Serves 10.

Apple & Cranberry Filling:

3	large apples, peeled, cored and thinly sliced
1	cup frozen cranberries
1/2	cup sugar
1	tablespoon grated lemon. (Use fruit, juice and peel. Remove any large pieces of membrane.)
2	tablespoons flour

In a large bowl, stir together all the ingredients until nicely mixed.

Thanksgiving Southern Pecan Pie

This is a terrific, classic pecan pie. If you are pressed for time, the prepared pie crust works well. However, if you prefer making your own great crust, recipe follows.

1   frozen 10-inch deep dish pie shell. Place on a cookie sheet and bake at 350° for 7 minutes or until dough looks set.

4	eggs
1 1/4	cups dark brown sugar
1/2	cup light corn syrup
1/3	cup melted butter
2	teaspoons vanilla
1/4	teaspoon salt
2	cups coarsely chopped pecans

Prepare pie crust and keep it on the cookie sheet. Beat together next 6 ingredients until nicely blended. Stir in the pecans. Pour mixture evenly into prepared crust and bake at 350° for about 40 minutes or until pie is set. Serves 10.

Flaky Cookie Pie Crust:

3/4	cup butter (1 1/2 sticks)
1 1/2	cups flour
3	tablespoons sugar
1	egg yolk
2	tablespoons water

In a food processor, blend butter, flour and sugar until butter particles are the size of small peas. (Do not overprocess.) Beat together egg yolk and water until blended. Add to the flour mixture and pulse 4 or 5 times, or until dough roughly clumps together, adding a few drops of water, if necessary. Place dough on floured wax paper and shape into a ball.

Press dough into a 10-inch deep-dish pie pan and bake at 375° for 20 minutes, or until crust is very lightly browned. Fill as described above.

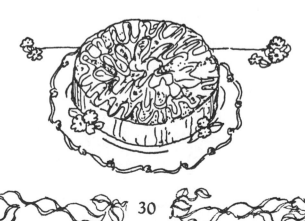

Spiced Pumpkin Cheesecake with Brown Sugar Creme Fraiche

Crust:
- 1 1/2   cups graham cracker crumbs
- 4   tablespoons butter, melted
- 1/2   cup chopped walnuts
- 4   tablespoons cinnamon sugar

Filling:
- 2   pounds cream cheese, at room temperature
- 1 1/2   cups sugar
- 5   eggs
- 1   cup sour cream
- 2   cups canned pumpkin puree
- 2   teaspoons pumpkin pie spice
- 2   teaspoons vanilla
- 1/4   cup flour
- 1   tablespoon grated orange zest (orange part of the peel)

To make the crust:
Combine crust ingredients and mix until blended. Butter the bottom of a 10-inch springform pan and line it with parchment paper. Press crumb mixture on the bottom and 1-inch up the sides of the pan.

To make the filling:
Beat cream cheese until creamy, about 2 minutes. Beat in remaining filling ingredients until blended. Pour mixture into prepared crust.

Bake at 325° for about 1 hour and 20 minutes or until center is still soft and a cake tester, inserted 1-inch off center, comes out clean. Do not overbake. (Top may crack. This is normal.) Allow to cool in pan and then spread top with Brown Sugar Creme Fraiche. Refrigerate for 6 hours or overnight.

Using the parchment paper to help you, carefully slide cheesecake onto a serving platter. Serves 12 to 16.

Brown Sugar Creme Fraiche:
- 3/4   cup sour cream
- 1/4   cup cream
- 2   tablespoons sifted brown sugar
- 2   sprinkles cinnamon

In a bowl, stir together all the ingredients and allow to stand at room temperature for several hours or until sugar is dissolved. Can be refrigerated at this point for several days until ready to spread on cheesecake.

Chocolate Chip Cookie Pie

The is a variation of the classic chocolate chip cookie made into a pie. We tasted one several years ago, but the restaurant wouldn't share the recipe. The following recipe will produce a pie, very similar in taste and texture, to the one we enjoyed years ago. This is rich, so keep the portions small.

1   9-inch deep-dish frozen pie shell. Place shell on a cookie sheet and bake at 350° for 7 minutes or until crust is set.

Filling:

2   eggs
1/2   cup melted butter (1 stick)
1/2   cup sour cream
1/2   cup flour
3/4   cup brown sugar, packed
1/4   cup sugar
1   teaspoon vanilla

1   cup semi-sweet chocolate chips
1   cup coarsely chopped walnuts

Prepare pie shell and leave it on the cookie sheet. Beat together first 7 filling ingredients until blended. Stir in chocolate and nuts. Pour mixture into prepared pie shell and bake at 325° for about 1 hour or until top is browned. If the edges start to darken place a sheet of aluminum foil loosely over the top. Serve warm. Serves 10.

"Come for a Bit of the Bubbly & A Spot of Dinner..."
An English Merry Christmas

———————————

Dilled Mousseline of Caviar with Creme Fraiche & Toast Points
Champagne

Lemon & Dill Mushroom & Onion Soup
Cheese Phyllo Roulades

Old English Prime Rib Roast & Horseradish Sauce with
Yorkshire Pudding

Instant Creamed Spinach or
French Peas with Butter & Shallots

Mushroom Persillade with Tomatoes, Onions & Garlic

Roasted Potatoes with Rosemary & Garlic or
Potato Fans with Chives & Cheese

Imperial White Chocolate Mousse on Almond Crust with
Raspberry Sauce or
Souffle au Chocolat with Creme Vanilla or
Cappuccino Ice Cream with Brandy Kahlua Sauce

This is a formal English Merry Christmas menu, but it is suitable for many other holidays and celebrations. The only recipe to be careful with is the Prime Rib. Be careful not to overcook.

The Mousseline of Caviar is a grand introduction, setting the mood for the good things to come. The Mushroom Soup is excellent and the Cheese Phyllo Roulades are the perfect accompaniments. Everyone will love them.

Prime Rib is majestically served on a large platter, surrounded by roasted potatoes. Yorkshire Pudding with Creamed Spinach would be my choices. (In the event you do not prepare the soup, the Mushroom Persillade is great to serve with the beef.)

Choose any of the desserts...they are all grand finales to this superb dinner.

Dilled Mousseline of Caviar with Whipped Creme Fraiche

Champagne with the ultimate romantic accompaniment, caviar, is great to serve at anytime; from brunch to a late evening get together, it is always a delight to enjoy. Serve it with triangle toasted points, very thinly spread with sweet butter. Lining the mold with plastic wrap makes unmolding the mousseline totally foolproof.

1	package (1 tablespoon) unflavored gelatin
1/3	cup cold water
1	cup cream
1	cup sour cream
4	tablespoons chopped chives
1/4	teaspoon dried dill weed
3	tablespoons lemon juice
1	jar (3 ounces) golden caviar or the best you can afford

In a metal measuring cup, soften gelatin in water. Place cup in a pan with simmering water, and stir until gelatin is dissolved. Set aside.

Beat cream until stiff. Beat in the sour cream, chives, dill weed and lemon juice until blended. Beat in the dissolved gelatin until blended. Very gently, stir in the caviar until blended.

Line a beautiful 4-cup heart mold (without a hole in the center) with plastic wrap. Spread mousseline into prepared mold, pressing lightly to remove any air bubbles. Cover mold with another sheet of plastic wrap and refrigerate until firm.

To serve, remove plastic cover, and invert mold on a serving platter. Remove the mold and carefully peel off the plastic lining. Decorate platter with bouquets of parsley and lemon slices sprinkled with dill weed. Serve with toast points.

To Make Toast Points:
Use a good quality, firm-textured, thinly-sliced white bread. Remove the crusts and cut each slice in half, on the diagonal. Toast bread slices in a 350° oven for about 10 minutes, or until the bread is lightly crisped. Spread with a thin layer of butter while still warm. These can be made earlier in the day and stored in a cannister with a tight-fitting lid.

Lemon & Dill Mushroom & Onion Soup with Cheese Phyllo Roulades

These light and delicate Cheese Phyllo Roulades paired with this incredible soup was my contribution to a recent "gourmet dinner." The results were smashing, so I thought you would enjoy them, too. As an introduction to a gala meal, it sets a great stage for the marvellous pleasures ahead.

1 1/2	pounds mushrooms, cleaned and very thinly sliced.
2	large onions, finely chopped
6	shallots, minced
4	cloves garlic, minced
6	tablespoons butter
1/4	cup dry white wine
3	tablespoons flour
4	cups rich chicken broth
1	cup cream
3	tablespoons lemon juice
1	teaspoon dried dill weed
	salt to taste

In a Dutch oven casserole, saute together first 5 ingredients until onions are soft and all the liquid rendered is evaporated. Stir in the wine and cook until it is evaporated. Add the flour and cook and stir for 2 minutes. Stir in the remaining ingredients and simmer soup for 10 minutes, stirring now and again. To serve, top with a teaspoon of Creme Fraiche and a faint sprinkling of dill weed. Serves 8.

Creme Fraiche:

1/4	cup sour cream
1/4	cup cream
1	teaspoon lemon juice

Stir together all the ingredients until blended. Allow to stand at room temperature for 2 hours and then refrigerate until serving time.

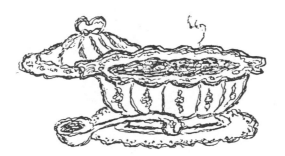

Cheese Phyllo Roulades

Fresh phyllo leaves can be purchased from Middle Eastern groceries. However, many supermarkets carry these pastry leaves frozen. If you buy these frozen, they must be defrosted overnight in the refrigerator. While they are delicate to handle, they are hardier than they appear. Have everything ready before starting.

12 sheets phyllo pastry leaves (about 11x14-inches). **Cover with wax paper and then a damp towel.**

6 tablespoons butter, melted

6 tablespoons grated Parmesan cheese

Preheat oven to 350°. Butter a 12x16-inch baking pan. Stack 2 phyllo leaves and brush top leaf with butter. Place about 8 tablespoons Cheese Filling along the 11-inch edge, leaving 1-inch on the sides without filling. Roll up 3 times, tuck in the sides, and continue rolling to the end. Place roulades in prepared pan and baste tops and sides with melted butter. Sprinkle each top with 1 tablespoon grated cheese.

Bake for about 30 minutes, or until pastry is crisp and golden. Allow to cool in pan. (Can be frozen or refrigerated at this point.) Before serving, cut each roulade into thirds, and heat at 350° for 12 to 15 minutes, or until heated through. Serve warm. Yields 18 3-inch roulades.

Cheese Filling:
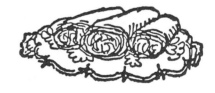

1/2 pound cream cheese, softened,
1 cup cottage cheese
1/2 cup grated Parmesan cheese
2 eggs
1/2 cup cracker crumbs

Beat together all the ingredients until blended.

Old English Prime Rib Roast with Yorkshire Pudding & Horseradish Sauce

1 standing prime rib roast. Ask your butcher to remove the chine bone, loosen the ribs and tie them back in place. Use a 6-pound roast (3 ribs) for 6 servings. Sprinkle with salt, pepper and garlic powder. Insert meat thermometer in the thickest part of the meat without touching a bone.

Place roast, bone-side down, in a roasting pan and roast in a 350° oven until meat thermometer registers desired doneness, about 1 1/2 hours for "rare".

Very rare	-	130°
Rare	-	140°
Medium Rare	-	150°
Medium	-	160° (not recommended)

Remove roast from the oven. Remove the strings and place on a serving platter. Carve at the table and serve with Old English Yorkshire Pudding and Creamy Horseradish Sauce on the side.

Old English Yorkshire Pudding

3 eggs
1 cup milk
1 cup flour
  pinch of salt

4 tablespoons hot melted butter

Beat together eggs, milk, flour and salt until blended. In a 9x13-inch roasting pan, evenly spread hot melted butter. Pour batter into pan and bake in 350° oven until puffed and golden, about 30 to 35 minutes. Cut into squares and serve at once. Serves 6.

Note: Yorkshire pudding can be heightened by adding 2 tablespoons chopped chives to the batter.

Creamy Horseradish Dressing:
Stir together 1/2 cup sour cream, 1/2 cup cream and 2 tablespoons (or to taste) prepared horseradish. Refrigerate for several hours or overnight. Serve on the side with roast beef.

Mushrooms Persillade
with Tomatoes, Onions & Garlic

1   pound mushrooms, thinly sliced
2   tablespoons butter
2   cloves garlic, finely minced

2   canned tomatoes, drained and finely chopped
2   green onions, finely chopped
2   tablespoons chopped parsley
1   tablespoon lemon juice
     salt and pepper to taste

In a saucepan, saute mushrooms and garlic in butter until mushrooms are tender. Add the remaining ingredients and simmer mixture until juices have evaporated and sauce has thickened. A sprinkling of grated Parmesan is lovely but optional. Serves 6.

Instant Creamed Spinach

2   packages (10 ounces, each) frozen chopped spinach, defrosted
       and pressed in a strainer to drain
2   packages (3 ounces, each) cream cheese
     salt to taste
     pinch of nutmeg

In a saucepan, place all the ingredients, and over low heat, cook and stir until cream cheese is melted and nicely blended. Serves 6.

French Peas with Butter & Shallots

3   tablespoons butter
1   tablespoon very finely minced shallots
1/4   cup chicken broth
1   teaspoon sugar
4   leaves butter lettuce, chopped
      salt and pepper to taste

2   packages (10 ounces, each) frozen petit peas

In a covered saucepan, cook together first group of ingredients until shallots are soft. Add the peas and continue cooking for 5 minutes, or until peas are tender. Serves 8.

Roasted Potatoes with Rosemary & Garlic

2 pounds small red potatoes, scrubbed and cut into fourths
6 cloves garlic, very thinly sliced
2 teaspoons dried rosemary, crumbled
2 tablespoons margarine, melted
1/4 cup chicken broth
salt and pepper to taste

In a 9x13-inch baking pan, toss together all the ingredients until potatoes are nicely coated. Roast them in a 350° oven for about 45 minutes, turning now and again, until potatoes are tender and golden brown. Serves 6.

Potato Fans with Chives & Cheese

6 large potatoes, peeled. Cut potatoes into 1/4-inch thick slices, crosswise, but do not cut through. Cut to within 1/4-inch from the bottom. Sprinkle with salt to taste.
1/4 cup butter (1/2 stick), melted

1/4 cup grated Parmesan cheese
1/3 cup chopped chives

Melt butter in a roasting pan that will comfortably hold the potatoes without crowding. Place potatoes in pan, fan side up and baste thoroughly with butter. Bake in a 350° oven for about 40 minutes, basting now and again. Sprinkle potatoes with the cheese and continue baking until potatoes are tender, about 20 minutes. Sprinkle with chives. Potatoes can be held for about 20 minutes in a low oven. Serves 6.

Imperial White Chocolate Mousse
with Almond Crust & Raspberry Sauce

If you are looking for a dessert to really impress, this is a great one to consider. While the preparation of this mousse is very unorthodox, it does produce a magnificent dessert. It is a dense mousse with a good deal of character...a bit more work to prepare, but truly worth every minute of it.

1	envelope unflavored gelatin (1 tablespoon)
1/4	cup rum
1/2	cup cream
1/4	cup butter (1/2 stick)
1/2	pound white chocolate, coarsely chopped
1	teaspoon almond extract
2	egg whites, beaten with 1 cup sifted powdered sugar until stiff
1	cup cream, beaten until stiff

In a metal measuring cup, soften gelatin in rum. Place cup in a pan of simmering water and stir gelatin until dissolved.

In the top of a double boiler, over hot water, heat cream with butter until butter is melted. Add the white chocolate and almond extract and stir until chocolate is melted. Place mixture into the large bowl of an electric mixer, and beat in the egg white mixture and cream until blended. Beat in the dissolved gelatin until blended.

Place mixture in prepared crust and refrigerate until firm, overnight is good, too. Decorate top with finely grated chocolate, or chocolate leaves. To serve, cut into wedges and spoon a little Raspberry Sauce on top. Memorable! Keep the portions small and serve 12.

Almond Crust:
Stir together 1 1/2 cups macaroon crumbs; 1/4 cup butter, melted; 1/4 cup finely chopped almonds until blended. Press mixture on the bottom of a 10-inch glass pie plate and bake in a 350° oven for 7 minutes. Allow to cool.

Raspberry Sauce:
Stir together 1 package (10 ounces) raspberries in syrup; and 3 ounces frozen orange juice concentrate until blended. Refrigerate until serving time.

Souffle au Chocolat with Creme Vanilla

This is one of my best inventions and I know I have given you this recipe before. However, in the event you do not own "The Love of Eating", I had to include it in my Holiday book. In this recipe, the very complicated souffle is amazingly simple and easy to prepare for a company dinner. Souffle can be assembled earlier in the day, refrigerated and baked before serving.

1 1/2 cups semi-sweet chocolate chips
1 cup cream

5 eggs, at room temperature
8 ounces cream cheese, cut into 8 pieces
pinch of salt
1 teaspoon vanilla or 1 tablespoon rum

Place chocolate chips in food processor bowl or blender. Heat cream to boiling point and pour into the processor. Blend for 1 minute, or until chocolate is melted. Beat in eggs, one at a time, while processor continues running. Continue blending, adding the remaining ingredients, until cream cheese is completely blended.

Pour mixture into a buttered and sugared 1 1/2-quart souffle dish and refrigerate. One hour before serving, bake at 375° for about 50 minutes to 1 hour. Top will be slightly cracked. Spoon into serving bowls with Creme Vanilla spooned on top. Serves 6.

Creme Vanilla:
1/2 cup cream
2 teaspoons sugar
1/2 teaspoon vanilla

1/2 cup vanilla ice cream, softened

Beat cream with sugar and vanilla until stiff. Fold in the ice cream. Refrigerate until ready to serve. Can be prepared 2 hours before serving.

Alternatively, cream can be whipped earlier in the day and stored in the refrigerator. Fold in the ice cream 1 to 2 hours before serving. Store sauce in the refrigerator until serving time.

To Prepare Individual Chocolate Souffles:
Divide mixture between 6 buttered and sugared ramekins and bake for about 20 minutes or until puffed and golden.

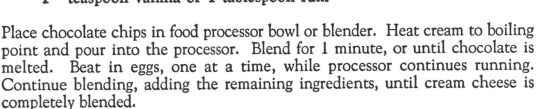

Cappuccino Ice Cream with Brandy Kahlua Sauce

3 egg whites
4 tablespoons sugar

1 cup cream
4 tablespoons sugar
1 tablespoon Cognac (or brandy)
1 tablespoon Kahlua liqueur
2 teaspoons powdered instant coffee

Beat egg whites until foamy. Gradually add the sugar and continue beating until whites are stiff and glossy.

In another bowl, whip the cream with the sugar until stiff. Add the Cognac, Kahlua and instant coffee and beat until blended.

Combine beaten egg whites and whipped cream mixture and beat together on low speed of your mixer until thoroughly combined. Divide mixture between 12 paper-lined muffin cups. Place in the freezer until firm. When frozen firm, store in double plastic bags.

To serve, remove the paper liners and place ice cream in a lovely stemmed glass or glass dessert dish. Spoon a little Brandy Kahlua Sauce over the top and sprinkle with chopped toasted almonds. Serves 12.

Brandy Kahlua Sauce:
1 cup sugar
3/4 cup water

1 tablespoon Cognac or brandy
1 tablespoon Kahlua liqueur
2 teaspoons instant powdered coffee

In a saucepan, heat together the sugar and water. Cook mixture over medium heat for about 7 minutes or until mixture is syrupy. Stir in the remaining ingredients until blended. Allow mixture to cool. Serve over ice cream. Yields 1 cup sauce.

The Best of Times...
A Dickens Christmas Dinner

American Blinis with Golden Caviar

Grand Holiday Cream of Mushroom & Chestnut Soup
Crusty Loaf of Bread

Honey Plum-Glazed Goose with
Apricot, Chestnut & Wild Rice Stuffing

Sweet & Sour Red Cabbage with Apples & Raisins
Brussels Sprouts with Lemon Garlic Crumbs

Imperial Cheesecake Mousse with Raspberries & Chocolate or
Apple, Apricot & Fig Christmas Tart

If you are looking to serve a memorable Christmas dinner in the spirit of Dickens, this is a good one to consider. I worked the Blinis so they could be made at any time with regular flour, as most pantries are not stocked with buckwheat. The Blinis are very delicious and everybody loved them at a recent party we gave. They can be prepared earlier in the day, wrapped in foil and heated before serving.

The soup is sturdy and wonderful. Purchase some crusty breads to serve with the soup. The Goose is deeply glazed with Honey & Plums and the Wild Rice Stuffing is flavored with Apricots and Chestnuts. Red Cabbage with Apples & Raisins and Brussels Sprouts are both nice accompaniments.

The Cheesecake Mousse is a light dessert, very delicious and satisfying. Accented with Raspberries and Chocolate it is memorable. The Christmas Tart with Apples, Apricots & Figs is a fine Winter dessert.

American Blinis with Golden Caviar & Creme Fraiche

I call these "American" because they are made with white flour instead of the usual buckwheat. These are interesting little rounds of dough and deeply flavorful and aromatic. Serve them with a dollup of Creme Fraiche and a dot of caviar or smoked salmon on top. A faint sprinkle of chopped chives or dill is very nice, also. Serve these warm. They can be prepared in advance and heated before serving.

1	package (1/4 ounce) dry yeast
1/2	teaspoon sugar
1/3	cup warm water (105°)

2 1/4	cups flour
1 3/4	cups warm milk (105°)
1	egg, beaten
1	teaspoon sugar
1/4	teaspoon salt
4	tablespoons butter, melted and cooled

1/4	cup water

In a small bowl, stir together yeast, sugar and water and set aside for 10 minutes. Yeast should start to bubble and foam, and if it does not, yeast is not active and should be discarded. This is called "proofing" the yeast.

In the large bowl of an electric mixer, beat together next 6 ingredients until blended. Add the proofed yeast and beat for 1 minute. Cover bowl with plastic wrap and refrigerate overnight. When ready to cook blinis, stir in the remaining 1/4 cup water.

On a hot and buttered griddle, for each blini, spoon 1 tablespoon of batter. (This will produce a 2-inch blini.) Cook until bottoms are browned, about 1 minute. Turn and brown other side about 1/2 minute. Place blinis in a 9x13-inch baking pan while you continue with the rest of the batter. Cover pan tightly with foil and refrigerate until serving time. To serve, heat blinis in a 350° oven until warm. Serve with a dollup of Creme Fraiche, a bit of caviar or smoked salmon and an optional sprinkle of chives or dill. Yields 48 blinis.

Toppings:
Creme Fraiche:
Stir together 1/3 cup cream and 1/3 cup sour cream until blended. Cover bowl with plastic wrap, allow to stand at room temperature for several hours and refrigerate until serving time. Yields 2/3 cup.

-3 ounces golden caviar--with a sprinkle of finely minced chives

-Small 1-inch squares of smoked salmon--with a little fresh dill

Grand Holiday
Cream of Mushroom & Chestnut Soup

*What a wonderful soup to serve for a festive holiday dinner. The flavor is superb...
rich and deep. Soup can be prepared earlier in the day and heated before serving.
Chestnuts sold in cans are a bit costly, but at holiday time, it's nice to splurge a
little. Canned chestnuts come in varied forms. Whole chestnuts come packed in
syrup or packed in water. Pureed chestnuts come sweetened or unsweetened.*

2	onions, finely chopped
4	shallots, minced
4	cloves garlic, minced
1/2	teaspoon dried thyme flakes
1/4	teaspoon ground poultry seasoning
4	tablespoons butter
1/2	cup dry white wine
2	tablespoons flour
3	cans (10 1/2 ounces, each) chicken broth
1	can (15 1/2 ounces) chestnuts, packed in water (not in syrup), drained and sliced
1	pound mushrooms, thinly sliced and tossed with 2 tablespoons lemon juice
2	tablespoons butter
1	cup cream or half and half
	salt to taste

In a Dutch oven casserole, saute together first 6 ingredients over low heat,
until onions are soft and liquid rendered is evaporated. Add the wine and
continue cooking, over medium heat, until wine is evaporated. Stir in the
flour and cook for 2 minutes, stirring. Add the broth and chestnuts and
simmer soup for 15 minutes. Puree soup in blender or food processor and
return to Dutch oven casserole.

Meanwhile, in a skillet, saute mushrooms in butter, over low heat, until
mushrooms are tender and liquid rendered is evaporated. Add mushrooms to
soup and simmer for 5 minutes. Add the cream, adjust seasoning, and
simmer soup for another 5 minutes. Decorate with a sprinkle of chopped
chives. Serves 8.

Honey Plum-Glazed Goose with Apricot, Chestnut & Wild Rice Stuffing

This is an exciting change from the usual roast turkey or ham traditionally served at Christmas dinner. Chestnuts are wonderful with the stuffing, but, in absence of these, 1 cup toasted pecans can be substituted. I prefer preparing the stuffing separately, as I have said so many times before. To reheat rice, sprinkle it with 2 tablespoons broth before reheating. Cover pan and use a low heat setting.

1   goose, about 12 pounds (fresh or frozen). If frozen, allow to defrost in the refrigerator overnight. Prick the skin on the back of the goose in 5 or 6 places to allow the fat to drip out. Cut a lemon in half and rub it on the goose, inside and out. Sprinkle with salt to taste. Place a meat thermometer in the middle of the upper thigh, not touching the bone. Place 1/2 sliced orange and 1/2 sliced apple in cavity. Tie the legs together.

Honey Plum Basting Mixture:
1/2   cup plum jam
3   tablespoons honey
2   tablespoons melted margarine
4   cloves minced garlic
1/2   cup dry white wine

Line a roasting pan with foil, and place prepared goose on a rack in pan. Tent pan loosely with foil. Roast goose at 350° for 1 1/2 hours. Heat together basting ingredients. Remove foil and baste goose with honey mixture. Continue baking for about 1 hour, basting every 15 minutes with the honey mixture until meat thermometer registers 180°. Remove the strings and discard the fruit from the cavity. Serve surrounded with Apricot, Chestnut and Wild Rice Stuffing. Serves 8.

Apricot, Chestnut & Wild Rice Stuffing

Granted they are expensive, using canned chestnuts makes this delicious stuffing easy to prepare. Not only is it time-saving, but peeling roasted chestnuts is really hard on your fingers. Chestnuts can be substituted with 1 cup chopped pecans. Stuffing can be prepared earlier in the day and placed in a heat and serve casserole. Sprinkle with 1 tablespoon water, cover tightly with foil and reheat in a 350° oven until heated through, about 25 minutes.

1 1/2	cups wild and brown rice
4	tablespoons butter
3 1/4	cups chicken broth
	salt to taste
4	tablespoons butter
1	onion, finely chopped
2	stalks celery, finely chopped
6	shallots, minced
4	cloves garlic, minced
1	can (1 pound) chestnuts, drained and coarsely chopped
3/4	cup dried apricots, chopped

In a saucepan, bring the first 4 ingredients to a boil, cover pan, lower heat, and simmer mixture for about 40 to 45 minutes, or until rice is tender.

Meanwhile, in a skillet, saute together next 5 ingredients until vegetables are tender. Add the chestnuts and apricots and continue cooking for 5 minutes, stirring every now and again. When rice is cooked, stir in the chestnut mixture. Serves 8.

Note: -*For a festive presentation, press the hot, cooked stuffing in a mold and invert onto the serving platter.*

Sweet & Sour Red Cabbage with Apples and Raisins

- 1 onion, chopped
- 1 clove garlic, minced
- 4 tablespoons butter

- 1 small head red cabbage, (about 1 1/4 pounds), cored and finely shredded
- 2 apples, peeled, cored and grated
- 1 cup drained sauerkraut
- 2 tablespoons brown sugar
- 3/4 cup apple juice
- 1/2 cup raisins
- salt and pepper to taste

In a Dutch oven casserole, saute together first 3 ingredients until onions are transparent. Stir in the remaining ingredients, cover pan, lower heat and simmer mixture for about 45 minutes or until cabbage is tender. To prevent scorching, add a little apple juice if cabbage appears dry. Serves 8.

Brussels Sprouts & Lemon Garlic Crumbs

- 2 packages (10 ounces, each) frozen Brussels sprouts
- 1/2 cup chicken broth
- 1 tablespoon lemon juice

- 2 cloves garlic, minced
- 1 tablespoon margarine
- 1/3 cup fresh bread crumbs
- salt and pepper to taste

In a saucepan, simmer Brussels sprouts in chicken broth and lemon juice until they are tender, and drain.

Meanwhile in a skillet, saute garlic in margarine for 2 minutes, but do not let garlic brown. Toss in the bread crumbs and seasonings. Toss crumb mixture with sprouts and heat through. Serves 8.

Imperial Cheesecake Mousse with Raspberries & Chocolate

This is a splendid dessert to serve for the finest occasion. The combination of raspberries and chocolate in a whipped cream cheese mousse is heavenly. As it does not have to be cooked, it is rather easy to prepare. If you are planning to serve this for a small group, this recipe can be halved.

1	tablespoon butter
3/4	cup vanilla wafer crumbs
1 1/2	tablespoons unflavored gelatin
1/3	cup water
2	packages (8 ounces, each) cream cheese, at room temperature
1/2	cup sugar
1	teaspoon vanilla
2	cups cream, whipped
1	package (10 ounces) frozen raspberries in syrup, defrosted
4	ounces semi-sweet chocolate, finely chopped

In a parchment-lined 10-inch springform pan, spread butter and sprinkle crumbs evenly. In a metal measuring cup, soften gelatin in water. Place cup in a larger pan with simmering water and stir until gelatin is dissolved. Set aside.

Beat cream cheese with sugar and vanilla until cream cheese is smooth and fluffy. Fold in the whipped cream, raspberries, chocolate and dissolved gelatin until blended. Pour mousse into the prepared crumbed pan and spread to even. Refrigerate until firm. Decorate top with raspberries and grated chocolate. To serve, using the parchment paper to help you, slide mousse onto a lovely serving platter. Serves 8 to 10.

Apple, Apricot & Fig Christmas Tart

Fresh apples and dried fruits make for a delicious contrast in taste and texture. This sturdy pie is, also, a good choice to serve after a day on the slopes or a trudge in the snow. The crust is filled with almonds and spice and is a delicious base for the dried fruit filling.

Filling:
- 2 apples, peeled, cored and thinly sliced
- 4 ounces, each, dried apricots and dried figs
- 3/4 cup yellow raisins
- 1 cup orange juice
- 3/4 cup sugar
- 1 teaspoon cinnamon
- 2 tablespoons lemon juice

Almond Custard:
- 1/2 cup cream
- 1 egg
- 3 tablespoons sugar
- 1/4 cup finely grated almonds (almond meal)
- 1/2 teaspoon almond extract

In a covered saucepan, cook together all the filling ingredients until fruit is soft, about 30 minutes, and drain. Beat together custard ingredients until blended. Place custard into prepared crust and place fruit decoratively on top. Bake in a 350° oven for 30 minutes, or until custard is set. Allow to cool in pan. Serve with hot cider. Serves 8.

Spicy Butter Crust:
- 1 1/2 cups flour
- 1 cup finely grated almonds (almond meal)
- 1/2 cup sugar
- 1 teaspoon pumpkin pie spice
- 1/2 cup butter, cut into 8 pieces

- 1 egg
- 3 tablespoons water
- 1/2 teaspoon almond extract

Beat together first 5 ingredients until mixture resembles coarse meal. Beat together egg, water and almond extract until blended, and add, beating until dough clumps together. Do not overbeat. Gather dough together and pat it on the bottom and 1-inch up the sides of a greased 10-inch springform pan. Bake in a 350° oven for 20 to 25 minutes, or until dough appears dry and is just beginning to take on color.

A Regal "White Christmas" Feast

Gravad Lax with Honey Dill Sauce
Red Cocktail Dipping Sauce for Shellfish
Crown Mold of Crabmeat Mousse Royale

Caramelized Onion & Mushroom Soup with
Croustades of Cheese & Chives

Crown Roast of Lamb with Mushroom Wine Sauce
Bulgur, Lamb, Lemon & Chive Stuffing
Sauteed Cucumbers with Chives & Dill
Glazed Carrots, or
Brussels Sprouts with Onions
Compote of Apples & Cranberries

Iced Lemon Cream with Raspberry Sauce
Easiest & Best Apricot Nut Torte with Whipped Creme Fraiche
The Ultimate Chocolate Cheesecake with Macaroon Crust

While, I do believe, this is an excellent menu for a White Christmas dinner, it is also great to serve at any time during the year. It is a menu that can be served in grand style and is a fine choice for a special celebration, birthday or anniversary. Every dish is just fabulous and delicious.

Follow the instructions carefully for the Crown Roast. Remove it from the oven as described and it will be a perfect pink when served. The Compote of Apples & Cranberries is loved by all. It adds the perfect fruitiness to the lamb and bulgur.

Desserts range from the marvelously light Lemon Cream with Raspberry Sauce to the more substantial Chocolate Cheesecake. The Apricot Nut Torte with Whipped Creme Fraiche, sparkled with apricots, is a poem of flavors and textures. Your guests will love it. What more can I add except "Enjoy!"

Gravad Lax with Honey Dill Sauce

Serving small squares of lox on wafer-thin slices of black bread with a dab of Honey Dill Sauce, transforms basic lox into Gravad Lax, an excellent hors d'oeuvre taken from the Swedish smorgasbord.

Honey Dill Sauce:
- 1/4 cup vinegar
- 2 tablespoons honey
- 1/2 cup salad oil
- 1/2 teaspoon dried dill weed (or to taste)
-   salt and pepper to taste

- 1/2 pound lox, cut into 1-inch squares

Beat together the vinegar and the honey. Gradually beat in the oil. Add dill and taste for salt and pepper. Serve lox with Honey Dill Sauce on wafer-thin slices of black bread. Serves 6.

Red Cocktail Dipping Sauce for Shellfish

This is another simple starter for a complex meal. Everybody loves this simple sauce. It can be prepared earlier in the day and stored in the refrigerator.

- 1 1/2 pounds crabmeat, picked over for bones

Red Cocktail Dipping Sauce:
- 1 cup ketchup
- 3 tablespoons lemon juice
- 2 tablespoons prepared horseradish
- 4 tablespoons finely chopped green onions

Stir together sauce ingredients and place in a decorative bowl. Cover bowl with plastic wrap and refrigerate until serving time. To serve, place bowl on a platter and surround with crabmeat chunks. Decorate lavishly with lemon slices, green onion frills and small cherry tomatoes. Place small plates and forks close by for guests to serve themselves. Serves 6.

Crown Mold of Crabmeat Mousse Royale

The flavor of lemon and dill is pronounced in this mold and it is a fine combination with the crabmeat. Work quickly when you stir in the gelatin so that it does not start to gel before it is evenly mixed.

1	package (1 tablespoon) unflavored gelatin
1/4	cup cold water
1/2	cup mayonnaise, at room temperature
1/2	cup low-fat sour cream
4	tablespoons lemon juice
1/2	cup finely chopped chives
1/2	teaspoon dried dill weed
2	tablespoons finely chopped parsley
	salt and pepper to taste
1/2	pound cooked crabmeat, picked over for bones and flaked

In a metal measuring cup, soften gelatin in cold water. Place cup in a pan with simmering water and stir until gelatin is dissolved. In a large bowl, toss together the remaining ingredients. Working quickly, stir in the dissolved gelatin and mix until all the ingredients are nicely combined.

Spread mixture into a 4-cup ring mold and refrigerate until firm. Unmold onto a serving platter and decorate with green onion frills, lemon slices sprinkled with parsley and cherry tomatoes. Serve with a bland soda cracker. Serves 8.

Note: -If you are using a mold without a hole in the center, line it with plastic wrap so that unmolding will be effortless.

Caramelized Onion & Mushroom Soup & Croustades of Cheese & Chives

4	medium onions, chopped
4	cloves garlic, minced
4	shallots, chopped
1	teaspoon honey
3	tablespoons butter
1	pound mushrooms, cleaned and very thinly sliced
2	tablespoons butter
1/4	cup dry white wine
	salt and pepper to taste
2	tablespoons flour
5	cups chicken broth
1/2	cup cream

In a Dutch oven casserole, over very low heat, cook together first 5 ingredients, stirring now and again, until onions are soft and golden (not fried), about 30 minutes.

Meanwhile, in a skillet, saute mushrooms in butter until mushrooms are tender. Add the wine and seasonings and cook until wine has evaporated. Add the flour and cook for 2 minutes, stirring.

Add the mushroom mixture to the onions in the casserole, and stir in the chicken broth. Simmer soup for 5 minutes and then add the cream. Simmer soup for another 2 minutes. Serve with Croustades of Cheese & Chives. Serves 8.

Croustades of Cheese & Chives:
8	thin slices good quality white bread, crusts removed. Brush with a little melted butter and bake for a few minutes in a 350° oven until slightly crisped, but not browned.
8	teaspoons sour cream
8	teaspoons grated Parmesan cheese
8	teaspoons finely chopped chives

Spread each slice of bread with a little sour cream, sprinkle with cheese and chives and cut each slice on the diagonal. Place on a cookie sheet and just before serving, place under the broiler for 1 minute to brown tops. Be careful as there are only a few seconds between brown and burned. Serves 8.

Crown Roast of Lamb with Bulgur, Lamb, Lemon & Chive Stuffing

This stuffing is so delicious, I can make a meal of it. The lamb is faintly sparkled with shallots, lemon and chives. The bulgur adds an interesting texture. The best way to make certain not to overcook the lamb is to remove it from the oven at 140° to 145° (rare), for it does continue to cook for several minutes and it will be a perfect medium rare when serving. Timing is extremely important with this recipe, for it is a real pity if the lamb is overcooked.

Bulgur & Lamb Stuffing:

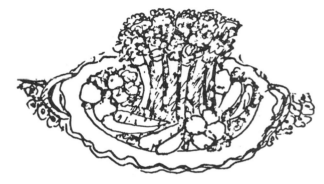

2	shallots
2	teaspoons margarine
1	pound lean ground lamb
1 1/2	cups bulgur (cracked wheat)
2	tablespoons margarine
3	cups chicken broth
2	tablespoons lemon juice
	salt to taste
1/2	cup chopped chives

Saute shallots lightly in margarine. Add the lamb and cook and stir until meat loses its pinkness. Set aside.

In a Dutch oven casserole, cook together bulgur and margarine, turning and stirring until bulgur is beginning to take on color. Stir in the chicken broth, lemon juice and salt to taste, cover pan and bring to a boil. Lower heat and simmer mixture for 15 to 20 minutes or until liquid is absorbed. Stir in the reserved lamb mixture and chives. Heat stuffing before serving.

2 racks of lamb, (14 chops total; about 3 1/2 pounds trimmed weight, i.e. fat trimmed, rib bones trimmed, chine bone removed). Ask butcher to tie racks into a crown roast. Place a meat thermometer in the thickest part of one rib eye without touching the bone. This will help to avoid overcooking. Cover the rib bones with foil to prevent burning.

4 cloves garlic, very finely minced

Place lamb in a 9x13-inch baking pan. Rub the lamb with garlic on all sides, cover loosely with plastic wrap and refrigerate for several hours. Preheat oven to 350°. Remove plastic wrap. To keep roast round, stuff center with foil. Roast lamb for about 1 hour, or until meat thermometer registers 140°, for rare. Remove lamb from oven, remove foil on ribs and center and fill center with **heated Bulgur & Lamb Stuffing**. Cover bones with decorative frills. With a flourish, carve roast at the table. Serve with Mushroom Wine Sauce on the side. Serves 6.

More→

Mushroom Wine Sauce:

- 1/2 pound mushrooms, sliced
- 2 cloves garlic, finely minced
- 2 shallots, finely minced
- 2 tablespoons butter

- 1/4 cup dry white wine
- 1 can (10 1/2 ounces) beef broth
- 1 teaspoon Bovril
- 2 teaspoons Sauce Robert
- 3 tablespoons chopped chives
- 1 tablespoon chopped parsley
  salt and pepper to taste

Saute together mushrooms, garlic and shallots in butter until mushrooms are tender. Add wine and simmer mixture until wines has almost evaporated. Add broth, Bovril, Sauce Robert, chives, parsley and salt and pepper to taste. Simmer sauce for 5 minutes. (Sauce can be prepared 1 day earlier and stored in the refrigerator. Heat before serving.)

Sauteed Cucumbers with Chives & Dill

- 3 medium cucumbers, peeled and cut in half, lengthwise. Scoop out the seeds with a spoon and slice the cucumbers, crosswise, into thin slices.

- 2 tablespoons butter
- 1 teaspoon chicken seasoned stock base
  salt and pepper to taste
- 3 tablespoons chopped chives
- 1 tablespoon chopped parsley
- 1/8 teaspoon dill weed

In a saucepan, melt butter with chicken stock base. Add the remaining ingredients and saute mixture for about 10 minutes or until cucumbers are tender and all the liquid rendered has been absorbed. Serves 6.

Compote of Apples & Cranberries

Apples with cranberries make a nice Winter compote. This one is fruity and on the tart side, and a lovely accompaniment to the lamb and bulgur. This can be served slightly chilled or at room temperature.

4	large apples, peeled, cored and sliced
3/4	cup orange juice
1/2	cup cinnamon sugar
2	tablespoons lemon juice
1 1/2	cups fresh or frozen cranberries

In a covered Dutch oven casserole, simmer together first 4 ingredients for 15 minutes. Add the cranberries and continue cooking for about 8 minutes or until cranberries are popped. Serves 6.

Brussels Sprouts with Onions

1	onion, finely chopped
2	cloves garlic, minced
2	tablespoons butter
1/4	cup chicken broth
2	tablespoons balsamic vinegar
	salt and pepper to taste
2	packages (10 ounces, each) frozen Brussels sprouts

In a saucepan, saute onion and garlic in butter until onion is soft, but not browned. Add the remaining ingredients, cover pan and simmer sprouts for 10 minutes or until tender. Serves 8.

Glazed Carrots

1 1/2	pounds fresh baby carrots, cooked in boiling water for 5 minutes and drained
2	tablespoons butter
1	tablespoon sugar
	salt to taste
2	tablespoons chopped parsley

In a large skillet, cook together first 4 ingredients until carrots are shiny and glazed. Place in a saucepan, toss with parsley and refrigerate until serving time. Add a few drops of water when reheating. Serves 6.

Iced Lemon Cream with Raspberry Sauce

There is no iced dessert that is easier or more beautiful than this one. It is a variation of a recipe I shared with you in "The Joy of Eating" except this one is made a little lighter with half and half. This is a great dessert to serve after a hefty meal.

2   packages (12 count, each) lady fingers, split in half. The lady fingers used to line the sides of the pan should be cut in half again. This is a low dessert.

1   cup whipping cream
1   cup half and half
4   tablespoons lemon juice
1/2   lemon, finely grated. Remove any large pieces of membrane.
1   cup sugar

Line an 8-inch springform pan with parchment paper. Now, line the bottom and sides of the pan with lady fingers, holding them in place with a smidge of butter.

In a bowl, place the remaining ingredients and stir until sugar is dissolved, about 1 minute. Pour this into the prepared pan, cover with plastic wrap and freeze until firm. Remove from freezer, and using the parchment paper to help you, slide dessert onto a serving platter. To serve, cut into thin wedges and spoon a little Raspberry Sauce on top. Serves 10 to 12.

Raspberry Sauce:
1   package (10 ounces) frozen raspberries in syrup, defrosted
1   tablespoon lemon juice

Simply stir ingredients together until blended. Store in the refrigerator until ready to serve.

Note: -Lemon cream can be divided between 12 paper-lined muffin cups and frozen until firm. To serve, remove the paper liners and place in a lovely stemmed glass. Spoon a little Raspberry Sauce on top.

The Ultimate Chocolate Cheesecake with Macaroon Crust

This is one IMPRESSIVE dessert that is immensely delicious. If you love cheesecake and are "mad" about chocolate, this is a little treasure you will use often. It is a dense filling, so please don't overbeat. You do not want too much air incorporated in the filling. Just beat until blended, no more.

1	tablespoon butter
1	cup macaroon cookie crumbs
1 1/2	pounds cream cheese, at room temperature (3 8-ounce packages)
1	cup sour cream, at room temperature
3	eggs, at room temperature
3/4	cup sugar
2	teaspoons vanilla
1	package (6 ounces) semi-sweet chocolate chips, melted

In a 10-inch springform pan, spread the butter on the bottom and sprinkle crumbs evenly over all. Set pan aside.

In the large bowl of an electric mixer, beat together, cream cheese, sour cream, eggs, sugar and vanilla until blended. Do not overbeat. Beat in the melted chocolate until blended. Pour mixture into prepared pan and bake at 350° for 45 minutes. Allow to cool and then refrigerate for at least 6 hours. Overnight is good, too. Decorate top with a generous sprinkling of grated chocolate. To serve, cut into wedges and keep the portions small. Serves 12.

Note: -Can be prepared 1 day earlier and stored in the refrigerator.
-2 tablespoons of Creme de Cacao can be added to the cream cheese mixture, if you enjoy the subtle addition of liqueur.

Easiest & Best Apricot Nut Torte with Whipped Creme Fraiche

Perhaps one of the easiest and most delicious desserts (if you love apricots and walnuts) is this marvelous chewy torte. It is tart and fruity, and the frosting is the perfect accompaniment. Pecans can be substituted for the walnuts.

3	egg whites
1/2	cup sugar
3/4	cup dried apricots
1/2	cup sugar
1	cup soda cracker crumbs
3/4	cup chopped walnuts
1	teaspoon vanilla

Beat together whites and sugar until mixture is creamy. (Do not beat to stiff peaks.)

In a food processor, chop apricots with sugar until apricots are finely chopped, but not pureed. Add apricots and remaining ingredients to beaten egg whites and stir to blend. Spread batter evenly into a greased 9-inch deep dish glass pie pan and bake in a 350° oven for 25 to 30 minutes, or until top is very lightly browned. Remove from oven and allow to cool in pan.

When cool, swirl top with Whipped Creme Fraiche. Decorate top with a sprinkling of finely grated toasted walnuts. Refrigerate for several hours. Overnight is good, too. Serves 8.

Whipped Creme Fraiche:
1/2	cup cream
1	tablespoon sugar
1/2	teaspoon vanilla
1/4	cup sour cream

Beat cream with sugar and vanilla, until cream is stiff. Beat in sour cream until blended. (Can be prepared in advance and stored in the refrigerator until ready to frost torte.)

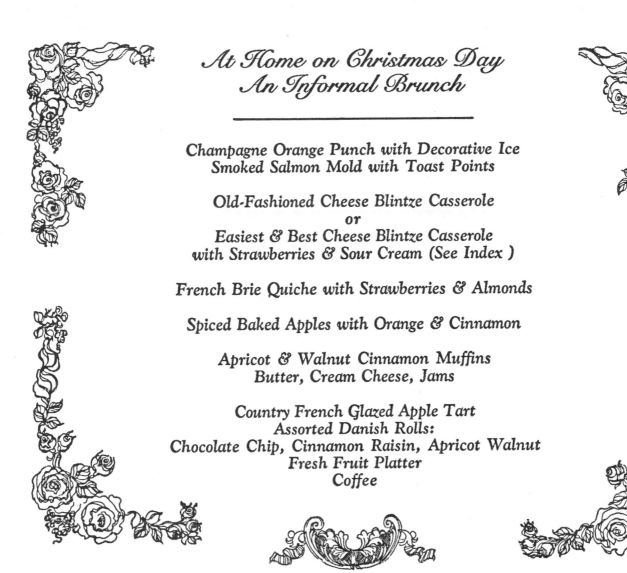

At Home on Christmas Day
An Informal Brunch

Champagne Orange Punch with Decorative Ice
Smoked Salmon Mold with Toast Points

Old-Fashioned Cheese Blintze Casserole
or
Easiest & Best Cheese Blintze Casserole
with Strawberries & Sour Cream (See Index)

French Brie Quiche with Strawberries & Almonds

Spiced Baked Apples with Orange & Cinnamon

Apricot & Walnut Cinnamon Muffins
Butter, Cream Cheese, Jams

Country French Glazed Apple Tart
Assorted Danish Rolls:
Chocolate Chip, Cinnamon Raisin, Apricot Walnut
Fresh Fruit Platter
Coffee

"Come for brunch on Christmas Day... and spend the afternoon with us."... is a delightful, informal way to entertain family and friends. It is an especially warm and friendly time, for brunch is a leisurely meal that slowly drifts into the afternoon, giving everyone a chance to relax and spend some good time together. Our very lovely family brunch should be unhurried, so linger awhile over the strawberry-studded Champagne, served with Smoked Salmon and delicate toast points.

Depending on the number of guests you are entertaining, choose a Cheese Blintze Casserole or French Brie Quiche. For more than 12 guests, I would suggest you prepare both.

Cut and place the French Apple Tart on a footed platter a day earlier and cover it with plastic wrap. Do the same with the Danish. Just before the guests arrive, stir the Champagne into the punch.

Planning is the key word for any party, but especially for brunch. As guests will usually be arriving around 11, it is important that linen, silver, serving pieces and table decorations be out and ready the day before. Allow only reheating and last minute touches for the day of your party.

Champagne Orange Punch

2 quarts orange juice
2 tablespoons lemon juice
1/4 cup sugar
  orange slices and lemon slices

2 bottles (25 ounces, each) Champagne, chilled

Strawberries
Decorative Ice Ring and Orange Juice Cubes

Combine orange juice, lemon juice, sugar and fruit in a large bowl and refrigerate. (If your punch bowl fits in your refrigerator, it can be used.) Just before serving, add the chilled Champagne and stir. Float in the strawberries and some Decorative Ice. Serve in a lovely stemmed glass with a strawberry floating on top. Yields 1 gallon punch and will serve 12 generously.

To make Decorative Ice:
1. Freeze 1 quart orange juice in an ice cube tray. These ice cubes will not dilute the punch.
2. Place 1 Maraschino cherry in each compartment of an ice tray, fill with orange juice or other juice and freeze.
3. Fill a ring mold with strawberries, lemon slices, orange slices or other fruit. Half-fill it with water, cover with foil and freeze. When frozen, fill the mold with additional cold water and freeze again. This will keep the fruit from floating to the top and melting into the punch too soon. If fruit pops up, press it back into the mold when it is partially frozen.
4. To unmold, dip mold into warm water for a few seconds and it will easily slip out.

Smoked Salmon Mold with Toast Points

2	packages (8 ounces, each) cream cheese. (Can use low-fat)
3	tablespoons lemon juice
1/2	cup finely chopped chives or green onions
1/1	pound smoked salmon, cut into 1-inch pieces
48	Toast Points made with 12 slices bread (see Index)

Beat cream cheese and lemon until blended. Beat in chives until blended. Beat in salmon just until blended. Do not overbeat. You want the salmon to be chunky, not pureed.

Line a 2-cup flower-mold with plastic wrap. Add cream cheese mixture into the mold and cover with another sheet of plastic wrap. Press gently on top to spread evenly and for the filling to take the shape of the mold. Refrigerate.

This is a snap to unmold. Remove the top piece of plastic wrap, invert mold onto a platter and then remove the remaining piece of plastic. Surround with parsley or green leaves, cherry tomatoes, chive-sprinkled lemon slices or green onion frills. Place Toast Points on a bread tray close by. This is a gorgeous mold and lovely to serve with the Champagne Punch. Serves 12.

Old-Fashioned Cheese Blintze Casserole

4	tablespoons butter, melted
12	cheese blintzes, purchased from a deli
4	eggs
1	pint sour cream
1/2	small orange, grated. (Use fruit, juice and peel, about 3 tablespoons.)
3/4	cup sugar
1	teaspoon vanilla
1/2	cup yellow raisins, plumped in orange juice
2	tablespoons cinnamon sugar

In a 9x13-inch baking pan, place melted butter and cheese blintzes. Beat together next 6 ingredients until blended and pour over the blintzes. Sprinkle top with cinnamon sugar. (Press down into the custard any raisins that have floated to the top.) Bake at 350° for 45 minutes or until custard is set and top is golden. Serve with a dollup of sour cream and fresh strawberries. Serves 6 to 12 depending on the accompaniments.

French Brie Quiche with Strawberries & Toasted Almonds

Brie, served with fresh fruit and almonds, is a lovely combination of flavors and colors. Here, they are combined in a quiche that has flair and panache. It can be prepared in advance and stored in the refrigerator. Heat through before serving.

1   deep dish frozen pie shell, baked in a 400° oven for about 8 minutes, or until just beginning to take on color. Leave shell in pan.

6   ounces French Brie. Remove the outer moldy rind and cut the remaining Brie into small dice.
1   package (3 ounces) cream cheese, cut into 1/2-inch dice

4   eggs
1   cup half and half

1/3   cup sliced almonds
1   cup strawberries sliced in halves

Place pie shell on a cookie sheet. Place Brie evenly in shell. Place cream cheese evenly in shell. Beat together eggs and half and half and pour evenly in shell. Bake at 350° for 30 minutes. Sprinkle top with almonds and continue baking for 15 minutes or until custard is set and almonds are toasted. Remove from the oven and place strawberries decoratively along the rim. Serves 6 to 8. Double the recipe for 12.

———————

Spiced Baked Apples with Orange & Cinnamon

6   medium apples, peeled 2-inches on the top, cut in half lengthwise and cored
1   cup orange juice
3   tablespoons grated orange
4   tablespoons cinnamon sugar

1/4   cup chopped walnuts, (optional)

Place apples, cut side down, in a 9x13-inch baking dish. Pour orange juice on the top and sprinkle with grated orange and cinnamon sugar. Bake at 350° for 30 minutes, baste tops with the juices in the pan and sprinkle with the optional walnuts. Continue baking until apples are tender, not mushy, about 10 minutes. Serve warm or chilled. Serves 12.

Country French Glazed Apple Tart

Crust:

1/2	cup butter (1 stick)
4	ounces cream cheese (1/2 of an 8-ounce package)
1	cup flour
4	heaping tablespoons sifted powder sugar

Filling:

1/2	cup apricot jam, warmed
4	apples, peeled, cored and cut in half vertically. Place cut ends down and cut into very thin slices.

Beat together butter and cream cheese until blended. Beat in flour and sugar just until blended. Do not overbeat. Dough is soft. Pat dough on the bottom and 1-inch up the sides of a greased 10-inch tart pan with a removable bottom and bake in a 350° oven for 25 minutes or until crust is just beginning to take on color.

Paint crust with half of the apricot jam. Fan apple slices on the top to resemble 8 petals and bake in a 350° oven for 40 minutes. Paint top with remaining apricot jam, increase temperature to 400° and continue baking for 10 minutes to set glaze. Serves 12.

Apricot & Walnut Cinnamon Muffins

1	egg
1	small thin-skinned orange, grated (about 4 tablespoons)
1/2	cup milk
1/2	cup sour cream
1/3	cup oil
3/4	cup sugar

2 1/4	cups flour
1	tablespoon baking powder
3/4	cup chopped dried apricots
1/2	cup chopped walnuts

In the large bowl of an electric mixer, beat together first 6 ingredients until blended. Stir in the remaining ingredients until blended. Do not overmix.

Divide batter between 12 paper-lined muffin cups and bake at 400° for 25 minutes, or until tops are browned and a cake tester, inserted in center, comes out clean. Allow to cool for 10 minutes, and then remove from pan and continue cooling on a rack. Brush tops with Apricot Glaze when cool. Yields 12 muffins.

Apricot Glaze: Stir together 1 tablespoon orange juice, 2 tablespoons minced dried apricots and 1/2 cup sifted powdered sugar until blended.

Danish Rolls

These freeze beautifully, wrapped in double thicknesses of wax paper and then foil. Do not sprinkle with powdered sugar before freezing. Sprinkle with sugar after defrosted.

Cream Cheese Pastry:
- 1   package (8 ounces) cream cheese
- 1   cup butter (2 sticks)
- 1   egg yolk
- 2   cups flour
- 1/8 teaspoon salt

In the large bowl of an electric mixer, beat together the butter and cream cheese until the mixture is blended. Beat in the egg yolk. Add the flour and salt and beat until blended. Do not overbeat. Turn dough out on a floured wax paper. Form dough into a circle, wrap it in the wax paper and refrigerate it for several hours or overnight.

Divide dough in fourths. Roll out one part at a time to measure a 10-inch square. Spread 1/4 of the Chocolate Quik over the dough. Sprinkle with 1/4 of the chocolate chips. Roll it up, jelly-roll fashion to measure a 10x3-inch roll. Place seam side down on a 12x16-inch teflon-coated baking pan. Repeat with the remaining 3 parts dough.

Bake in a preheated 350° oven for 30 minutes or until the top is lightly browned. Cool in pan. Cut into slices and sprinkle tops generously with sifted powdered sugar. Yields 24 to 28 slices.

Chocolate Chip Filling for 4 rolls:
- 12   tablespoons Nestle's Chocolate Quik
- 6   ounces semi-sweet chocolate chips
- 1/2 cup chopped walnuts (optional)

Cinnamon Raisin Nut Filling for 4 rolls:
- 4   tablespoons cinnamon sugar
- 3/4 cup yellow raisins
- 3/4 cup chopped walnuts

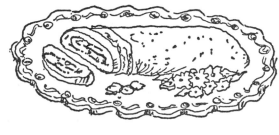

Apricot Jam & Walnut Filling for 4 rolls:
- 1   cup apricot jam
- 1   cup chopped walnuts

Divide filling ingredients between the 4 rolls.

A Toast to the New Year
A Black Tie New Year's Eve Celebration

Royal Gateau Souffle with Pink Caviar & Dill
Champagne

Marscapone & Chevre Layered with Pesto, Sun-Dried Tomatoes & Chives
Toast Points (see Index), Small Soda Crackers, Crackling Frosted Grapes

Cream of Apple & Chestnut Soup or
French Mushroom Salad with Dijon Dressing
Burgundian Cheese & Chive Gougere or
Croissants

Burgundian Paupiettes of Beef with Mushroom Wine Sauce
Casserole of Wild Rice with Apples & Chives

Creamed Mushrooms with Butter, Garlic & Herbs or
Honey-Glazed Baby Carrots

Honey Baked Onions in Butter & Broth or
Roasted Red Onions

Cognac Mousse with Ladyfingers, Raspberries & Chocolate, or
Souffle Cakes with Chocolate Ganache, or
Chocolate Decadence with Fudge Glaze
Coffee, Espresso or Cappuccino (see Index)

It often feels so nice to dress up in an especially festive manner, and New Year's Eve is certainly one of those times. It is a time of toasting to health, happiness and peace in the New Year. Tomorrow we will think of the practical...resolutions and goals... but tonight is filled with the hope and promise of all good things. This is a good menu to consider for any formal celebration, for it is appropriate to serve any time during the year.

The Gougere can be baked earlier in the day and heated before serving. It will settle a little, but the taste will still be wonderful. It is excellent to serve with the Layered Cheese, soup or salad. Choose either the Mushroom Salad or the mushroom vegetable. Prepare the mushrooms for the salad and the Dijon Dressing 1 day earlier, but toss them together before serving. All the other dishes can be prepared 1 day earlier and heated before serving.

For dessert, the Cognac Mousse is marvelously light. The Souffle Cakes are very attractive and very new. They can be prepared 1 day earlier and heated lightly before serving. The Chocolate Decadence is just that. Choose the dessert that best matches your guests' tastes.

Royal Gateau Souffle with Pink Caviar & Dill

This is a spectacular small entree. It serves like a beautiful layer cake, abundantly decorated with green leaves, lemon slices and cherry tomatoes. The recipe that follows is my adaptation of the classic roulade souffle. Preparing it as a gateau (layer cake) is easier to handle and serve. It is one of the most elegant, festive and exciting small entrees. The layers are delicate in texture and subtle in taste. The filling is a marvelous balance. Caviar can be substituted with finely chopped smoked salmon. The layers are very thin, so don't think anything went wrong.

Gateau Souffle:

4	tablespoons butter
1/2	cup flour
2	cups milk
4	egg yolks
4	egg whites, beaten with 1 teaspoon sugar until stiff, but not dry

Lightly grease 2 10-inch springform pans and line them with wax paper. Grease the paper.

In a saucepan, cook together flour and butter for 2 minutes, stirring all the while. Add the milk and continue cooking and stirring for about 5 minutes, or until mixture is thickened. Remove from heat and beat in the egg yolks. Gently fold in the beaten egg whites. Divide mixture between the 2 prepared pans and bake at 350° for about 30 minutes, or until top is lightly browned. Allow to cool in pan. When cool, remove from pan and remove paper lining.

Place one layer on a serving plate and spread with half of the Pink Caviar Filling. Top with second layer and spread top and sides with remaining filling. Decorate platter with green leaves and lemon slices sprinkled with dill. Cut into wedges to serve. Serves 12.

Pink Caviar Filling:

1	packages (8 ounces) cream cheese, softened
1/2	cup sour cream
1/3	cup finely minced chives
3	tablespoons lemon juice
1/2	teaspoon dried dill weed
4	ounces pink caviar

Beat together cream cheese and sour cream until blended. Beat in chives, lemon juice and dill until blended. Gently stir in caviar until blended.

Marscapone & Chevre Layered with Pesto, Sun-Dried Tomatoes & Chives

This very interesting and delicious cheese loaf is also a beautiful hors d'oeuvre. Everyone loves the subtle flavor. Serve it with a bland soda cracker. I know I have allowed for a larger amount than you will need, so if you do not want leftovers, recipe can be halved.

Sun-Dried Tomato Mixture:
- 2/3 cup minced sun-dried tomatoes, packed in oil and drained
- 2 tablespoons lemon juice

Cheese Mixture:
- 2 pounds Marscapone (soft Italian cheese) or cream cheese
- 1 pound Chevre (goat cheese), crumbled
- 1/2 cup chopped chives

Pesto Mixture:
- 1 cup sweet basil leaves
- 2 cloves garlic
- 1/4 cup pine nuts
- 2 tablespoons olive oil

Line an 8x4-inch loaf pan with plastic wrap. Mix together Sun-Dried Tomato ingredients and spread on the bottom of the pan.

Beat together Cheese Mixture ingredients until blended. Press 1/2 Cheese Mixture over the tomato layer.

In a food processor, chop together Pesto Mixture until it is very finely chopped and spread it over the cheese. Press remaining Cheese Mixture over the Pesto.

Cover pan with plastic wrap and press down to smoothen it out. To serve, remove plastic cover, invert mold onto a serving platter, and then remove plastic lining. (Sun-dried tomatoes will be on top.) A few extra toasted pine nuts can be sprinkled on top (optional.)

Serve with small soda crackers or thin slices of French bread. Decorate platter with an abundance of various colored Crackling Frosted Grapes. Yields 3 pounds of cheese and will serve 24.

Cream of Apple & Chestnut Soup

This is not the usual soup...not in taste or texture. It is exceedingly glamorous and will certainly create high interest. Double the recipe to serve 12.

1   apple, peeled, cored and grated
1   small onion, chopped
3   shallots, minced
1   can (1 pound) chestnuts, drained and chopped
3   cups chicken broth
3   tablespoons honey
1   teaspoon pumpkin pie spice
    salt to taste

1   cup half and half

6   teaspoons sour cream
6   sprinkles cinnamon

In a Dutch oven casserole, simmer together first group of ingredients until onion is soft. Puree mixture in a food processor, using some of the broth to help you. Return mixture to Dutch oven, add half and half and heat through. Serve with a dollup of sour cream and a faint sprinkle of cinnamon. Serves 6.

Roasted Red Onions

6   medium red onions, peeled and cut into thin slices.
        Separate slices into rings.
1/2 cup chicken broth
2   tablespoons oil
2   tablespoons vinegar
1   teaspoon dried sage flakes
    salt and pepper to taste

In a 9x13-inch baking pan place the onions. Stir together the remaining ingredients and pour evenly over the onions. Toss and turn onions until they are evenly coated. Cover pan with foil and bake at 350° for about 45 minutes, or until onions are soft. Remove foil and broil onions, 6 inches from the heat, turning and tossing until onions are flecked with brown. Serves 12.

Crackling Frosted Grapes

It's nice to use these grapes as a lavish garnish. Use seedless red, black or green grapes or a little of each. Small Champagne grapes are especially gorgeous.

- 1 egg white
- 1 pound seedless grapes, cut into small clusters
  sugar for coating the grapes

Beat egg white until foamy. Brush grapes on all sides with the egg white and place grapes on a wax paper-lined platter. Sprinkle with sugar on all sides. Allow the sugar coating to dry for several hours at room temperature. Do not refrigerate as it may cause the fruit to sweat. Use to decorate serving platters.

French Mushroom Salad with Dijon Dressing

For subtlety and delicacy, this is one of the best salads. It is marvelous served with the Gougere. Double the recipe to serve 12.

- 1 pound mushrooms, cleaned and thinly sliced
- 1/2 cup chopped chives
- 2 tablespoons minced parsley leaves

Dijon Dressing:
- 1 egg yolk
- 1/4 cup red wine vinegar
- 1 tablespoon Dijon-style mustard
- 1 teaspoon sugar

- 1/2 cup oil
  salt and pepper to taste

Place mushrooms, chives and parsley in a bowl. To make the dressing, in a blender or food processor, beat first 4 ingredients for 15 seconds. Slowly, with motor running, drizzle in the oil, until dressing is creamy and oil is thoroughly incorporated. Stir in seasonings. Toss dressing to taste over the mushrooms until they are nicely coated. Serve on a bed of red-leaf or butter lettuce. (Unused dressing can be stored in the refrigerator for 1 week.) Yields about 1 cup dressing. Serves 6.

Burgundian Cheese & Chive Gougere

A Gougere is an incredible bread-like pastry that is great with a glass of wine and to accompany a delicate pate or a mild cheese. It can be prepared in a round or oval porcelain baker. Freshly baked, it puffs up and is gorgeous to behold. If it is prepared earlier in the day, it settles somewhat, but it is still beautiful. Serve it warm, not hot.

1	cup milk
4	tablespoons butter
1	cup flour
4	eggs, at room temperature
1/4	cup chopped chives
4	tablespoons grated Parmesan cheese
1	teaspoon Dijon mustard
	pinch of salt

In a saucepan, heat milk and butter until mixture comes to a boil. Stir in the flour and cook and stir for 2 minutes, or until a dough forms and pulls away from the side of the bowl. Place dough in the large bowl of an electric mixer. Beat in the eggs, one at a time, beating well after each addition. Beat in the remaining ingredients until blended.

Spoon the dough along the edge of a greased 10-inch round porcelain baker to form a 1 1/2-inch ring. Bake at 400° for 15 minutes. Lower heat to 350° and continue baking for about 30 minutes or until Gougere is puffed and golden brown. To serve, cut with a sharp serrated knife into 1-inch wedges. Yields about 24 1-inch wedges and serves 12.

Honey Baked Onions in Butter & Broth

Somehow, onions are often neglected as a vegetable. These are delicious and very easy to prepare. The honey will glaze them to a rich caramel color. Onions can be prepared earlier in the day and heated before serving.

6	large onions, peeled, stemmed and cut into halves, crosswise
4	tablespoons butter, melted
4	tablespoons honey
2	tablespoons tomato sauce
1/2	cup chicken broth
1/4	teaspoon paprika
	salt to taste

In a 9x13-inch roasting pan, place onions, cut side down. Stir together the remaining ingredients and pour over the onions. Cover pan tightly with foil and bake in a 350° oven for 1 hour, or until onions are tender. Serves 12.

Burgundian Paupiettes of Beef with Mushroom Wine Sauce

This is a great dish to consider for a party. It can be prepared in advance, it is a medley of flavors and textures and it is delicious. This is not a difficult recipe, but it is a little more work...what with the stuffing and flaming. However, it cooks up in minutes, so that's the trade-off. Seasoned flour can be stored in the freezer indefinitely. It is good to have on hand for chicken or fish. The Mushroom Wine Sauce can be prepared a day earlier and heated before serving. Preparing 18 paupiettes is more than adequate for 12 servings. Leftovers are great the next day.

18	slices Spencer steaks (cut from the small end of a boneless rib roast.) Ask your butcher to cut these just under 1/4-inch thick. This will add up to about 2 1/2 pounds.
1	package (6 ounces) chicken flavored stuffing mix, prepared according to the directions on the package
1	egg, beaten
1/4	teaspoon thyme flakes
1/4	teaspoon sage flakes
1/2	cup butter or margarine
1/4	cup Cognac

Stir together stuffing mix, egg and herbs until blended. Place 1 tablespoon stuffing on the end of each steak, roll it up and fasten it with a toothpick. Roll it in Seasoned Flour. Melt 3 tablespoons butter in a skillet and saute the rolls until meat loses its pinkness, about 2 minutes on each side. Do not crowd the pan and do not overcook. (These steaks are exceedingly tender.)

Place beef rolls in a 9x13-inch metal baking pan. Warm the Cognac in a brandy warmer, ignite and carefully pour over the beef rolls. (Can be held at this point in the refrigerator.) Before serving, bring to room temperature and heat in a 300° oven until heated through. To serve, spoon a little sauce on top and pass the remaining sauce at the table. Serves 12.

Seasoned Flour:
Combine in a plastic bag and shake until blended, 1 cup flour, 2 teaspoons garlic powder, 1 tablespoon paprika, 1/2 cup grated Parmesan cheese and 1 teaspoon salt. Unused Seasoned Flour should be stored in the freezer.

More→

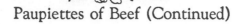

Mushroom & Wine Sauce:

1/2	pound mushrooms, sliced
2	cloves garlic, minced
1	shallot, finely chopped
3	tablespoons butter

1/4	cup dry white wine
1	can (10 1/2 ounces) beef broth
1	teaspoon Bovril (beef-seasoned stock base)
1	tablespoon Sauce Robert (from the market's gourmet section)
2	tablespoons chopped chives
1	tablespoon chopped parsley leaves
	salt and pepper to taste

In a saucepan, saute together first 4 ingredients until mushrooms are tender and liquid has evaporated. Add the wine and cook until the wine has evaporated. Stir in the remaining ingredients and simmer sauce for 5 minutes.

Creamed Mushrooms with Butter, Garlic & Herbs

This is a delightful dish to serve with roast chicken or veal.. The mushrooms are lavished with herbs and cream and sparkled with garlic.

1	pound mushrooms, cleaned and sliced
2	tablespoons lemon juice
1	onion, finely minced
4	shallots, finely minced
3	cloves garlic, finely minced
2	tablespoons butter

1/4	cup chopped parsley
1/4	cup chopped chives
1/2	teaspoon thyme
1/2	teaspoon poultry seasoning
	salt and pepper to taste

1/4	cup cream or half and half

In a large skillet, saute together first 6 ingredients until mushrooms are tender, onion is soft and all the liquid has evaporated.

Add the remaining ingredients and turn heat to moderately high. Mixture will bubble briskly and cream will evaporate into a shiny sauce. Serves 6.

Honey-Glazed Baby Carrots

Fresh baby carrots are sweet and tender and can be found in most supermarkets. There was a time when they were only available frozen, but now they are plentiful. These can be prepared earlier in the day and heated before serving.

2 pounds baby carrots

2 tablespoons butter
1 tablespoon honey
3 tablespoons minced parsley leaves
salt to taste

Cook baby carrots in boiling water for 8 minutes or until tender and drain. In a large skillet, place carrots and the remaining ingredients and cook and stir until carrots are all coated. Continue cooking and stirring for about 5 minutes, or until carrots are glazed. You may want to add a little butter and honey. Serves 12.

Casserole of Wild Rice with Apples & Chives

Wild rice, faintly sweetened with apple and sparkled with chives is a nice accompaniment to beef. This can be prepared earlier in the day and heated before serving.

1 cup wild rice
1 cup long-grain brown rice
4 cups chicken broth
2 tablespoons butter or margarine
salt and pepper to taste

1 apple, peeled, cored and grated
1 tablespoon butter

3 tablespoons chopped chives

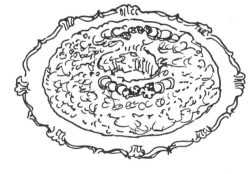

In a covered saucepan, place first group of ingredients, and simmer mixture for about 40 to 45 minutes, or until rice is tender. In a skillet, saute apple in butter until apple is tender. When rice is cooked, fluff it up with a fork and stir in the apple and chives. Serves 12.

Cognac Mousse with Ladyfingers, Raspberries & Chocolate

This is one of those grand desserts, light, delicious and memorable. It is great as a winter or summer dessert. I have served it so many times in the past, and the applause is always very flattering. This can be prepared 1 day earlier, covered with plastic wrap and stored in the refrigerator. If you prepare this dessert during the summer months, when raspberries are in season, decorate the top with a ring or two of fresh raspberries.

2   packages (12, each) ladyfingers, split in half. You will have 48 halves.

Cognac Mousse:
     2   tablespoons unflavored gelatin
1/2   cup Cognac

     2   cups cream, beaten until stiff

     6   eggs, at room temperature
3/4   cup sugar

Raspberry & Chocolate Toppings:
     1   package (10 ounces) frozen raspberries in syrup, defrosted

1/4   cup grated chocolate

Line the bottom of a 10-inch springform pan with parchment paper. Press 24 ladyfinger halves along the sides. Cover the bottom with the remaining ladyfingers. You will have to cut and patch a little to cover the bottom.

In a metal measuring cup, soften gelatin in Cognac. Place cup in a pan with simmering water and stir until gelatin is liquefied. Set aside. Beat cream until stiff and set aside.

Beat eggs with sugar until eggs are thick and lemon colored, about 8 minutes. Working quickly beat in the gelatin mixture and cream until blended.

Pour mousse into prepared springform pan and spread evenly. Refrigerate until firm. When firm, trim the tops of the ladyfingers and fold the tops over the mousse. This will create a scallop along the edge. Sprinkle top with grated chocolate. Refrigerate until serving time. To serve, cut into wedges and serve with a spoonful of raspberry sauce on top. Serves 12.

Soufflé Cakes with Chocolate Ganache

This is a great dessert…easy to prepare and easy to serve. Little soufflé cakes, set on a creamy chocolate sauce and topped with a little vanilla ice cream is simply lovely. An extra bonus…eggs do not have to be separated and best of all the soufflés can be prepared in advance. We had a very similar dessert at a restaurant recently, but they wouldn't share the recipe. This is an exact duplicate and probably a lot easier to prepare.

3	eggs, at room temperature
4	teaspoons sugar
2/3	cup semi-sweet chocolate chips, melted
1	teaspoon powdered (instant) espresso mixed with 1 tablespoon warm water
1	tablespoon rum

Butter 4 8-ounce ramekins and sprinkle with sugar to coat. Preheat oven to 375°. In the large bowl of an electric mixer, beat eggs until foamy. Gradually beat in the sugar and continue beating, at high speed, until eggs have tripled in volume, about 5 minutes.

Meanwhile, in the top of a double boiler, over hot, not boiling water, melt the chocolate. Slowly beat the chocolate into the egg mixture, until nicely blended. Beat in the coffee and rum just until blended.

Divide mixture between the 4 ramekins, place ramekins on a cookie sheet and bake at 375° for 20 minutes. Allow to cool. Cakes will settle and firm up a little. Run a knife along the edge and remove cakes to a porcelain baker. To serve, warm them at 350° for 5 minutes.

Place 1 cake on each plate, drizzle a little Chocolate Ganache on the side and place 2 small scoops of ice cream on the Ganache. Serves 4.

Chocolate Ganache:

3	tablespoons cream
1/3	cup semi-sweet chocolate chips
1	teaspoon rum

In a saucepan, heat cream. Add the chocolate and stir until melted. Stir in the rum. Serve sauce warm.

Note: -Recipe can be doubled or tripled.

Chocolate Decadence with Fudge Glaze

Deep, dark, delicious and totally decadent, is this moist chocolate cake, sparkled with the flavor of apricot and chocolate and beautiful with its dark, shiny chocolate glaze. Save this recipe for special moments, as this is what chocolate dreams are made of.

1/2	cup butter, (1 stick), softened
1	cup sugar
4	eggs
1/2	cup cocoa
1/2	cup water, at room temperature
2/3	cup flour
1 1/2	teaspoons baking powder
3/4	teaspoon baking soda
	pinch of salt (optional)
1/2	cup apricot jam

Cream butter with sugar. Beat in eggs, one at a time, beating well after each addition. Stir together cocoa and water and add, beating until blended. Stir together next 4 ingredients and add, all at once, beating until blended.

Divide batter between 2 parchment-lined 10-inch springform pans and bake at 350° for about 25 minutes, or until a cake tester, inserted in center, comes out clean. Allow to cool in pan.

When cool, place one layer on serving platter and spread top with apricot jam. Place second layer over and spread evenly with Fudge Glaze. Allow to set at room temperature. Cut into wedges to serve. Serves 12.

Fudge Glaze:
1/2	cup sugar
1/2	cup cream
1/2	cup cocoa, sifted
1/4	cup butter (1/2 stick)

In a saucepan, heat together all the ingredients, and simmer mixture, stirring, for about 5 minutes, or until glaze has thickened slightly. (If you own a candy thermometer, temperature should reach 236°.) Allow glaze to cool slightly before frosting cake.

New Year's Day Royal Champagne Brunch
A Toast to a New Year

Golden Caviar on Toast Points
Smoked Salmon Paté Cheesecake
Champagne

Scrambled Eggs with Brie, Raisins & Pine Nuts
Apricot Glazed Canadian Bacon
Spiced Apricots or Peaches with Walnuts
Croissants with Butter & Jams

Petite Breakfast Crescents with Walnuts & Raisins

Assorted Sweet Breads
Grand Banana Chocolate Chip Bread
Darling's California Carrot Bread
Country Pumpkin Bread
Coffee - Tea

Glamorous and exciting best describes this beautiful brunch. Sipping Champagne with golden caviar and smoked salmon cheesecake is a grand way to start a New Year. Everything on this menu can be prepared in advance except for the scrambled eggs which takes minutes to assemble.

Actually, the whole table can be set in advance the day before. Petite Breakfast Crescents and the sweet breads can be on their serving platter, wrapped in double thicknesses of plastic wrap. Spiced apricots or peaches can be place on a lovely rimmed platter and stored in the refrigerator. Canadian Bacon can be prepared and sliced the day before and stored in the refrigerator. Reheat before serving. Jams can also be ready in their servers the day before. Croissants can be purchased from your local bakery.

Planning is the key...as with all parties. But especially at brunch when guests are arriving early, do not leave anything for the last minute except the eggs and reheating the Canadian bacon. Spend the morning relaxing and feeling happy for the good time to come.

Golden Caviar on Toast Points

This is the easiest way to serve caviar, and to my taste, one of the best. Bland toast points, spread with the faintest amount of butter will allow the full flavor of the caviar to come through. Alternatively, serve with a dollup of Creme Fraiche or sour cream. Creme Fraiche can be prepared 2 days in advance.

    1   jar (3 1/2 ounces) golden or pink caviar

To make Toast Points:
    8   slices, thinly sliced good quality white bread, crusts removed
        butter

With a rolling pin, flatten bread slightly. Spread each slice with a thin coating of butter, and cut on the diagonal into 4 triangles. Place bread on a cookie sheet and bake at 350° until the first sign of color. They should be just lightly crisped, so do not allow to brown. Remove from oven and allow to cool. Store in a sealed plastic bag. Yields 32 toast points.

To make Creme Fraiche:
    1/3   cup sour cream
    1/3   cup cream

Stir together sour cream and cream until blended. Allow to stand at room temperature for 3 hours or until thickened. Refrigerate until serving time. Yields 2/3 cup.

Scrambled Eggs with Brie, Currants & Pine Nuts

Please don't be alarmed. This can partly be made in advance, then popped into a chafing dish, to keep warm. The touch of currants and pine nuts is a lovely complement to the Brie. Black currants can be plumped in boiling water for 5 minutes and then drained.

    2   tablespoons butter
    8   eggs, thoroughly beaten

    8   ounces Brie, cut off the rind and coarsely chop
    1/4   cup black currants, plumped
    1/4   cup pine nuts

In a large skillet, heat the butter until it is sizzling hot, but not brown. Add the eggs and stir gently until eggs are half set. Add the remaining ingredients and continue to cook and stir until eggs are almost completely set and cheese is melted. Transfer eggs to a heated chafing dish to keep warm. Yields 8 servings.

Smoked Salmon Paté Cheesecake in Cheese & Dill Cracker Crust

This is delicately flavored with salmon and dill with just a hint of garlic and herbs. While it is simple to prepare, it does serve in a grand manner. Decorated with rosettes of cream cheese and a sprinkle of dill and surrounded with cherry tomatoes and chive-sprinkled lemon slices, it is beautiful and delicious. This can be prepared a day earlier and stored in the refrigerator.

1	package (4 ounces) cream cheese with garlic and herbs. (Sold as Boursin or Rondole or Alouette.)
4	ounces cream cheese
1/4	cup chopped chives
1/2	teaspoon dried dill weed (or 2 teaspoons fresh dill weed)
3	eggs
3/4	cup cream
2	tablespoons lemon juice
2	ounces smoked salmon, cut into 1-inch pieces

Beat together first 7 ingredients until blended. Stir in the salmon. Spread mixture evenly into prepared crust and bake at 350° for 25 minutes, or until filling is set about 1-inch off center. Allow to cool and then refrigerate.

Carefully remove from pan and place on a platter. Decorate top with rosettes of Whipped Cream Cheese and Chives and a sprinkling of dill weed. Garnish platter with lemon slices sprinkled with chopped chives and cherry tomatoes. Serves 8 generously.

Cheese & Dill Cracker Crust:

1 1/2	cups cracker crumbs. (Use a tasty cracker like Waverly or Ritz)
1/4	cup grated Parmesan cheese
6	tablespoons melted butter
1/2	teaspoon dried dill weed

Stir together all the ingredients until blended. Pat mixture on the bottom of a 9-inch springform pan and bake at 350° for 8 minutes. Allow to cool for 10 minutes before filling.

To make Whipped Cream Cheese & Chives:
Beat a 3-ounce package of cream cheese until light and fluffy. Beat in 1 tablespoon chopped chives and 1 tablespoon lemon juice until blended. Place in a pastry bag with a star tip and pipe rosettes decoratively on top.

Apricot Glazed Canadian Bacon

2 pounds Canadian bacon or boneless ham round (ready to eat)

1/2 cup apricot jam
1/4 cup honey
1 tablespoon prepared mustard

Combine apricot jam, honey and mustard and heat until blended. Spread mixture over bacon or ham. Bake in a 375° oven for about 30 minutes or until meat is glazed. Cool. Slice thinly, reshape and place in a porcelain baker. Can be prepared a day earlier and reheated at time of serving. Serve garnished with Glazed Brandied Apricots. Serves 8.

Glazed Brandied Apricots:
12 dried apricots
1/4 cup orange juice
2 tablespoons sugar
1 tablespoon Apricot Brandy

In a saucepan, simmer together all the ingredients for 5 minutes, or until apricots are softened and mixture is syrupy.

Spiced Apricots or Peaches with Walnuts

8 fresh apricots or peaches, cut in half and pits removed
1/4 cup orange juice
1/2 teaspoon vanilla

3 tablespoons sugar or to taste
1/2 teaspoon cinnamon
pinch of nutmeg
pinch of ground cloves

1/3 cup chopped walnuts (optional but recommended)

Place apricots, cut side down, in a 9x13-inch baking dish. Stir together orange juice and vanilla and pour over the apricots. Stir together sugar and spices and sprinkle over the top. Bake at 350°, basting now and again, for about 15 minutes. Sprinkle nuts on top and continue baking for 10 minutes, or until apricots are tender and juices are syrupy. Serve warm or chilled. Serves 8.

Petite Breakfast Crescents with Walnuts & Raisins

These delicate little crescents are assembled in minutes and look and taste as if they were made with yeast. The dough is easily handled and very easy to work with.

1 cup cottage cheese
3 ounces butter (3/4 stick)
1 cup flour

Filling Ingredients:
1/2 cup finely chopped walnuts
1/2 cup finely chopped raisins
1/2 cup sugar
1 teaspoon cinnamon

cinnamon sugar

Beat together cottage cheese and butter until blended. Beat in flour until blended, about 1 minute. Shape dough into a ball and sprinkle with a little flour to ease handling. Cut dough into thirds. In a bowl stir together filling ingredients until blended.

Roll each third out on a floured pastry cloth to measure a 10-inch circle. Sprinkle 1/3 the filling ingredients over the dough, and cut dough into 8 triangular wedges. Roll each triangle from the wide end toward the center and curve into a crescent. Sprinkle with cinnamon sugar and place on a lightly buttered cookie sheet. Repeat with remaining dough.

Bake at 350° for about 30 to 35 minutes, or until tops are golden brown. Remove from the pan and allow to cool on brown paper. Yields 24 crescents.

To make Cinnamon Sugar:
In a glass jar with a tight-fitting lid, shake together 1/2 cup sugar with 2 teaspoons cinnamon until blended. Unused Cinnamon Sugar can be stored indefinitely.

Grand Banana Chocolate Chip Bread

1/2	cup butter, softened
1	cup sugar
2	eggs
1/2	cup sour cream
1	teaspoon vanilla

1 3/4	cups flour
1	teaspoon baking powder
1	teaspoon baking soda
	pinch of salt

1/2	cup semi-sweet chocolate chips
1/2	cup chopped walnuts
1	cup ripe coarsely mashed bananas (about 2 medium-sized)

Beat together first 5 ingredients until blended. Beat in next 4 ingredients just until blended. Do not overbeat. Divide batter between 4 greased mini-loaf foil pans (6x3x2-inches), place pans on a cookie sheet and bake at 325° for 45 to 50 minutes, or until a cake tester, inserted in center comes out clean.

Allow to cool in pans for 15 minutes, and then, remove from pans and continue cooling on a rack. Sprinkle with a little sifted powdered sugar. Or drizzle tops with Cream Glaze. Yields 4 loaves.

Cream Glaze:

2	tablespoons cream
3/4	cup sifted powdered sugar
1/4	teaspoon vanilla

Stir together all the ingredients until blended.

Darling's California Carrot Bread

1   package (3 ounces) cream cheese, softened
2   eggs
1   cup sugar
1/2   cup oil
3   small carrots, peeled and grated (about 1 1/2 cups)
1   teaspoon vanilla

1   cup flour
1   teaspoon cinnamon
1   teaspoon baking powder
1/2   teaspoon baking soda
  pinch of salt
1   cup chopped walnuts

Beat together first 6 ingredients until blended. Stir in the remaining ingredients just until blended. Do not overmix.

Divide batter between 4 greased mini-loaf foil pans (6x3x2-inches), place pans on a cookie sheet and bake at 350° for 45 minutes, or until a cake tester, inserted in center comes out clean.

Allow to cool in pans for 15 minutes, and then remove from pans and continue cooling on a rack. Sprinkle with a little sifted powdered sugar. Or swirl tops with Cream Cheese Frosting. Yields 4 loaves.

Cream Cheese Frosting:
1/4   cup butter
1/4   pound cream cheese
1 1/2   cups sifted powdered sugar
1   teaspoon vanilla

Beat together butter and cream cheese until blended. Beat in sugar and vanilla until blended.

Country Pumpkin Bread

1/4	cup butter, softened
1	cup sugar
2	eggs
1/3	cup orange juice
2	tablespoons grated orange (1/2 small orange, grated)
1	cup canned pumpkin puree
1/3	cup chopped raisins

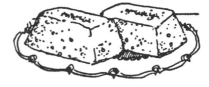

2	cups flour
2	teaspoons baking powder
1/2	teaspoon baking soda
2	teaspoons pumpkin pie spice
1	teaspoon cinnamon
1/4	teaspoon salt

Beat together first 7 ingredients until blended. Beat in remaining ingredients just until blended. Do not overbeat.

Divide batter between 4 greased mini-loaf foil pans (6x3x2-inches), place pans on a cookie sheet and bake at 350° for 45 minutes, or until a cake tester, inserted in center comes out clean.

Allow to cool in pans for 15 minutes, and then, remove from pans and continue cooling on a rack. A faint sprinkle of powdered sugar is nice. Or brush tops with Orange Peel Glaze. Yields 4 loaves.

Orange Peel Glaze:
1	tablespoon grated orange (use fruit, juice and peel)
1	tablespoon orange juice
1/2	cup sifted powdered sugar

Stir together all the ingredients until blended.

I'm Yours, Be Mine, Sweet Valentine
St. Valentine's Midnight Supper

Caviar with Toast Points

Russian Mini-Muffins with Smoked Salmon &
Creme Fraiche with Lemon & Dill

Champagne

Chocolate Walnut Torte with Cocoa Buttercream, or
Chocolate Fudge & Almond Torte with Chocolate Satin Glaze

This is a very simple but wonderful menu for Valentine's Day. It does not require a great deal of work...for this is a time when all the attention should be on you. All the recipes can be prepared in advance, and a day earlier. It does not require a lot of preparation time, but it can be expensive. If you own a heart-shaped 10-inch cake mold (with a removable bottom) it would be nice to use. But don't overdo the heart shapes. If you prepare the heart-shaped toast points, that's enough. Purchase the best Caviar and Champagne your budget will allow. And serve, of course, with an elegant air, with your best crystal and silver.

Caviar with Toast Points

Caviar should be served in your most glamorous crystal server. Surround it with Toast Points on a silver tray. No fussing this evening. All the attention should be on you. However, if you must fuss a little, Toast Points can be shaped into hearts, using a heart-shaped cookie cutter.

1   jar (2 ounces) caviar, the best you can afford

To Make Toast Points:
4   slices thinly sliced good quality white bread, crusts removed
    sweet butter

With a rolling pin, flatten bread slightly. Spread each slice with a thin coating of butter and cut it on the diagonal into 4 triangles. Place bread on a cookie sheet and bake at 350° until slightly crisped. Do not allow to brown. Remove from the oven and allow to cool. Store in a sealed plastic bag. Yields 16 Toast Points.

Russian Mini-Muffins with Salmon
& Creme Fraiche with Lemon & Dill

While this recipe yields more muffins than you will need, unused muffins can be frozen. Mini-muffins are served warm, not hot or cold. Room temperature is O.K. Creme Fraiche can be made with the light cream and light sour cream. However, non-fat sour cream cannot be substituted.

2	eggs, beaten
1	cup small curd cottage cheese
2	tablespoons sour cream
1	tablespoon melted butter
1	teaspoon sugar
1/2	teaspoon vanilla
1/2	cup Bisquick

Accompaniments:
2   ounces smoked salmon, thinly sliced and cut into 1-inch squares
1/2   cup Creme Fraiche with Lemon & Dill

Beat together all the ingredients until blended. Do not overmix. Grease small hors d'oeuvre-size teflon-lined muffin pans. Fill 1/2 full with batter. Bake at 350° for 25 minutes or until puffed and lightly browned. Tops will settle when cool. Serve warm with a dollup of Creme Fraiche with Lemon & Dill and a thin slice of smoked salmon. Caviar is also an excellent accompaniment. Yields 24 to 30 muffins.

Creme Fraiche with Lemon & Dill:
1/4   cup cream (or half and half)
1/4   cup sour cream (or low-fat sour cream)
1   tablespoon lemon juice
1/4   teaspoon dried dill weed

In a glass jar, stir together all the ingredients until blended. Allow to stand at room temperature for 2 hours and then, cover jar and refrigerate. Can be prepared 2 days earlier. Yields 1/2 cup.

Chocolate Walnut Torte with Apricot & Cocoa Buttercream

This is one of the finest tasting chocolate tortes. It presents beautifully, yet only takes minutes to prepare. This will give you plenty of time during the day to luxuriate in free time and to look and feel beautiful.

4	eggs
1	cup sugar
1	cup walnuts
1	teaspoon vanilla
2	tablespoons cocoa
1	teaspoon baking powder

1/3   cup finely chopped walnuts

1/3   cup heated apricot jam

In a food processor, beat together first 6 ingredients until the walnuts are almost pureed (just a little texture should remain), about 1 minute. Stir in the finely chopped walnuts. Pour batter into a greased 10-inch springform pan and bake at 350° for 20 to 25 minutes, or until a cake tester, inserted in center, comes out clean. Allow to cool in pan.

When cool, remove from pan and spread warmed apricot jam over the cake. Swirl Cocoa Buttercream on top and sides in a decorative fashion. Serves 8.

Cocoa Buttercream:
1	cup butter (2 sticks), softened
3/4	cup sifted powdered sugar
3	tablespoons sifted cocoa
1	teaspoon vanilla

Beat butter until light and creamy. Beat in the remaining ingredients until thoroughly blended.

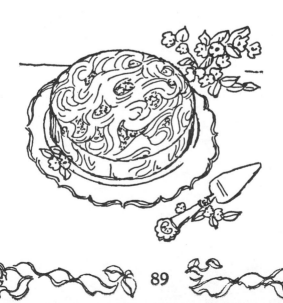

Chocolate Fudge & Almond Torte with Chocolate Satin Glaze

The words "sinful, decadent, devilish" are often used to describe chocolate dreams. Well, all of these adjectives can be used to describe this little fantasy. It is rich and delicious and should be prepared for a special occasion. Keep the portions small.

4	ounces almond paste
1/2	cup butter, at room temperature
1/2	cup sugar
3	eggs
2/3	cup (4 ounces) semi-sweet chocolate chips, melted
1/2	cup flour
1	teaspoon baking powder
1	teaspoon almond extract

Cream together almond paste, butter and sugar until mixture is light and fluffy. Beat in eggs, one at a time, beating well after each addition. Beat in the melted chocolate until blended. Beat in the remaining ingredients until blended.

Spread mixture into a greased 10-inch springform pan and bake at 350° for about 40 minutes, or until a cake tester, inserted in center, comes out clean. Allow to cool in pan. When cool, spread Chocolate Satin Glaze evenly over the top and allow it to stay at room temperature until serving. Serves 10.

Chocolate Satin Glaze:
In a blender or food processor, place 2/3 cup semi-sweet chocolate chips and 1 teaspoon vanilla. Bring 1/3 cup cream to a boil and pour over the chocolate. Blend until chocolate is melted and smooth.

Note: - If this is prepared 1 day earlier, it can be refrigerated. Allow to come room temperature before serving.

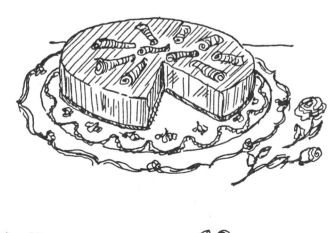

Four Family Dinners
to Celebrate Easter Sunday

Country Vegetable Soup
Baby Muffins with Cheese & Chives

Honey Baked Ham with Glazed Cinnamon Apple Rings
Noodle Pudding with Apples & Raisins
or
Honey Baked Ham
Apple & Pecan Cornbread Pudding
or
Butterflied Leg of Lamb with Lemon, Garlic, Dill Sauce
Bulgur Pilaf
or
Rosemary Lamb with Tomatoes, Lemon & Garlic
Toasted Barley with Mushrooms & Onions

Country Corn Pudding
Glazed Brandied Carrots

Royal Peach Tart on Butter Cookie Crust with Lemon Cream
Chocolate Chip & Pecan Pie
Hungarian Walnut & Apricot Squares on Lemon Shortbread
Torta de Pascal (Easter Lemon Ricotta Pie)

In this "Sky's the Limit" menu, vegetables are served early, in the soup, so you can get on to the wonderful dishes ahead. The muffins are made small so that appetites don't jade at the very start.

Lots of choices on this Holiday. Traditional Honey Baked Ham surrounded by beautiful Glazed Apple Rings, sparkled with a touch of cinnamon. Or a Honey Baked Ham with Apple & Cornbread Pudding. Two lamb roasts accompanied with bulgur or toasted barley are also lovely.

Glazed carrots are sparkled with Brandy. If Brandy is a problem, it can be omitted. The Glazed Carrots stand alone quite well. You will love the Corn Pudding. It is the essence of simplicity but so delicious.

A few desserts to choose from. The Chocolate Chip Pecan Pie is one of the best and I promise, everyone will ask for the recipe. The Royal Peach Tart is truly fit for a king and the Hungarian Walnut & Apricot Squares with the tart Lemon Glaze will please the most discriminating nut lover. Torta de Pascal is a lemony cheesecake pie and so appropriate this holiday. Enjoy.

91

Country Vegetable Soup

The only hard part in this recipe is chopping the vegetables. You can grate them in a food processor, but they are more attractive if you chop them by hand.

- 3   medium onions, finely chopped
- 3   shallots, finely chopped
- 6   cloves garlic, minced
- 3   carrots, very thinly sliced
- 4   tablespoons butter

- 5   cups chicken broth (can use 4 cans (10 ounces, each) chicken broth)
     salt and pepper to taste

- 1   package (10 ounces) frozen baby peas

In a Dutch oven casserole, saute together first 5 ingredients until onions are transparent. Add the broth and seasonings and, and simmer soup, with cover slightly ajar, for 30 minutes or until vegetables are tender. Add the peas and simmer for an additional 10 minutes. Serve in small bowls with Baby Muffins as an accompaniment. Serves 8.

Baby Muffins with Cheese & Chives

- 2   eggs, beaten
- 1   cup small curd cottage cheese
- 2   tablespoons sour cream
- 1   tablespoon oil
- 1   teaspoon sugar
- 1/2   cup grated Parmesan cheese
- 1/4   cup chopped chives
- 1/2   cup Bisquick, prepared biscuit mix

In the large bowl of an electric mixer, beat together all the ingredients until blended. Butter 24 teflon-coated hors d'oeuvre-size muffin cups and fill 1/2 full with batter. Bake at 350° for 25 minutes, or until puffed and golden. Yields 24 small muffins.

Honey Baked Ham
with Glazed Cinnamon Apple Rings

This is a traditional recipe for baked ham, sparkled with brown sugar, mustard and cloves. The apple rings are a nice accompaniment.

1 ready-to-eat ham, about 12 pounds, with bone in. With a sharp knife, remove the skin and fat, leaving a thin layer of fat to keep meat moist while baking. Score surface of ham in a diamond pattern, without cutting into the meat.

3 tablespoons Dijon mustard
whole cloves
1 cup brown sugar
1/2 cup honey

1 1/2 cups apple juice

Place ham in a roasting pan. Brush it with mustard and place a whole clove in half of the diamonds. Combine sugar and honey and spread over the ham. Pour apple juice into the pan. Bake in a 325° oven for 1 1/2 hours, basting now and again with the juices in the pan, or until a meat thermometer, set in the thickest part (not touching the bone), registers 160°. Serve ham surrounded with Glazed Apple Rings. Serves 12.

Glazed Cinnamon Apple Rings

4 large apples, cored and sliced into 3/4-inch rings
1/2 cup apple juice
3 tablespoons cinnamon sugar
pinch of nutmeg and cloves

1/2 cup chopped pecans

Place apple rings in a 9x13-inch baking pan, drizzle with apple juice, sprinkle with cinnamon sugar and spices. Bake in a 350° oven for 20 minutes, sprinkle top with pecans and continue baking for 10 minutes. Serves 8.

Honey-Baked Ham with
Apple & Pecan Cornbread Pudding

This is a grand way to serve ham, accompanied with a deeply fragrant apple and pecan pudding. The pudding is basically a stuffing baked in a separate pan. This is good served with chicken or turkey.

1	canned ham (about 5 pounds). Score top of ham in a diamond pattern with the tip of a knife. Do not cut deep into the meat. Place 1 clove in every other diamond.
1/2	cup honey
1/4	cup apple cider
1	teaspoon Dijon mustard
1/2	cup brown sugar

Bake ham according to the directions on the can. About 45 minutes before ham is finished cooking, combine honey, cider, mustard and sugar and brush this mixture on the ham.

Return ham to oven and continue baking until ham is finished cooking, basting once or twice. (Meat thermometer should register 170°.) Allow ham to rest for about 10 minutes to facilitate carving. Serve with Apple & Pecan Cornbread Pudding on the side.

Apple & Pecan Cornbread Pudding

1	package (8 ounces) cornbread stuffing mix
2	apples, peeled, cored and grated
1	cup chopped pecans
1	cup yellow raisins
2	teaspoons pumpkin pie spice
	pinch of powdered cloves
2	eggs, beaten
1	cup apple cider
1/2	cup honey or sugar
2	tablespoons melted butter

In a bowl, toss together first 6 ingredients until thoroughly mixed. Beat together the remaining ingredients and stir into fruit and nut mixture.

Place in a buttered 10-inch porcelain baker and bake in a 350° oven for 30 minutes or until top is just beginning to color. Serve with ham or chicken. Serves 8.

Butterflied Leg of Lamb with Lemon, Garlic & Dill Sauce

Tender spring lamb is another great dish to celebrate Spring. Lamb can be marinated in the refrigerator overnight. Sauce can be made 1 day earlier and stored in the refrigerator.

1   leg of lamb, (about 6 pounds), boned and trimmed of fat. Ask the
    butcher to cut into the thicker sections to make lamb as even
    as possible.

4   tablespoons oil
4   tablespoons lemon juice
6   garlic cloves, minced
1   teaspoon dried dill weed
    salt and pepper to taste

In a glass or enamel pan, place lamb. Combine the remaining ingredients and pour evenly over the lamb. Cover pan and allow to marinate in the refrigerator for several hours, or overnight turning now and again.

Remove lamb from marinade and place on broiler rack. Broil for about 15 minutes on each side, and about 6 inches from the heat. Broil until lamb is pink, or check with a meat thermometer in the thickest part of the meat. It should register 150° for medium-rare or 165° for medium.

To serve cut into slices and serve with Lemon, Garlic & Dill Sauce on the side. Serves 8.

Lemon, Garlic & Dill Sauce:
    2   tablespoons butter
    3   shallots, minced
    4   cloves garlic, minced

1/4   cup dry white wine
3/4   cup canned beef broth
  1   teaspoon Bovril (beef extract)
  1   tablespoon lemon juice
1/2   teaspoon dried dill weed
  1   tablespoon chopped chives
  1   teaspoon minced parsley

In a saucepan, saute together first 3 ingredients until shallots are soft. Add the wine and simmer mixture until wine has evaporated. Add the remaining ingredients and simmer sauce for 3 minutes. Cover pan and refrigerate until serving time. Heat before serving. Yields 1 cup.

Bulgur Pilaf with Red Peppers

1 1/2   cups bulgur (cracked wheat)
1   tablespoon margarine

3   cups chicken broth
1   tablespoon lemon juice
    salt to taste

1   medium red pepper, cored and diced
2   teaspoons butter

In a saucepan, saute bulgur in margarine, turning and stirring, until bulgur is beginning to take on color. Stir in the next three ingredients, cover pan, and bring to a boil. Lower heat and simmer mixture for 15 to 20 minutes, or until liquid is absorbed. Meanwhile, saute red pepper in butter until it is soft. When bulgur is cooked, stir in the cooked red pepper. Serves 8.

Noodle Pudding with Apples & Raisins

4   large apples, peeled, cored and grated
1/4   cup orange juice
1   tablespoon grated orange peel
4   tablespoons cinnamon sugar
1/2   cup yellow raisins

1   package (8 ounces) medium noodles, cooked and drained
1/4   cup melted butter

4   eggs, beaten
1/2   cup sugar
1 1/2   cups low-fat sour cream
1   teaspoon vanilla
    salt to taste

In a saucepan, cook together first 5 ingredients until apples are soft, about 20 minutes. In a 9x13-inch pan, toss together noodles and butter. Toss in apple mixture. Beat together the remaining ingredients until blended and pour evenly over the noodles. (Ease the noodles, here and there, so that the egg mixture is even.) Bake at 350° for about 1 hour or until top is golden and custard is set. Cut into squares to serve. Serves 12.

Glazed Brandied Carrots

1 1/2   pounds fresh baby carrots

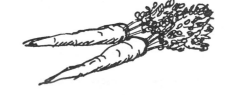

3   tablespoons butter
3   teaspoons sugar
1   tablespoon Cognac or Brandy
2   tablespoons chopped parsley

Cook carrots, covered in boiling water, until tender, about 15 minutes and drain. In a large skillet, heat together the remaining ingredients, add the carrots, and cook, tossing and turning, until carrots are shiny and glazed. Serves 8.

Country Corn Pudding

2   packages (10 ounces, each) frozen corn kernels, defrosted and
        patted with paper towelling to soak up moisture

3   eggs
1   cup half and half (or cream, if you can splurge a little)
1   tablespoon sugar
     salt to taste

Prepare corn. With a fork, beat eggs with the remaining ingredients just until blended. Stir in the corn. Place mixture into a 12x2-inch oval porcelain baker and bake at 350° for 35 to 40 minutes, or until custard is set. Serve it straight from the porcelain baker. Serves 8.

Rosemary Lamb
with Tomatoes, Lemon & Garlic

1   leg of lamb (about 6 or 7 pounds), boned, rolled, tied and trimmed of all visible fat.

1   can (1 pound 12 ounces) Italian plum tomatoes, undrained and coarsely chopped

20   cloves of garlic, peeled and left whole

1/4   cup lemon juice

1   teaspoon crumbled dried rosemary

salt and pepper to taste

Insert meat thermometer in thickest part of lamb and place in roasting pan. Stir together the remaining ingredients and place around the lamb. Bake at 425° for 20 minutes, lower heat to 350° and continue roasting for about 1 1/2 hours or until thermometer registers 150° for medium rare. (During this time, baste lamb with the juices in the pan and keep garlic covered with the tomatoes to make certain the garlic does not burn.)

Remove meat from pan and place on a serving platter. Surround with the tomato/garlic mixture. Garlic is very sweet at this point. Slice at the table. Serves 8.

Toasted Barley with Mushrooms & Onions

1 1/2   cups toasted egg barley

2   cups beef broth (canned or homemade)

1   cup water

1   tablespoon oil

salt and pepper to taste

1/2   pound mushrooms, sliced

1   large onion, chopped

2   tablespoons butter

In an 8x3-inch round baking pan, stir together first 6 ingredients, cover pan tightly with foil and bake at 350° for 45 to 50 minutes, or until barley is tender and liquid is absorbed. Meanwhile, in a large skillet, saute together next 3 ingredients until onion is soft and most of the liquid rendered is absorbed. Fluff barley with a fork and stir onion mixture into the barley. Nice to serve with lamb. Serves 8.

Royal Peach Tart on Butter Cookie Crust with Lemon Cream

This is a great tart to serve after a holiday dinner. It is truly delicious. If you can't find ripe peaches at this time of year, use the frozen peaches. Using frozen peaches, you can make this tart at any time of the year. This is best prepared on the same day as serving. It can be prepared earlier in the day and stored in the refrigerator. Fruit can weep and soften crust if prepared 1 day earlier.

Butter Cookie Crust:

2	cups flour
1/4	cup sugar
1	cup butter (2 sticks), softened
1	egg
3	tablespoons cream

Beat together flour, sugar and butter until mixture resembles fine meal. Beat together egg and cream and add, beating until just blended. Do not overbeat. Pat dough on the bottom and 1-inch up the sides of a greased and parchment-lined 10-inch springform pan and bake at 350° for 20 minutes, or until top looks dry and is just beginning to take on color.

Lemon Cream Filling:

1 1/2	pounds fresh peaches, peeled, stoned and sliced (or 1 pound frozen peaches, thinly sliced and drained)
1 1/2	cups sour cream
1	egg
6	tablespoons sugar
2	tablespoons grated lemon
1	teaspoon almond extract

Layer peaches into prepared crust, in a decorative manner. Beat together the remaining ingredients and pour evenly over the peaches. Bake at 350° for about 35 minutes, or until custard is set and just beginning to brown. Allow to cool in pan. When cool, remove from pan and cut into wedges to serve. Serves 8 to 10.

Chocolate Chip & Pecan Pie

Children love this pie...children of all ages, that is. This is a homey pie, easy to prepare and great for family dinners. It can look exciting if the top is decorated with rosettes or swirls of frosting. Sprinkle top with a faint spray of finely chopped chocolate. Vanilla wafers can be made into crumbs in a food processor. Chocolate chips can be finely chopped in a food processor.

3	eggs
1/2	cup sugar
2	cups vanilla wafer crumbs
1/2	cup sugar
1	teaspoon baking powder
1	teaspoon vanilla
1	cup coarsely chopped pecans
1	cup semi-sweet chocolate chips

Beat eggs with sugar until light and fluffy, about 5 minutes. Fold in the remaining ingredients until blended. Pour batter into a buttered 9-inch pie plate and bake at 350° for 30 minutes. Frost with rosettes of Chocolate Chip Cream and sprinkle top with a teaspoon of finely chopped chocolate. Refrigerate overnight. Serves 8.

Chocolate Chip Cream:

3/4	cup cream
1	tablespoon sugar
3	tablespoons finely chopped chocolate chips

Beat cream with sugar until stiff. Beat in chocolate chips.

Hungarian Walnut & Apricot Squares on Lemon Shortbread Cookie Crust

This is an adaptation of a delicious cookie my mother-in-law made often. She used apricot jam, but raspberry jam works very well, too. It is important to heat the jam as it will spread easily and will avoid tearing the crust. The Lemon Glaze is the perfect accent.

Lemon Shortbread Cookie Crust:

2	cups flour
1	cup sugar
1	cup cold butter (2 sticks), cut into 8 pieces
1	tablespoon grated lemon zest
1/2	cup apricot jam or raspberry jam, heated

In the large bowl of an electric mixer, beat together first 3 ingredients until mixture resembles fine meal. Toss in the lemon peel until blended. Pat dough on the bottom and 1-inch up the sides of a greased 9x13-inch baking pan and bake at 350° for 20 minutes, or until crust is just beginning to take on color.

Spread warmed jam evenly on crust. Pour Walnut Filling over the jam and smooth to spread evenly. Return pan to 350° oven and bake for another 30 minutes, or until a cake tester, inserted in center, comes out clean. Allow to cool in pan. Drizzle top with Lemon Glaze. Cut into small squares. Yields 48 cookies.

Walnut Filling:

4	eggs
2	cups brown sugar
1/4	cup flour
2	teaspoons vanilla
1	teaspoon baking powder
2	cups chopped walnuts

Beat together first 5 ingredients until nicely blended. Beat in the walnuts until blended.

Lemon Glaze:
Stir together 1 1/2 tablespoons lemon juice and 3/4 cup sifted powdered sugar. Add a little lemon juice or sugar to make glaze a drizzling consistency.

Torta de Pascal
(Easter Lemon Ricotta Pie)

Butter Cookie Crust:

1 1/2	cups flour
3/4	cup butter (1 1/2 sticks)
3	tablespoons sugar
2	tablespoons grated lemon
1	egg yolk
2	tablespoons water

In a food processor, beat together flour, butter and sugar until mixture resembles coarse meal. Pulse in the grated lemon only until blended. Beat together egg yolk and water and add, all at once, pulsing only until blended and dough holds together. Add a few drops of water, if necessary, to make a soft dough.

Pat dough on the bottom and 1-inch up the sides of a greased and parchment paper-lined 10-inch springform pan. Bake at 350° for 20 minutes or until crust is just beginning to take on color.

Spread Ricotta Filling evenly over the crust, return pie to oven and continue baking for 35 to 40 minutes, or until filling is set and lightly browned. Allow to cool in pan. Using the parchment paper to help you, slide pie onto a serving platter and cut into wedges to serve. Serves 10.

Ricotta Filling:

1	pound Ricotta cheese
1	package (8 ounces) cream cheese, at room temperature
1	cup sugar
1	tablespoon vanilla
3	eggs, at room temperature
1/2	lemon grated. (Use fruit, juice and peel. Remove any large pieces of membrane.)

Beat together first 4 ingredients until blended. Beat in eggs, 1 at a time, until blended. Beat in lemon until blended.

A Joyous Passover Seder

Seder Plate
Haroses
Roasted Shank Bone
Moror-Bitter Herbs (Parsley or Romaine Lettuce)
3 Matzas
Roasted Egg
Karpas-Green Vegetable
Salt Water

*

Delicate Mushroom & Lemon Soup
Poppyseed Onion Rolls for Passover

*

Easiest & Best Roast Chicken, or
Roasted Turkey Breast Roll, or
Chicken with Mushrooms, Lemon & Dill
Confit of Honeyed Onions
Roasted Garlic Potato Boats
or
Brisket with Peaches & Sweet Potatoes

*

Macaroons with Apricots, Coconut & Chocolate Dip
Chocolate Chip & Walnut Meringue Passover Pie
or Sour Cherry, Raisin, Apricot or Date Pie

Passover is one of the most celebrated of Jewish holidays. While different nations and cultures prepare foods in the mood of their country, the Seder plate is an ancient tradition. The Seder is a joyous meal where family and friends join together to celebrate the liberation of the Jewish people.

This menu is in the Greek mood with the accents of lemon and dill. The Mushroom Soup is one of the best, and lovely accompanied with little Passover rolls. Choose from chicken, turkey or brisket. The brisket is a meal unto itself, filled as it is with vegetables, fruit and sweet potatoes. The Macaroons are one of my favorites and the Chocolate Chip & Walnut Meringue Passover Pie will truly surprise you for its uniqueness. The many variations included produce a totally different pie in flavor and character.

Haroses

You will enjoy this Sephardic-style haroses. It is so delicious and versatile, you will enjoy using this on toast or muffins throughout the year. Also, very good on ice cream or frozen yogurt.

1/2	cup orange juice
3	medium apples, peeled, cored and grated
1	cup dried apricots, chopped (4 ounces)
1/2	cup yellow raisins
1/4	cup sugar
1	tablespoon lemon juice
1/2	cup chopped toasted walnuts

In a saucepan, simmer together first group of ingredients for about 30 minutes or until apples are soft. Stir in toasted walnuts.

Delicate Mushroom & Lemon Soup

1 1/2	pounds mushrooms, cleaned and thinly sliced
6	shallots, minced
6	cloves garlic, minced
2	tablespoons margarine
1/4	cup lemon juice
1/2	teaspoon dried thyme flakes
1/4	teaspoon ground poultry seasoning
1/3	cup dry white wine
1/2	teaspoon dried dill weed
	salt and pepper to taste
4	cups chicken broth

In a Dutch oven casserole, over low heat, saute together first group of ingredients until vegetables are softened, about 10 minutes. Stir in the next group of ingredients, cover pan, and continue to simmer for 20 minutes. Stir in the broth and simmer soup, uncovered, for 5 minutes. Serves 8.

Poppyseed Onion Rolls for Passover Holiday

Bread for Passover? No way you say. But these are actually made with matza meal, instead of flour. They are leavened with eggs and delicious to serve at any time of year. It is important to wet your hands while shaping the rolls. This will allow the rolls to expand. These are also wonderful when made with garlic and rosemary. Recipe follows.

1/2	cup margarine (1 stick), softened
1	cup water
2	tablespoons dried onion flakes
2	cups matza meal
1/2	teaspoon salt
1	tablespoon sugar
4	eggs
1	teaspoon poppy seeds

In a saucepan, bring margarine, water and onion flakes to a boil. Stir in matza meal, salt and sugar until blended. Cook for 1 minute, stirring.

Place dough into the large bowl of an electric mixer and beat in eggs, one at time, beating well after each addition. Beat in the poppy seeds.

With moistened hands, shape dough into 12 rolls and place on a greased cookie sheet. Cut a cross on the top of each roll. Bake in a 350° oven for about 50 minutes to 1 hour or until tops are golden brown. Yields 12 rolls.

Passover Rolls with Rosemary & Garlic:
Substitute 1/2 teaspoon coarsely ground garlic powder for the onions. Substitute 4 tablespoons crumbled rosemary for the poppy seeds.

Easiest & Best Roast Chicken

When you serve chicken with another main course, it usually means a big family dinner, where you are trying to please different palates. This is a very easy way to prepare chicken, and easily one of the best. The Basting Mixture produces the finest tasting chicken and turkey. Unused Basting Mixture can be stored in the refrigerator for 2 weeks.

    2   fryer chickens (about 3 pounds, each), cut into serving pieces
    1/2 cup chicken broth

Basting Mixture:
    1/2 cup margarine (1 stick)
    1   teaspoon garlic powder
    1   teaspoon onion powder
    2   teaspoons paprika

Place chicken pieces in 1 layer in a 12x16-inch baking pan. In a small saucepan, heat Basting Mixture ingredients and simmer for 1 minute. With a brush, baste chicken until nicely coated. Bake at 350° for 30 minutes. Add chicken broth to the pan and continue baking for 30 minutes, or until chicken is tender. Baste every 20 minutes during baking time. Serves 8.

Roasted Turkey Breast Roll

To assure that the turkey does not turn out dry and tasteless, do not overbake it. Most meat thermometers recommend poultry temperatures at 185° or 190°, but that is too high for the delicate breast. I have found that by removing it from the oven at 170° or 175°, it is juicy, succulent and delicious. As our family prefers the white meat, I always make an extra breast in addition to the big bird.

    1   boned turkey breast, rolled and tied (3 to 4 pounds net weight)
    1/4 cup chicken broth

Basting Mixture:
    1/2 cup margarine (1 stick)
    1   teaspoon garlic powder
    1   teaspoon onion powder
    2   teaspoons paprika

In a 9x13-inch baking pan, place turkey and broth. Brush turkey on all sides with Basting Mixture. Insert a meat thermometer in the thickest part of the roast, and bake at 350° until thermometer registers 170°. Allow to stand for 5 minutes, and then cut into slices. The gravy is a rich and delicious broth and does not need to be thickened. Serves 8.

Brisket with Peaches & Sweet Potatoes

- 4 pounds brisket of beef, trimmed of all fat
- 6 cloves garlic, minced
- 2 onions, chopped
- 4 carrots, cut into 1-inch pieces
- 1 package (6 ounces) dried peaches
- 12 pitted prunes
- 2 sweet potatoes, peeled and cut into 1-inch slices

- 1/2 cup peach jam
- 4 tablespoons brown sugar
- 1/4 cup ketchup
- 1 1/4 cups beef broth
- 1/2 cup white wine
  salt and pepper to taste

In a 12x16-inch baking pan, evenly place first 7 ingredients. Stir together the remaining ingredients and pour evenly over all. Cover pan tightly with foil and bake in a 350° oven for about 2 1/2 hours, or until meat is tender. Remove from the oven, allow to cool and then refrigerate.

When meat is cold, remove every trace of fat that has congealed on top. Slice the meat and return it to the pan with the fruit and vegetables. When ready to serve, heat in a 350° oven, covered with foil, until heated through, about 35 minutes. Serve surrounded with the fruit and vegetables. Serves 8.

Chicken with Mushrooms, Lemon & Dill

Mushroom, Lemon & Dill Sauce:
- 1/2 pound mushrooms, thinly sliced
- 4 shallots, minced
- 2 garlic cloves, minced
- 2 tablespoons margarine

- 1/3 cup dry white wine
- 1 cup rich chicken broth
- 1/2 teaspoon dried dill weed
- 2 tablespoons lemon juice
  salt to taste

Saute together first 4 ingredients until mushrooms are tender. Add the wine and cook until wine is almost evaporated. Add the remaining ingredients and simmer sauce for 10 minutes or until slightly reduced.

- 8 chicken breast halves, sprinkled with paprika, garlic and onion powders. Brush lightly with 3 tablespoons melted margarine.

Bake chicken at 350° for 20 minutes, or until just cooked through. Do not overbake. Place chicken on a serving platter and spoon a little sauce on top. Pass the remaining sauce at the table. Serves 8.

Confit of Honeyed Onions

        4   large onions, thinly sliced
        3   tablespoons oil

      1/3   cup dry white wine
        1   tablespoon sherry
        3   tablespoons honey
        2   tablespoons vinegar

In a large skillet, over low heat, cook onions in oil, stirring now and again, until onions are very soft and limp, but not fried. Add the wine, and continue cooking until most of the wine has evaporated. Stir in the remaining ingredients and cook and stir for another 2 minutes. Serve with roast chicken or meats. Serves 8.

Roasted Garlic Potato Boats

Potato boats are simply unpeeled potatoes that are cut into long wedges that resemble boats. They are seasoned and baked as you would any other roasted potato, but the shape adds a little interest. Garlic Potatoes have a wonderful flavor. Chicken broth replaces some of the oil.

        4   large potatoes (about 4 pounds), thoroughly scrubbed. Do not
              peel. Cut each potato in half, lengthwise, and cut each half
              into long wedges, about 3/4-inch thick.

        3   tablespoons oil
      1/2   cup chicken broth
        6   cloves garlic, finely minced
              salt and pepper to taste

Place potatoes in one layer in a 9x13-inch pan, standing them up as boats. Stir together the remaining ingredients and brush on the potatoes. Cover pan with foil and bake at 350° for 20 minutes. Remove foil, baste potatoes and continue baking and basting for 25 to 30 minutes, or until potatoes are lightly browned and crisped. Serves 8.

Macaroons with Apricots & Coconut with Chocolate Dip

These macaroons are a delicious choice for a Passover dessert. If you want to gild the lily, which I recommend, then dip the bottoms in chocolate. Use coconut flakes as shredded coconut is not fine enough. If you use shredded coconut, then finely chop it into flakes in the food processor before you begin. These can be prepared 1 day earlier and stored in an airtight container.

3	egg whites
3/4	cup sugar
1/2	cup dried apricots
1	teaspoon vanilla
2	cups coconut flakes
3	cups coconut flakes

In a food processor, finely chop the first 5 ingredients. Add the remaining coconut flakes and process for 30 seconds until mixture is very finely chopped. Place heaping tablespoons of macaroon mixture on a parchment-lined 12x16-inch baking sheet and bake for about 15 minutes or until tops are browned. Allow to cool on the parchment paper.

When macaroons are cool, dip the bottoms of the macaroons into Chocolate Dip, place them on a wax-paper-lined pan and refrigerate for 30 minutes or until chocolate is firm. Remove from wax paper and place on a serving platter. Can be stored at room temperature, in an airtight container, if preparing ahead. Do not refrigerate again. Yields 30 macaroons.

Chocolate Dip:

1/2	cup semi-sweet chocolate chips
2	tablespoons margarine

In the top of a double boiler over hot, not boiling water, melt chocolate with margarine. Stir until nicely mixed. Remove pan from heat and dip the macaroons.

To melt chocolate in the microwave:
Place chocolate and margarine in a small bowl and microwave mixture for 3/4 of a minute. Turn the bowl and microwave again for an additional 1/2 minute. Stir until everything is nicely mixed.

Chocolate Chip & Walnut Meringue Passover Pie

What a surprise this pie will be for a Passover dinner. It should be prepared 1 day earlier and stored in the refrigerator to allow meringue to soften. The chocolate chips used to decorate the pie can be chopped in a food processor.

3	egg whites
	pinch of salt
1	cup sugar
1	cup matza meal
3/4	cup chopped walnuts
3/4	cup semi-sweet chocolate chips

In the large bowl of an electric mixer, beat egg whites with salt until foamy, Slowly add the sugar and continue beating until whites are stiff, but not dry. On low speed, beat in the remaining ingredients. Place mixture into a 9-inch pie plate and bake at 350° for 25 to 30 minutes, or until top is lightly browned. Allow to cool in pan. When cool, frost with Whipped Dzertwhip and decorate with finely chopped chocolate chips on top. Serves 10.

To make Whipped Dzertwhip:
Beat 1 cup Dzertwhip until it is as thick as whipped cream. Dzertwhip is a trade name for a non-dairy whipped topping. While it may not be available in all parts of the country, a similar product should be available in most supermarkets. Dzertwhip, is treated just like cream and should be whipped until spreading consistency. It comes sweetened, so it is not necessary to add sugar.

Note: If preparing this for a dessert table, then 1/2 cup cream whipped with 1 teaspoon sugar can be substituted for the Dzertwhip.

To Make Sour Cherry & Walnut Pie:
Delete chocolate and add 1 cup canned and pitted sour cherries, drained.

To Make Raisin & Walnut Pie:
Delete chocolate and add 1/2 cup yellow raisins and 1/2 teaspoon cinnamon.

To Make Apricot & Walnut Pie:
Delete chocolate and add 2/3 cup chopped dried apricots.

To Make Date & Walnut Pie:
Delete chocolate and add 2/3 cup chopped dates.

Rosh Hashanah
Two Menus for "A Sweet New Year"

Best Challah Bread with Poppy Seeds
Holiday Raisin Challah

❧

The Best Chopped Liver
Cocktail Rye Bread

❧

Petite Knishes with Potatoes & Onions
Beef & Barley Mushroom Soup

❧

Holiday Brisket of Beef
Tzimmes
Large Potato Pancake, or
Individual Potato Pancakes
Orange Applesauce
or
Old-Fashioned Stuffed Roast Chicken
Sweet Potato Pancake with Cinnamon, Orange & Apples, or
Roasted Potatoes with Onions & Tomatoes, or
Roasted Potatoes with Peppers & Onions

❧

Brussels Sprouts with Garlic & Dill
Honey Glazed Carrots with Shallots & Dill

❧

Easiest & Best Old-Fashioned Orange & Lemon Sponge Cake
Easiest & Best Date Nut Chewies
Apricot Nut Chewies
Chocolate Chip Chewies
The Best Mandelbread

This menu has some of the best traditional recipes and can be used for many holidays. All of the dishes have been coordinated so that you can choose either the Brisket or Chicken menu with any of the accompaniments. If you choose not to bake the Challah, then purchase the best you can find. Chopped Liver, Knishes, Beef & Barley Soup, all my interpretations of the classic favorites.

Brisket served with Tzimmes, Potato Pancakes, Orange Applesauce are very traditional. Chicken served with a Kugel, made with sweet potatoes and fruit is really great...as are the 2 very excellent potato casseroles. Choose one now...there is always next year. Pick a few cookies. Make these earlier in the month, for they freeze well. Enjoy.

Best Challah Bread with Poppy Seeds

This is a divine loaf. Baking bread is like a religious experience. Enjoying it with sweet butter is the stuff poetry is made of. It is a little more work, but worth every bit of it, I promise you. You must use a paddle beater, or a dough hook. The rotary beaters will not work for this method of preparation.

1	package dry yeast
1	cup warm water (105°)
2	heaping tablespoons sugar
2	cups flour
3/4	teaspoon salt
3/4	cup butter or margarine, softened
4	eggs
3	cups flour
1	egg yolk mixed with 1 teaspoon water for egg wash
	poppy seeds

In the large bowl of an electric mixer, place yeast, water and sugar. Allow to rest for 10 minutes or until yeast is dissolved and starts bubbling. Add the 2 cups of flour and salt and beat for 30 seconds. Beat in butter and eggs, beating well after each addition. Beat for 3 minutes using the paddle beater.

Beat in 2 cups of the remaining flour and beat another 3 minutes. Add the remaining 1 cup of flour and beat another 3 minutes. Place dough in an oiled bowl and then turn, so that it is oiled on top. Cover with a towel and allow to rise in a warm place until it is doubled in bulk, about 1 hour. Punch dough down and cut off 1/4 of it. Now, cut the larger piece and the smaller piece into 3 sections. Roll each piece into a rope, 12-inches long.

Braid the 3 larger ropes, tuck in the ends and place on a greased cookie sheet. Braid the 3 smaller ropes and place on top of the larger braid. Baste the top and sides with the egg wash and sprinkle generously with poppy seeds. Allow to rise again, for 1 hour or until doubled in bulk. Bake in a 400° oven for 35 minutes or until top is golden brown and bread sounds hollow when thumped. If bread is browning too quickly, tent loosely with foil. Allow to cool in pan and cut into slices with a serrated knife. Yields 1 large 12-inch loaf.

To make Holiday Raisin Challah:
Add 1 cup yellow raisins to the dough and substitute sesame seeds for the poppy seeds. Everything else remains the same.

The Best Chopped Liver

The difference between paté and chopped liver is "panache." This is the homey kind, filled with the tastiest fried onions. While it appears to be made with an inordinate number of onions, do no despair. The end result is delicious. Leave the thin layer of fried onions on the bottom as a surprise.

6	large onions, chopped
6	tablespoons margarine
1 1/2	pounds chicken livers, connective membranes removed, and cut into 1-inch pieces
2	tablespoons margarine
4	hard-boiled eggs

In a large skillet, over high heat, fry onions in margarine until onions are a deep golden brown. Place 3/4 of the onions in a food processor and reserve 1/4 of the onions.

Saute chicken livers in margarine until meat loses its pinkness. Do not over cook, but do not undercook, either. Place chicken livers and eggs in the food processor with the onions. Pulse mixture until everything is very finely chopped, but not pureed.

Line a 4-cup mold with plastic wrap and press chopped liver evenly into it. Place reserved onions on the top. Cover mold with plastic wrap and refrigerate for several hours. Overnight is good, too.

To unmold, remove plastic cover, invert mold onto a serving platter, and remove plastic lining. Voilá, the most intricate mold is uncovered, intact and without fuss. (This is the easiest and best way to unmold patés and sticky fillings.) Serve with thin slices of cocktail rye bread. Champagne Crackers are very good, too. Yields about 4 cups.

Petite Knishes with Potatoes & Onions

Let me say, right at the start, that the Potato & Onion Filling gives these the name of "knishes." Fill them with mushrooms and they become Piroshkis. These little knishes have to be one of the best-tasting hors d'oeuvres. They are also a great accompaniment to a hearty soup, like Mushroom Barley. I recently prepared these for a Super Bowl game and everybody loved them. Traditionally made with a heavy-duty dough, making these with puff pastry truly elevates them to gastronomical heights. I have further simplified preparation using the potato flakes. This is o.k. as the flavor of the onions takes over.

Onion Potato Filling:
- 3   large onions, chopped
- 3   tablespoons margarine

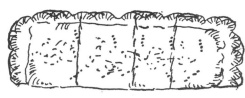

- 3   cups instant mashed potato flakes
- 3   cups boiling water
- 3   tablespoons margarine
-     salt and freshly ground pepper to taste

Saute onions in margarine for about 20 minutes, or until onions are lightly browned. (Careful not to burn or onions will be bitter.) Meanwhile, add the boiling water to the potato flakes, stir in the margarine and salt with a good grind of pepper. Add a few more potato flakes, if necessary, to form a stiff filling. Stir in the browned onions. Allow mixture to cool.

Puff Pastry:
- 1   package (17 ounces) Pepperidge Farms Puff Pastry (2 sheets)
- 1   egg, beaten
- 12   tablespoons grated Parmesan cheese

Cut pastry sheets in thirds on the fold. Cut each third in half crosswise. You will have 12 pieces. On a floured pastry cloth, roll out each piece to measure 4x8-inches. Place a few tablespoons Potato Onion Filling along the 8-inch side, fold dough over and press edges down with the tines of a fork. Scallop the edges.

Place knishes on a greased cookie sheet, brush tops with beaten egg and sprinkle with cheese. Pierce tops in 4 or 5 places with the tines of a fork. Bake at 400° for 25 to 30 minutes, or until tops are nicely browned. Remove from pan and allow to cool on brown paper.

To reheat, place knishes on a cookie sheet, cut each into 4 pieces and heat in a 350° oven for 15 minutes, or until heated through. Yields 48 knishes.

Beef & Barley Mushroom Soup

This is a nice, thick, homey soup that is a good choice for an informal Sunday night dinner with family and friends. It can be prepared earlier in the day and heated before serving.

- 2 cans (10 1/2 ounces, each) beef broth
- 1 cup chicken broth
- 1 large onion, finely chopped
- 2 carrots, grated
- 1/2 cup pearl barley
- 1/2 pound boneless chuck, cut into 1/2-inch cubes

- 1/2 pound mushrooms
- 2 teaspoons oil

- 1 tablespoon chopped parsley
- salt and pepper to taste

In a covered Dutch oven casserole, place first group of ingredients and simmer mixture until barley and beef are tender, about 1 hour. Meanwhile, saute mushrooms in oil until they are tender and add to soup. Stir in the parsley and seasonings and heat through. Serves 8.

Brussels Sprouts with Garlic & Dill

- 2 packages (10 ounces, each) frozen Brussels sprouts
- 1/2 cup chicken broth
- 1 tablespoon lemon juice
- 1/4 teaspoon dried dill weed

- 2 cloves garlic, minced
- 1 tablespoon margarine
- 1/3 cup fresh bread crumbs
- salt and pepper to taste

In a saucepan, simmer together first 4 ingredients until sprouts are tender and drain.

Meanwhile in a skillet, saute garlic in margarine for 2 minutes, but do not let garlic brown. Toss in the bread crumbs and seasonings. Toss crumb mixture with sprouts and heat through. Serves 8.

Holiday Brisket of Beef

This is a basic preparation for brisket. For the best flavor, onions should be sauteed until a dark color. Gravy is delicious and does not need to be thickened. Entire dish can be prepared 1 day earlier and reheated at the time of serving with excellent results. Beer can be substituted with white wine or beef broth.

4	pounds brisket of beef, lean and trimmed of all visible fat, and sprinkled with salt, pepper and garlic powder

4	medium onions
3	tablespoons oil
1 1/2	cups beer or white wine or beef broth
3/4	cup ketchup
1/2	cup brown sugar

Place brisket in a 9x13-inch roasting pan. In a large skillet, saute the onions in oil until onions are beginning to brown. Place onions on brisket. Combine remaining ingredients and pour over the meat.

Cover pan tightly with foil and bake in a 350° oven until fork tender, about 2 1/2 hours. Remove from the oven and allow to cool in the refrigerator for several hours.

When cold, remove any fat that has congealed on top. Slice meat and return to pan with gravy. When ready to serve, heat in a 350° oven, covered with foil, for about 45 minutes or until meat is tender. Serves 8.

Honey Glazed Carrots with Shallots & Dill

4	shallots, minced
2	teaspoons margarine
2	package (1 pound, each) baby carrots
4	teaspoons honey
2	tablespoons chopped parsley
1	cup chicken broth
	salt and pepper to taste
1/2	teaspoon dried dill weed

In a saucepan, saute shallots in margarine until transparent. Add the remaining ingredients, cover pan and cook over low heat, until carrots are tender. Serves 8.

Tzimmes

(Sweet Potatoes, Carrots & Dried Fruit Casserole)

This is an unusual Tzimmes recipe, in that it is made without meat. It is great to serve with brisket, roast chicken, or pot roast. This is actually very simple to prepare...boil the carrots, soften the dried fruit and assemble the casserole. It can be prepared 1 day earlier, stored in the refrigerator and heated before serving.

1 package (1 pound) baby carrots

1 can (1 pound 12 ounces) sweet potatoes, drained and cut into 1-inch thick slices

1 package (1 pound) mixed dried fruits-a combination of dried apricots, peaches, apples, pears and prunes. (Make certain that the prunes are pitted.)

1 1/2 cups orange juice

4 tablespoons cinnamon sugar

6 sprinkles ground cinnamon or to taste

In a saucepan, cook carrots in boiling water until tender, about 15 minutes. Place carrots evenly in a 9x13-inch baking pan. Place sweet potatoes evenly over the carrots.

In a saucepan, simmer together dried fruits, orange juice and cinnamon sugar, until fruits are tender, about 10 minutes. Place fruits and juice evenly over the sweet potatoes. Sprinkle top lightly with cinnamon. Can be held at this point, covered, in the refrigerator. Before serving, add a little orange juice if casserole appears dry. Heat, loosely tented with foil, in a 350° oven for 30 minutes, or until piping hot. Serves 12.

Large Potato Pancake with Orange Applesauce

If you find that you do not have enough time to prepare individual potato pancakes, this can be made in a 9x13-inch baking pan and cut into squares to serve. It can be prepared earlier in the day, chilled and cut into squares. Reheat in a 400° oven until hot and crisped. Recipe for individual pancakes follows.

6	potatoes, peeled and grated
3	small onions, grated
2	eggs, beaten
1/2	cup matza meal
	salt and pepper to taste
2	tablespoons salad oil
1	tablespoon salad oil

Grate potatoes just before preparation so that the batter does not darken. If you grate potatoes earlier, cover them with cold water and drain in a collander, place on a kitchen towel and pat dry before using.

In a large bowl, combine potatoes, onions, eggs, matza meal and seasonings. Spread 2 tablespoons oil in a 9x13-inch baking pan. Add potato mixture and spread evenly. Drizzle 1 tablespoon oil over top.

Bake at 350° for about 1 hour or until top is crusty and browned. Cut into squares to serve. Serve with Orange Applesauce on the side. Serves 12.

Orange Applesauce:
1   jar (1 pound) unsweetened applesauce
6   tablespoons concentrated orange juice, undiluted

Stir together applesauce and orange juice until blended.

To Prepare as Individual Potato Pancakes:
In a skillet, heat 2 tablespoons oil until sizzling hot. Form pancakes with 1/4 cup potato mixture. Do not crowd pan. When bottom is browned, turn and brown other side. Place in a jelly roll pan in one layer. Continue with remaining potato mixture, adding a little oil as necessary. To retain crispness, when reheating, do not stack the pancakes, but heat them in one layer. Reheat at 400° until hot and crusty. Yields 24 pancakes.

Old-Fashioned Stuffed Roast Chicken, Seasoned with Herbs & Spices

1   large roaster chicken (about 5 pounds)
1   package (12 ounces) Herb-Seasoned Stuffing Mix

1   onion, finely chopped
1/2 cup celery, finely chopped
1/4 cup margarine (1/2 stick)
1/4 pound mushrooms, thinly sliced

1   egg, beaten
3   tablespoons, chopped parsley
1   teaspoon chicken seasoned stock base
1   teaspoon poultry seasoning
    salt and pepper to taste
3   cups chicken broth. (Use only enough to hold stuffing together.)

Place stuffing mix in a large bowl and set aside. Saute onion and celery in margarine until soft. Add mushrooms and saute until mushrooms are tender. Add vegetables to stuffing mix. Add remaining ingredients using only enough chicken broth to hold stuffing together. Set aside

Baste entire chicken, inside and out with Basting Mixture. Stuff and skewer chicken (see below) and baste again. Roast in a 350° oven for about 2 hours, basting every 15 to 20 minutes. Remove from oven, cut string and remove pins and string. Serve with hot biscuits and gravy. Serves 8.

Basting Mixture:
   1/3 cup melted margarine
   1/8 teaspoon salt
   1/8 teaspoon pepper
1 1/2 teaspoons paprika
   3/4 teaspoon garlic powder
   3/4 teaspoon onion powder

In a bowl, stir together all the ingredients.

To Stuff and Skewer Chicken:
Place stuffing loosely into neck and body of chicken. Pull neck skin over to back and skewer it down. Skewer body opening with 2 or 3 poultry pins. Lace strings around pins, back and forth. At the last turn, bring the string under the legs and tie them together. Tuck wings under.

To Make Gravy:
In a saucepan, place all the juice from the drippings from which all the fat has been removed. Add 1 cup of chicken broth and simmer mixture for 5 minutes. This is not a heavy gravy, but light, fresh and more like a broth. It can be thickened by stirring in 1 tablespoon flour, but not recommended.

Sweet Potato Pancake
with Cinnamon, Orange & Apples

This is one of my best inventions. If you are looking for a new and delicious way to prepare sweet potatoes, please don't wait for a holiday, but make this casserole soon. Grated sweet potatoes, flavored with orange and apples and sparkled with cinnamon is truly fit for a king. It is especially good to serve with turkey, brisket, or roast chicken. Potatoes and apples can be grated in a food processor. Orange should be grated, with short strokes, on the 3rd largest side of a 4-sided grater.

2	pounds sweet potatoes, peeled and grated.
2	medium apples, peeled, cored and grated
1	medium orange, grated, (about 6 tablespoons fruit, juice and peel)
1/2	cup orange juice
1/2	cup matza cake meal
3	eggs, beaten
1/2	cup Cinnamon Brown Sugar
	salt to taste
1/4	cup melted margarine
4	tablespoons Cinnamon Brown Sugar

In a large bowl, mix together first 8 ingredients until blended. Place melted margarine into a buttered 9x13-inch baking pan and spread potato mixture evenly in pan. Sprinkle top with Cinnamon Brown Sugar. Bake at 350° for 1 hour, or until potatoes are tender and top is browned. Cut into squares to serve. Serves 8.

To Make Cinnamon Brown Sugar:
In a glass jar with a tight-fitting lid, shake together 1 cup sifted brown sugar and 1 tablespoon sifted cinnamon.

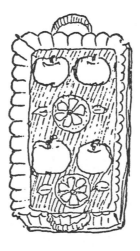

Roasted Potatoes with Onions & Tomatoes

This is one of the easiest casseroles to prepare and one of the most delicious to serve. It is great with roasted meats or poultry.

1/4 cup olive oil
2 pounds potatoes, peeled and thinly sliced
3 medium onions, thinly sliced and separated into rings
4 tomatoes (about 1 pound) thinly sliced

1 can (10 1/2 ounces) chicken broth
6 cloves garlic minced
1 teaspoon dried thyme flakes
salt and pepper to taste

In a 12x16-inch roasting pan, spread olive oil evenly. Layer potatoes, onions and tomatoes evenly on top. Mix together the broth, garlic, thyme and seasonings and pour evenly over all. Tent loosely with foil and bake at 350° for about 1 hour or until potatoes are tender. Serves 8.

Roasted Potatoes with Peppers & Onions

1/4 cup olive oil
2 pounds potatoes, peeled and thinly sliced
2 medium onions, thinly sliced and separated into rings
2 green bell peppers, cored, seeded and cut into strips
2 red bell peppers, cored, seeded and cut into strips

1 can (10 1/2 ounces) chicken broth
6 cloves garlic minced
1 teaspoon dried thyme flakes
salt and pepper to taste

In a 12x16-inch roasting pan, spread olive oil evenly. Layer potatoes, onions and peppers evenly on top. Mix together the broth, garlic, thyme and seasonings and pour evenly over all. Tent loosely with foil and bake at 350° for about 1 hour or until potatoes and peppers are tender. Serves 8.

Easiest & Best Old-Fashioned Orange & Lemon Sponge Cake

The classic sponge cake requires separating eggs, beating yolks and whites separately, delicately folding both together. My sponge cake eliminates all these steps and is truly wonderful.

6   eggs
1   cup sugar

1   cup sifted flour

3   tablespoons grated orange (about 1/2 medium orange)
2   tablespoons grated lemon
2   teaspoons vanilla

In the large bowl of an electric mixer, beat eggs and sugar at high speed until eggs have tripled in volume and are light and frothy, about 6 to 8 minutes. On low speed, beat in flour just until blended. Do not overbeat. Fold in the remaining ingredients until blended.

Spread batter evenly into a 10-inch ungreased tube pan (one with a stand for inverting) and bake at 350° for 40 to 45 minutes or until a cake tester, inserted in center, comes out clean. Do not overbake. Remove from the oven, invert, and allow to cool.

When cool, remove from pan, place on a lovely platter and serve with a dollup of frozen yogurt or non-dairy whipped topping with a spoonful of strawberries in syrup. Serves 12.

To Make Passover Sponge Cake:
In the above recipe, use 1/2 cup matza cake meal and 1/2 cup potato starch instead of the flour. Cake will not rise as high.

Easiest & Best Date Nut Chewies

This homey cookie always gets more compliments. Somehow, every one loves the texture and taste of these simple-to-prepare cookies. I hope you agree.

2	eggs
1/2	cup oil
1	teaspoon vanilla
3/4	cup flour
1/2	teaspoon baking powder
	pinch of salt
3/4	cup sugar
1	cup chopped pitted dates
1	cup coarsely chopped walnuts

Beat together first 3 ingredients until blended. Beat in next 4 ingredients until blended. Beat in dates and walnuts until blended. Spread mixture into a lightly greased 12x7-inch baking pan and bake at 350° for 25 minutes.

Allow pan to cool until able to handle. Cut into 1-inch squares while warm. Remove cookies from pan and allow to cool on brown paper. When cool, store in an airtight container. Sprinkle faintly with sifted powdered sugar to serve. Yields 72 small cookies.

To Make Easiest & Best Apricot Nut Chewies:
Substitute 1 cup chopped dried apricots for the dates.

To Make Easiest & Best Raisin Cookies:
Substitute 1 cup raisins for the dates.

To Make Easiest & Best Chocolate Chip Chewies:
Substitute 1 cup semi-sweet chocolate chips for the dates.

The Best Mandelbread

Traditionally, mandelbread is shaped by hand into flat loaves. Using the foil pans insures uniformity. This is my favorite mandelbread. While it is crisp, it is also chewy and the flavor is sublime. Nuts can be varied...pecans, almonds, hazelnuts are all good. Cherries can be substituted with any number of dried or glaceed fruits. Chocolate chips and pecans are great, too. As these cookies freeze beautifully, I have balanced the recipe to yield 6 dozen cookies. Freeze in double plastic bags. Recipe can be halved. To facilitate removing the warm loaves, be certain to use foil pans.

1	cup butter (2 sticks)
2	cups sugar
6	eggs
2	teaspoons vanilla
4	cups flour
1	tablespoon baking powder
2	cups chopped walnuts
2	cups glaceed cherries, coarsely chopped

Cream together butter and sugar until creamy. Beat in eggs, one at a time, beating well after each addition. Beat in vanilla until blended. Combine flour and baking powder and beat in until blended. Beat in walnuts and cherries until blended.

Divide dough into 6 greased and lightly floured foil loaf pans, 9x5-inches. Bake at 350° for about 30 minutes or until tops are lightly browned. Remove from the oven and allow to cool until pans can be handled.

Ease loaves out of the pans and place on a cutting board. Use a very sharp knife to cut into 3/4-inch slices. Place mandelbread slices on a cookie sheet and return to oven to lightly toast on both sides. Yields 6 dozen cookies.

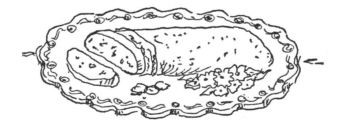

After Taxes Party
April 16th

Tomato & Red Onion Salad with Basil, Lemon & Cheese, or
Broiled Marinated Vegetable Salad

Old-Fashioned Meat Loaf
Easiest & Best Mashed Potatoes
Red Cabbage with Apples & Raisins

Family Chocolate Bread Pudding with Creme Vanilla

This is an informal, inexpensive dinner to serve after April 15th. It is a fun dinner, too. Meat Loaf is getting more and more popular lately. I guess, every so often it feels good to go back to basics. The Mashed Potatoes are traditional. Garlic Mashed Potatoes (see Index) are so delicious, you may want to substitute them.

Chocolate Bread Pudding is a great dessert and the Creme Vanilla is actually Whipped Creme Fraiche. So while this is a homey dinner, it is sparkled with some elegant touches.

Tomato & Red Onion Salad
with Basil, Lemon and Cheese

6   tomatoes, thinly sliced
6   thin slices red onion, separated into rings

1/4 cup grated Parmesan cheese
2   tablespoons olive oil
4   tablespoons lemon juice
1   clove garlic, put through a press
2   tablespoons parsley leaves
1   teaspoon sweet basil leaves
    salt and freshly ground pepper to taste

Place tomatoes and onion in a bowl. In a jar, shake together the remaining ingredients. Pour dressing over tomatoes and onions and toss to coat well. Refrigerate salad for several hours to allow flavors to blend. Serves 6.

Red Cabbage with Apples & Raisins

1   red cabbage, (about 1 pound), remove the hard central core and
        grate. This can be done in a food processor.
2   large apples, peeled, cored and grated
1   large onion, chopped
1   cup chicken broth
     salt and pepper to taste

3   tablespoons lemon juice
1   tablespoon honey
1/2   cup yellow raisins

In a covered Dutch oven casserole, simmer together first group of ingredients
for 40 minutes. Stir in the next 3 ingredients and continue cooking for 10
minutes, uncovered, or until cabbage is very tender. Serves 6.

Broiled Marinated Vegetable Salad

*This is an interesting colorful salad, very delicious, and very filling. It is glamorous
served warm and delicious when served cold. If you plan to serve this on a buffet,
then cut the vegetables into smaller pieces.*

4   zucchini, cut in half lengthwise. Do not peel.
4   yellow zucchini, cut in half lengthwise. Do not peel.
1   red bell pepper, cut into 8 wedges
1   green bell pepper, cut into 8 wedges
1   small onion, cut into rings
3   cloves garlic, minced
1/4   cup lemon juice
1   tablespoon red wine vinegar
1   tablespoon water
2   tablespoons olive oil
     pinch of salt
     black pepper to taste

In a 9x13-inch baking pan, toss together all the ingredients, until everything
is nicely mixed. Allow mixture to stand in the refrigerator for several hours.
Broil vegetables, about 4-inches from the heat, for about 8 minutes. Toss and
turn the vegetables and continue broiling for another 6 to 8 minutes, or until
vegetables are tender and flecked with brown. Serve hot or cold. Serves 8.

Old-Fashioned Meat Loaf

Ground turkey can be substituted in this very juicy and succulent meat loaf. It is important to grate the onion. If you do not grate the onion, then mince it finely. Onion can be grated in a food processor.

Meat Loaf:
- 1 1/2 pounds ground beef
- 1 medium onion, grated. Reserve 2 tablespoons for the sauce.
- 4 slices egg bread, crusts removed. Dip in water and squeeze dry.
- 1 egg
- 1 clove garlic, pressed
  - salt and pepper to taste

Combine all the meat loaf ingredients and mix lightly, until thoroughly blended. Place meat mixture into a 9x5-inch loaf pan. Pour Tomato Sauce Topping on the top. Bake in a 350° oven for about 1 hour. Serves 6.

Tomato Sauce Topping:
- 1 can (8 ounces) tomato sauce
- 2 tablespoons reserved grated onion
- 1 clove garlic, minced
- 1 teaspoon sugar
- 1/2 teaspoon Italian Herb Seasoning
  - salt and pepper to taste

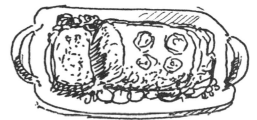

Stir together all the ingredients until blended.

Easiest & Best Mashed Potatoes

- 6 medium potatoes, peeled and cut into 1/2-inch thick slices

- 4 tablespoons butter
- 1/2 cup half and half or more, to make a creamy consistency
  - salt and pepper to taste

- 1 can (about 3-ounces) French-Fried Onions

Cook potatoes in boiling water until tender. With a potato masher, mash potatoes with butter. Keep mashing as you add the cream and seasonings. Potatoes should be creamy. Place potatoes in a 10-inch round porcelain baker and press French-Fried Onions over the top. Cover with foil and refrigerate until serving time. To reheat, remove the foil and bake at 350° until heated through and top is a little crusty, about 25 minutes. Serves 6.

Family Chocolate Bread Pudding
with Creme Vanilla

This is a nice economical dessert that is easily prepared and enjoyed by all. It is homey and informal, yet when prepared in individual ramekins, it can be quite elegant. The Creme Vanilla will surprise you. It is easy and very delicious.

8	thick slices day-old egg bread, remove crusts and tear into pieces
1/2	cup semi-sweet chocolate mini-chips

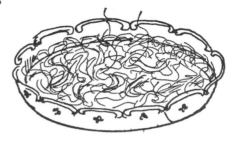

2 1/2	cups half and half or milk
1/3	cup sifted cocoa
1	cup sugar

4	eggs
1	tablespoon vanilla
1	tablespoon rum (optional)

Place bread in a buttered 12-inch oval porcelain baker. In saucepan, heat together milk, cocoa and sugar until cocoa and sugar are dissolved. Allow to cool and beat in eggs, vanilla and rum until blended. Pour mixture over the bread pieces and allow to stand for 30 minutes or until liquid is evenly absorbed. Bake at 350° for about 1 hour or until custard is set. Serve warm or chilled, not hot or cold. Spoon a little Creme Vanilla on top when serving. Serves 8.

Creme Vanilla:
1/2	cup cream, whipped
1/2	cup vanilla ice cream
1/2	teaspoon vanilla
1	teaspoon rum, optional

Combine all the ingredients and stir until blended. Yields 1 cup sauce. Prepare about 1 hour before serving and store in the refrigerator.

To Prepare in Individual Ramekins:
Divide bread between 8 individual ramekins. Divide milk mixture evenly between the ramekins. Place ramekins on a cookie sheet and bake at 350° for 25 minutes or until custard is set.

A Celebration for the Queen of Hearts
A Mother's Day Champagne Breakfast

Mimosas (Orange Juice with Champagne)

Compote of Mixed Berries
Easiest & Best Cheese Blintze Casserole with
Strawberries & Sour Cream

Crescents with Lemon Cream Cheese & Lemon Glaze
Apricot Walnut Cookies on Lemon Cookie Crust

Coffee

Breakfast Sampler

Scones & Biscuits
Wimbledon Cream Scones with Currants
Buttery Scones with Apricots
Buttery Raisin Scones with Walnuts
Devonshire-Style Cream
Breakfast Biscuits with Currants & Oats

Pancakes & French Toast
German Apple Pancake with Sour Cream & Lingonberry Jam
Dutch Babies - Popover Pancakes
Cottage Cheese Pancakes with Strawberries & Cream or
Cinnamon & Apple Sauce
French Orange Toast with Country Orange Marmalade
Royal French Toast
French Raisin Toast with Cinnamon & Orange Honey

Toppings
Cinnamon Sugar
Apples & Raisins
Strawberry & Orange Topping
Cinnamon & Apple Sauce
Orange Honey

The menu for Mother's Day was kept simple to assure success. Mimosas are nice as starters. The Cheese Blintze Casserole is delicious and satisfying and a great breakfast dish. It is foolproof to prepare. The Compote of Mixed Berries is great with the casserole. Little Danish Crescents and Apricot Walnut Cookies are good with coffee.

As Mom deserves the "very best of the best", I have included a few extra options that you may wish to add for this special day. Scones, biscuits, glamorous pancakes and French toast, and a few great toppings will offer many choices for your "Queen of Hearts."

Mimosas

For each serving, in a stemmed glass, mix 3 ounces of orange juice, 3 ounces of champagne and 2 ice cubes. Float a strawberry on top.

Compote of Mixed Berries & Peaches

I am offering this recipe with frozen fruit as fresh berries may be difficult to find in early May. If fresh berries are available, they are preferred, of course.

- 1/2 cup orange juice
- 4 tablespoons sugar
- 1 thin slice of lemon (about 1/8-inch thick)
- 1 cup frozen strawberries
- 1 cup frozen raspberries
- 1 cup frozen blackberries
- 1 cup frozen blueberries
- 1 cup frozen sliced peaches

In a Dutch oven casserole, simmer together all the ingredients for 5 minutes. Remove lemon slice and refrigerate compote until serving time. Serves 10.

Easiest & Best Cheese Blintze Casserole with Strawberries & Sour Cream

This is an oldie but goodie. Nothing could be easier to prepare than this delicious casserole. It has all the character and flavor of cheese blintzes with none of the work. This is a good choice for a breakfast or brunch, as it can be prepared in advance and heated before serving. The original of this recipe appeared in my newsletter in 1968. To this day, it is still enjoyed by everyone. This version is a little lighter.

Batter:

1/2	cup (1 stick) butter or margarine, melted
1/2	cup sugar
2	eggs
1	cup flour
1/2	cup milk
3	teaspoons baking powder
1	teaspoon vanilla
1	tablespoon cinnamon sugar

In the small bowl of an electric mixer, beat together all the ingredients (except the cinnamon sugar), until the mixture is nicely blended. Spread 1/2 the batter in a buttered 9x13-inch baking pan. Spoon the Lemon Cream Cheese Filling evenly on the top and cover it with the remaining batter. Sprinkle top with cinnamon sugar.

Bake at 350° for 45 minutes, or until top is browned. Cut into squares and serve warm with a dollup of low-fat sour cream and a spoonful of crushed strawberries or raspberries. A teaspoon of frozen strawberries or raspberries is very good, too. Serves 10.

Lemon Cream Cheese Filling:

1	package (8 ounces) cream cheese, at room temperature
1	cup small curd low-fat cottage cheese
1	egg
1/3	cup sugar
3	tablespoons lemon juice

Beat cream cheese until lightened, about 1 minute. Beat in remaining ingredients until blended.

Danish Pastry Crescents with Lemon Cream Cheese Filling & Lemon Glaze

These wonderful melt-in-your-mouth crescents are like a cheese Danish and a delight to serve for breakfast or brunch. The dough handles very easily and produces an exquisite yeast-like pastry. If cream cheese runs a little, trim it off.

1/2	cup butter (1 stick), softened
1	cup small curd cottage cheese
1	cup flour

Lemon Cream Cheese Filling:

4	ounces cream cheese
1/4	cup sugar
1	tablespoon grated lemon zest (yellow part of the peel)

Lemon Glaze

In the large bowl of an electric mixer, beat together butter and cottage cheese until blended. Beat in the flour until blended. Shape dough into a 6-inch circle and wrap in floured wax paper. Refrigerate for 1 hour.

Beat cream cheese, sugar and lemon zest until blended.

Divide dough into thirds. Roll each third out on a floured pastry cloth until circle measures about 9-inches. Spread 1/3 of the Lemon Cream Cheese Filling over the dough and cut circle into 8 triangular wedges. Roll each triangle from the wide end toward the center and curve slightly into a crescent. Sprinkle with a generous shake of sifted powdered sugar.

Place crescents on a lightly buttered cookie sheet and bake at 350° for about 30 minutes or until they are golden brown. Remove from pan and allow to cool on brown paper. When cool, sprinkle with sifted powdered sugar or brush with Lemon Glaze. Yields 24 crescents.

Lemon Glaze:
Stir together 1 tablespoon lemon juice with about 1/2 cup sifted powdered sugar until glaze is a drizzling consistency. Add a little lemon juice or powdered sugar if needed.

Apricot Walnut Cookies on Lemon Cookie Crust

A chewy apricot/nut topping on a lemon cookie crust makes this a truly marvelous cookie. The balance of sweet and tart, with the texture of fruits and nuts, is divine. The cookie crust is sparkled with lemon. Of course, you can tell, these are one of my very favorite cookies.

Crust:

2	cups flour
1/2	cup sugar
3/4	cup butter
2	tablespoons grated lemon (about 1/2 of a whole lemon)

Filling:

1	cup sugar
1/3	cup brown sugar
1	package (6 ounces) dried apricots
3	eggs
2	teaspoons vanilla
3	tablespoons flour
1 1/2	teaspoons baking powder
1	cup chopped walnuts

In the food processor, combine all the crust ingredients, and pulse until mixture is blended, about 30 seconds. Press dough evenly on the bottom of a greased 9x13-inch baking pan and bake at 350° for 25 minutes, or until very lightly browned.

Meanwhile, in the food processor, blend together apricots and sugars until apricots are finely chopped. Beat together next 4 ingredients until blended. Stir in apricots and walnuts. Pour mixture evenly over prepared crust and bake at 350° for about 25 minutes, or until top is golden brown. Allow to cool in pan and then cut into 1 1/2-inch squares. Yields 48 cookies.

Wimbledon Cream Scones with Currants

This is a variation of my Victorian Cream Scones. Serve it with Devonshire Cream and Strawberries for an English breakfast treat. This recipe is a little more moist and tender than the traditional scone. Chopped dried apricots can be substituted for the currants. As a variation, add 2 tablespoons of chopped almonds.

3	cups flour
3	teaspoons baking powder
1/4	teaspoon salt
2/3	cup sugar
1/2	cup cold butter or margarine, cut into 4 pieces
1/2	cup dried currants or dried apricots
2	eggs
1	cup cream

In the large bowl of an electric mixer, beat together first 5 ingredients until butter resembles fine meal. Beat in currants. Thoroughly beat together eggs and cream and, with the motor running, slowly add to the flour mixture just until blended. Do not overbeat. Spread dough evenly into a greased 10-inch springform pan. Bake at 350° for 30 minutes or until top is golden brown. To serve, cut into thin wedges. Yields 16 slices.

Buttery Scones with Apricots

2	cups flour
2 1/2	teaspoons baking powder
2/3	cup sugar
1/3	cup butter
1/2	cup finely chopped dried apricots
2	eggs
1/2	cup sour cream
1	teaspoon vanilla
1	teaspoon sugar

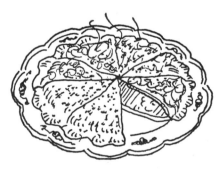

Beat together first 4 ingredients until mixture resembles coarse meal. Stir in dried apricots. Beat together eggs, sour cream and vanilla until blended, and add, all at once, to the flour mixture. Beat only until blended and do not overbeat.

Spread batter, (it will be very thick,) into a greased 10-inch springform pan and sprinkle top with 1 teaspoon sugar. Bake at 350° for 25 to 30 minutes, or until top is nicely browned. Allow to cool in pan. When cool, remove from pan and cut into wedges to serve. Serves 10.

Buttery Raisin Scones with Walnuts

This is one of the tastiest scones, so good with cream cheese and jam, or a few fresh sliced strawberries and chopped walnuts. It is not prepared with the traditional ingredients, but the end result is truly marvelous. Raisins can be substituted with black currants or dried apricots. Walnuts can be substituted with pecans.

2	cups flour
2	teaspoons baking powder
2/3	cup sugar
1/3	cup butter
1/2	cup raisins
1/4	cup chopped walnuts
2	eggs
1/2	cup sour cream
1	teaspoon vanilla

Beat together first 4 ingredients until mixture resembles coarse meal. Beat in raisins and walnuts. Beat together eggs, sour cream and vanilla until blended and add, all at once, to flour mixture. Beat just until blended. Do not overbeat.

Spread batter (it will be very thick) into a greased 10-inch springform pan and sprinkle top with 1 teaspoon sugar (optional but nice). Bake in a 350° oven for 25 to 30 minutes, or until top is browned and a cake tester, inserted in center, comes out clean. Allow to cool in pan. When cool, remove from pan and cut into wedges to serve. Serves 8.

Devonshire-Style Cream

8	ounces cream cheese, softened
1/4	cup cream
1/4	cup sour cream
2	tablespoons sifted powdered sugar
1/2	teaspoon vanilla

Beat cream cheese until light and fluffy. Beat in remaining ingredients until blended. Place mixture in a bowl, cover securely with plastic wrap and refrigerate for 4 to 6 hours. Overnight is good, too. Yields 1 1/2 cups.

German Apple Pancake
with Sour Cream & Lingonberry Jam

2 apples, peeled and grated and tossed with 2 tablespoons
    lemon juice
1/2 cup yellow raisins
1/2 cup chopped walnuts
1/4 cup sugar
1/4 teaspoon cinnamon
4 tablespoons butter

3 eggs
1 cup flour
1 cup milk
2 tablespoons melted butter
2 tablespoons sugar
1/2 teaspoon vanilla

In a 10-inch, round baking pan (or skillet that can go into the oven), saute together the first 6 ingredients, until apples are softened.

Meanwhile, beat together the remaining ingredients until nicely blended. Pour batter evenly over the apple mixture and bake in a 350° oven until puffed and golden, about 30 minutes.

Sprinkle top with cinnamon sugar, and dot with sour cream and lingonberry jam. Strawberry jam is excellent, too. Fresh lingonberries are very nice but not often available. Serves 4.

Cottage Cheese Pancakes
with Strawberries & Sour Cream

1 cup non-fat cottage cheese
3 eggs
    pinch of salt
2 tablespoons sugar
2 tablespoons melted butter
1/3 cup flour
1 teaspoon baking powder
1/2 teaspoon vanilla

In a mixing bowl, whisk together all the ingredients until blended. Batter will be thick. Do not overmix. Spread about 2 tablespoons batter on a buttered, preheated non-stick griddle and press gently to flatten. When bottom of pancake is golden brown and bubbly on top, turn and brown other side. Keep warm in a 200° oven. Serve with a dollup of sour cream and sliced fresh strawberries. Applesauce with a sprinkling of cinnamon is also nice. Yields 12 small pancakes and serves 4.

Dutch Babies - Popover Pancakes

Dutch Babies are giant popovers that are puffed and golden and then settle into a bowl shape. They can be served simply with different syrups or honey. Sour cream and strawberry syrup, fresh fruit, a sprinkling of cinnamon sugar...a few suggestions appear below.

1/4   cup butter (1/2 stick)

1   cup flour
1   cup milk
1/4   teaspoon salt
4   eggs

Melt butter in a 10-inch, round baking pan (or skillet that can go into the oven) and spread evenly. Beat together the flour, milk, salt and eggs until thoroughly blended. Pour batter into prepared pan.

Bake in a 400° oven for about 30 minutes or until pancake is puffed and golden. Sprinkle generously with sifted powdered sugar and serve with one of the following toppings. Serves 6.

Orange Honey:
Heat together 1 cup honey and 3 ounces concentrated orange juice until blended. Spoon over pancake to taste. Unused Orange Honey can be stored in the refrigerator.

Yogurt and Fresh Strawberries:
Serve pancake with a dollup of yogurt and sliced fresh strawberries.

Cinnamon Sugar:
Sprinkle top with cinnamon sugar to taste and serve with a dollup of sour cream and strawberry jam.

Apples and Raisins:
Cook together 3 thinly sliced apples, 1/2 cup yellow raisins, 1/2 cup sugar, 1/2 cup orange juice, 2 tablespoons grated lemon and 1 teaspoon vanilla until apples are soft, about 30 minutes. Sprinkle top of pancake with cinnamon sugar and serve with cooked apples.

Sour Cream and Strawberry Orange Topping:
In a bowl, combine 1 package (10 ounces) frozen sweetened strawberries with 3-ounces concentrated frozen orange juice. Serve pancake with a dollup of sour cream and a few tablespoons of Strawberry Orange Topping.

Sour Cream with Cinnamon Sugar:
Sour cream can be flavored with a little brown sugar and cinnamon to taste.

French Orange Toast
with Country Orange Marmalade

8   1-inch slices French bread

3   eggs
1   cup cream or half and half
2   tablespoons grated orange zest (orange part of the peel)
1/4 cup cinnamon sugar

butter
Country Orange Marmalade

In a 9x13-inch pan, place bread slices in one layer. Beat together eggs, orange juice, cream and cinnamon sugar until blended. Pour egg mixture evenly over the bread. Allow bread to soak up egg, turning now and again until evenly moistened.

In a large skillet, heat 1 tablespoon butter until sizzling hot. Saute bread slices until golden brown on both sides. Use more butter as needed. Serve with Country Orange Marmalade or your favorite syrup. Serves 4.

Note: -The French toast can be baked in the oven for a slightly different effect. After the eggs are nicely soaked up, place pan in a 350° oven and bake until bread is golden and puffed. The toast will not be as tender as when sauteed on the stove.

Country Orange Marmalade

This little gem produces the finest tasting marmalade. The lemon adds a beautiful flavor to the orange, the walnuts add texture and the cherries add color. I hope you try it soon. This is also a lovely gift from your kitchen.

1   cup orange marmalade
2   tablespoons lemon juice
4   tablespoons chopped walnuts
3   tablespoons yellow raisins
2   tablespoons chopped Maraschino cherries

Combine all the ingredients and stir until blended, Store in the refrigerator until ready to use.

Royal French Toast

3   eggs
1/2   cup milk
1/2   cup sour cream
3   tablespoons cinnamon sugar
8   slices cinnamon bread

Beat eggs with milk, sour cream and cinnamon sugar. Dip bread slices in egg and saute them in a skillet with a small amount of butter until they are golden brown. Turn and brown other side. Serve warm with maple syrup, honey or cinnamon sugar. A dot of strawberry jam and sour cream is good, too. Serves 4.

French Raisin Toast with Cinnamon & Orange Honey

3   eggs
1   cup half and half or milk
3   tablespoons cinnamon sugar
1/2   teaspoon vanilla

8   slices raisin bread

Beat eggs with cream or milk, cinnamon sugar and vanilla until eggs are light, about 1 minute.

Dip bread slices into egg mixture and let it soak up the egg. In a buttered skillet or griddle, cook the bread slices until golden brown. Turn and brown other side. Keep warm in a low oven until all the bread is sauteed. Serve warm with Orange Honey. Serves 4.

Orange Honey:
1   cup honey
2   teaspoons grated orange peel
1/4   cup orange juice concentrate

In a saucepan, heat together all the ingredients until they are well blended.

Breakfast Biscuits with Currants & Oats

These are nice to serve at breakfast, with sweet butter and jam. Preparing them in a food processor is totally foolproof...although they can be prepared in a mixer, using a paddle beater. Do not overbeat. This is not a fluffy biscuit, so don't think anything went wrong.

1/2	cup butter, cut into 8 pieces
2	cups flour
1/2	cup quick-cooking oats
1/4	cup sugar
2	teaspoons baking powder
1/3	cup milk
1	egg
1/2	cup dried black currants

Place first 5 ingredients in the bowl of a food processor and process for 10 on/off impulses, or until mixture resembles coarse meal.. Beat together milk and egg, and add, all at once, with the dried currants. Process for another 5 on/off impulses, or until dough clumps together around the center.

Place dough on a floured pastry cloth and pat into a 3/4-inch thick circle. Cut into 2-inch rounds with a biscuit cutter, and place on an ungreased cookie sheet. Collect the scraps and cut into additional rounds. Bake in a 400° oven for about 15 minutes, or until biscuits are puffed and golden. Yields 20 biscuits.

Note: -At teatime, these are nice to serve with Lemon Devonshire-Type Cream, and topped with a few chopped, toasted pecans and sliced strawberries.

Lemon Devonshire-Type Cream:
Beat together 1 package (8 ounces) cream cheese, softened; 2 tablespoons cream; 1 tablespoon sour cream; 2 tablespoons sifted powdered sugar; and 1 tablespoon lemon juice until blended. Refrigerate for several hours or overnight.

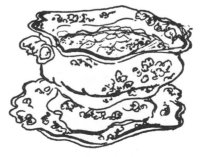

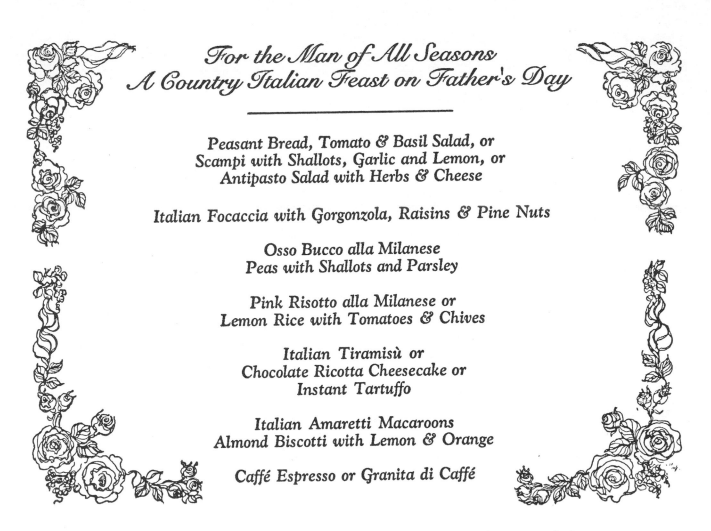

For the Man of All Seasons
A Country Italian Feast on Father's Day

Peasant Bread, Tomato & Basil Salad, or
Scampi with Shallots, Garlic and Lemon, or
Antipasto Salad with Herbs & Cheese

Italian Focaccia with Gorgonzola, Raisins & Pine Nuts

Osso Bucco alla Milanese
Peas with Shallots and Parsley

Pink Risotto alla Milanese or
Lemon Rice with Tomatoes & Chives

Italian Tiramisù or
Chocolate Ricotta Cheesecake or
Instant Tartuffo

Italian Amaretti Macaroons
Almond Biscotti with Lemon & Orange

Caffé Espresso or Granita di Caffé

Dad deserves "the best." Period. This is a wonderful informal dinner to celebrate his day. While it is certainly very appealing for youngsters and grown-ups alike, men seem to especially love these stout-hearted and robust dishes. They love to dip the crusty Italian bread into the delicious sauce and soak up the succulent gravy. And then, with gusto, they pick the meat off the veal shanks and scoop out every last morsel of marrow. The Focaccia is excellent, but you may want to purchase a few interesting crusty breads and rolls with a soft crumb to serve with this meal.

In addition, the dinner is a delight to prepare and very easy to serve. All the dishes can be prepared a day earlier, with the exception of the shrimp (which can be assembled earlier.) Have the shrimp ready, the sauce assembled and then broiling is just a matter of minutes. The veal shanks should be prepared a day earlier to allow the flavors to blend.

Many desserts to choose from. Tiramisù and Ricotta Cheesecake can be prepared a day earlier and refrigerated overnight. Tartuffo, Amaretti, Biscotti...all can be prepared days earlier.

Caffé Espresso is made with very finely ground Italian coffee, and is served in a demitasse or Espresso glass. In the absence of an Espresso coffee maker, you can purchase Instant Espresso in gourmet markets. Traditionally served with a twist of lemon peel, I very much prefer the addition of a dash of Kahlua and a dollup of whipped cream. On a hot night, serve the Granita.

Peasant Bread, Tomato & Basil Salad

An Italian bread salad is more than a salad sprinkled with croutons. The bread is deeply flavored with olive oil and vinegar. The Italian bread should be stale but not so dry as to be brittle. You want a firm "spring" to it.

Salad:
- 1/2 loaf (about 8 ounces) 2-day old Italian bread, crusts removed, sliced and cut into 1-inch squares.
- 3/4 pound Italian plum tomatoes, cut into 1/2-inch slices
- 1 small cucumber, peeled and thinly sliced
- 6 thin slices red onion, separated into rings
- 1/4 cup chopped fresh basil

Dressing:
- 1/4 cup olive oil
- 1/3 cup red wine vinegar
- 1/4 cup tomato juice
- 1/4 cup minced green onions
- salt and pepper to taste

In a large bowl, toss together salad ingredients. In a glass jar with a tight-fitting lid, shake together dressing ingredients. About 1/2 hour before serving, pour dressing to taste over the salad and toss until nicely mixed. Cover bowl and refrigerate until serving time. Serves 6.

Antipasto Salad with Herbs & Cheese

Herb & Cheese Dressing:
- 1 cup tomato juice
- 1/4 cup grated Parmesan cheese
- 1/4 cup oil
- 1/4 cup lemon juice
- 1/8 teaspoon garlic powder
- 1 teaspoon oregano flakes
- 1 teaspoon sweet basil flakes
- salt and pepper to taste

Combine all the dressing ingredients in a glass jar with a tight-fitting lid and shake until blended. Store in the refrigerator for several hours before using. Dressing will last for 2 weeks in the refrigerator. Yields about 2 cups.

Salad:
Depending on the number of people you are serving, use lettuce, tomatoes, black pitted olives, shredded Mozzarella cheese, garbanzos, shredded Italian salami, artichoke hearts in any combination or quantity.

Scampi with Shallots, Garlic and Lemon

Perhaps one of the easiest and best ways to prepare shrimp is to broil them for a few minutes in a rich garlic and lemon sauce. Serve with a loaf of crusty Italian bread to dip in the delicious sauce.

1 1/2 pounds large shelled shrimp, peeled and deveined

Garlic & Lemon Sauce:
- 2 tablespoons melted butter
- 2 tablespoons olive oil
- 6 cloves garlic, minced
- 4 shallots, minced
- 3 tablespoons lemon juice
- 3 tablespoons minced parsley leaves
  salt and freshly ground pepper to taste

In a saucepan, cook together sauce ingredients until onions are transparent, about 3 minutes. Place shrimp in a 10-inch round baking pan and pour sauce over the shrimp, making certain that the shrimp are well coated.

Broil shrimp 6-inches from the heat, a few minutes on each side and only until shrimp turn pink and become opaque. Watch carefully so that the shrimp do not overcook. Serve at once with the sauce spooned over the top. Serves 6 as a first course, or 4 as a main dish.

Note: - Sauce ingredients can be prepared earlier in the day. Entire dish can be assembled 30 minutes before broiling. Broil just before serving.

Peas with Shallots & Parsley

- 1/4 cup butter
- 3 shallots, finely chopped
- 1/2 teaspoon sugar
- 3 tablespoons finely chopped parsley
  salt and pepper to taste

- 2 packages (10 ounces, each) frozen baby peas

In a saucepan, saute together first 6 ingredients until shallots are tender. Add the peas and cook for 2 minutes, or until peas are tender but firm. Serves 6.

Note: - Entire dish can be prepared earlier in the day and refrigerated and reheated before serving.

Italian Focaccia with Gorgonzola, Raisins & Pine Nuts

This bread will add excitement to the most sedate party. Truly a masterpiece of taste, it will transform the most ordinary salad into an exciting course. No butter is necessary, just slice and enjoy.

2	eggs, beaten
1/3	cup oil
2	tablespoons sugar
1/2	cup sour cream
2	cups self-rising flour
1/2	teaspoon baking powder
1/2	cup crumbled gorgonzola cheese
1/4	cup grated Parmesan cheese
1/3	cup yellow raisins
1/3	cup toasted pine nuts
2	teaspoons sweet basil flakes (or 2 tablespoons fresh basil)

In the large bowl of an electric mixer, beat together first 4 ingredients until blended. Beat in the flour and baking powder until nicely blended, about 1/2 minute. Stir in remaining ingredients until blended.

Spread batter into an oiled 12-inch round baking pan and brush top with 2 teaspoons of oil. Sprinkle top with additional grated Parmesan cheese.

Bake at 350° for about 40 minutes or until top is browned. Allow to cool in pan. Serve warm or at room temperature. Yields 12 slices

Easiest & Best Osso Bucco alla Milanese

Try this marvelous recipe one night soon. It is such fun to pick the succulent meat off the bones and to scoop out every morsel of delicious marrow. Sauce is delicious and does not need to be thickened. The aroma is fabulous and will truly delight your family and friends. Traditionally served with Risotto alla Milanese, I prefer to add a little tomato to the rice, and I call it "Pink Risotto alla Milanese."

3	veal shanks (also called shinbones) about 6 pounds. Ask butcher to saw them into 3-inch pieces. Sprinkle them with salt and pepper and dust them lightly with flour.
6	medium onions, cut into fourths
2	cans (1 pound, each) stewed tomatoes, chopped and seeded. Do not drain.
1	can (6 ounces) tomato paste
1	cup dry white wine
2	teaspoons beef stock base
1	carrot, grated
1	teaspoon sugar
2	tablespoons olive oil
6	cloves garlic, minced
1/2	teaspoon each, oregano, basil and thyme flakes or 1 1/2 teaspoons Italian Herb Seasoning
	salt and freshly ground pepper to taste

Place veal shanks in a 12 x 16-inch roasting pan marrow side down (bone upright.) Scatter onions evenly over all.

Stir together the remaining ingredients and pour sauce evenly over the veal. Cover pan tightly with foil and bake in a 350° oven for about 2 hours or until veal is tender. Sauce should be quite thick. Pink Risotto is a delicious accompaniment. Serves 6.

Note: - Best made a day earlier to allow flavors to blend.
- Just before serving you can sprinkle a little Gremolada over the veal. This consists of mixing together 1 tablespoon grated lemon zest, 3 tablespoons minced parsley, 2 cloves minced garlic, and 1 mashed anchovy.

Pink Risotto alla Milanese
(Pink Rice with Parmesan)

This is one of the prettiest rice dishes and is great to serve with Osso Bucco. Please add the tomato, even if you are a purist. It adds a lovely depth to this dish. Can be prepared earlier in the day and reheated, over low heat, before serving. Sprinkle rice with a few drops of water or broth before reheating.

2 tablespoons butter
1 small onion, finely chopped

1 1/4 cups rice
2 cans (10 1/2 ounces, each) chicken broth
1 teaspoon ground turmeric
1 large tomato, peeled, seeded and chopped
salt and pepper to taste

4 tablespoons grated Parmesan cheese (or more to taste)

Saute onion in butter until onion is soft. Stir in next 6 ingredients, cover pan and simmer rice for about 30 minutes or until rice is tender and liquid is absorbed. Toss in cheese before serving. Serve with Osso Bucco. Serves 6.

Lemon Rice with Tomato & Chives

1 1/3 cups rice
2 cans (10 1/2 ounces) chicken broth
2 tablespoons lemon juice
1 tomato, peeled, seeded and finely chopped (or 1 canned tomato, finely chopped)
2 tablespoons oil
salt and pepper to taste

1 tablespoon chopped parsley
3 tablespoons chopped chives

In a covered saucepan, simmer together first 7 ingredients for 30 minutes, or until rice is tender and liquid is absorbed. Stir in the remaining ingredients, and heat through. Serves 6.

Italian Tiramisù
(Ladyfingers Layered with Cream Cheese & Chocolate)

Tiramisù has become a most popular dessert in Italian restaurants everywhere. And it is interesting to note, that most restaurants prepare it in a different fashion. I have tasted it with sponge cake layers, pound cake and ladyfingers. The fillings have varied also...from Mascarpone, ricotta and cream cheese. So with this in mind, this is my version of Tiramisù, using the traditional flavors of espresso, rum, and chocolate and the easiest (and most delicious) version I could muster.

Coffee Mixture:
- 1 cup brewed espresso; or 1 cup boiling water with
  - 2 tablespoons instant espresso coffee.
- 1/4 cup rum
- 1 tablespoon sugar

- 3 packages (12 each) ladyfingers, split. You will have 72 halves.

To Prepare Ladyfingers:
In a bowl, stir together Coffee Mixture until sugar is dissolved. Brush ladyfingers halves with a little Coffee Mixture.

Cheese Mixture:
- 1 pound cream cheese or 1 pound Mascarpone cheese
- 1/2 cup sifted powdered sugar

- 1 cup cream, whipped
- 2 tablespoons sweet Marsala (optional)
- 1/2 cup semi-sweet chocolate, grated or chopped
- 1 teaspoon vanilla

  Unsweetened cocoa for sprinkling on top

To Prepare Cheese Mixture:
Beat cream cheese and sugar until fluffy and smooth. Beat in next 4 ingredients until blended.

To Assemble:
Lightly butter the bottom and sides of a 10-inch springform pan and line it with parchment paper. (The butter will hold paper and ladyfingers in place.) Place 24 ladyfingers upright, along the edge, with the split-side toward center. Line the bottom of the pan with ladyfingers in a spoke fashion.

Place half the Cheese Mixture over the ladyfingers in pan. Place another layer of coffee-brushed ladyfingers over the cheese in a spoke fashion. Spread remaining Cheese Mixture on top. Sprinkle top generously with sifted cocoa.

Cover pan tightly with plastic wrap and refrigerate for several hours or overnight. To serve, remove outer ring of pan, and using the parchment paper to help you, ease the dessert onto a serving platter. Serves 12.

Chocolate Ricotta Cheesecake with Chocolate Cookie Crust

If you are passionate about chocolate, as you know I am, I know you will enjoy this glorious chocolate cheesecake. Filling ingredients should be at room temperature to avoid lumps.

Chocolate Cookie Crust:

1	cup chocolate wafer crumbs
1/4	cup butter, melted
1/2	cup finely chopped walnuts

Combine crumbs, butter and walnuts and mix until blended. Press the mixture on the bottom of a parchment-lined 10-inch springform pan.

Chocolate Ricotta Filling:

1/4	cup cream
8	ounces semi-sweet chocolate chips
1/2	pound Ricotta cheese, at room temperature
2	packages (8 ounces, each) cream cheese, at room temperature
1	cup sugar
3	eggs, at room temperature
1	cup sour cream, at room temperature
2	teaspoons vanilla

In a small saucepan heat the cream. Add the chocolate chips and stir until chocolate is melted. Do this over low heat so that the chocolate does not scorch. Set aside.

Beat together the Ricotta, cream cheese, sugar, eggs, sour cream and vanilla until the mixture is thoroughly blended. Beat in the melted chocolate. Pour cheese mixture into the prepared pan and bake in a 350° oven for 50 minutes. Do not overbake. Allow to cool in pan and then refrigerate for about 4 to 6 hours. Overnight is good, too. Garnish top with chocolate curls or grated chocolate. Remove from refrigerator 20 minutes before serving. Serves 12.

Note: - To make chocolate curls, take a vegetable peeler and run it down the sides of a chocolate bar that is at room temperature.
-Chocolate can be grated or very finely chopped in a food processor.

Caffé Espresso

Caffé Espresso is made with very finely ground Italian coffee, and is served in a demitasse or Espresso glass. In the absence of an Espresso coffee maker, you can purchase Instant Espresso in most markets. Traditionally served with a twist of lemon peel, I very much prefer the addition of a dash of Kahlua Liqueur and a dollup of whipped cream.

Instant Tartuffo

This is a really quick way to make Tartuffos. Generally, they are coated by dipping balls of ice cream in chocolate, which can be a little tricky. Using a muffin cup as a base makes it fool-proof. In many restaurants, Tartuffos are made with scoops of chocolate ice cream rolled in semi-sweet chocolate chips. It is the easiest method and, while not traditional, still satisfying.

- 1 package (12 ounces) semi-sweet chocolate chips
- 4 tablespoons butter

- 12 medium scoops of chocolate ice cream, just a little smaller than the muffin cup. Shape the scoops and return them to the freezer while you prepare the chocolate. These should not be softened.

In the top of a double boiler over hot water, melt chocolate with butter. Allow to cool for 3 minutes. Paper-line a muffin pan with 12 muffin cups.

Place 1 tablespoon chocolate and then a scoop of chocolate ice cream in each paper-lined cup. Working quickly, drizzle chocolate over the ice cream until the scoops are nicely coated on top and sides. (Chocolate will firm up as it touches the ice cream.)

Place pan in freezer until chocolate is firm. Remove paper liner and wrap each Tartuffo in plastic wrap. Store in a plastic bag in the freezer until ready to serve. Serves 12.

Granita di Caffé

This is a refreshing granular ice, served in lovely stemmed glasses with a short decorative straw. It is a nice alternative to the Caffé Espresso.

- 1 cup water
- 1/4 cup sugar
- 4 cups strong espresso coffee

In a 2-quart jar, stir together water and sugar until sugar is melted. Stir in the coffee. Place mixture in ice cube trays and freeze, stirring from time to time, to form a granular ice. If it freezes solid, crush the coffee cubes in a blender before serving. Serve with a splash of Kahlua and a tablespoon of cream. Serves 6.

Italian Amaretti Macaroons

2 cups grated blanched almonds
1 cup sifted powdered sugar
1 tablespoon cornstarch

4 egg whites
1/8 teaspoon cream of tartar
   pinch of salt
3/4 cup sugar

1 teaspoon almond extract
   coarse sugar crystals to sprinkle on top

Stir together first 3 ingredients until blended and set aside. Beat the egg whites with the cream of tartar and salt until foamy. Slowly add the sugar and continue beating until whites are stiff and glossy. Fold in the almond mixture and almond extract until blended.

Spoon meringue, by the tablespoonful, onto a parchment-lined cookie sheet and sprinkle tops with coarse sugar. Bake at 300° for 30 minutes, turn off the oven and leave cookies in oven to dry out for 15 minutes longer. Yields about 60 cookies.

Almond Biscotti with Lemon & Orange

1 cup butter
1 1/2 cups sugar

6 eggs
2 teaspoons vanilla

4 cups flour
1 tablespoon baking powder

1 cup chopped blanched almonds
2 tablespoons grated orange zest (orange part of the peel)
1 teaspoon grated lemon zest (yellow part of the peel)

Beat together butter and sugar until creamy. Beat in eggs, one at a time, beating well after each addition. Beat in vanilla until blended. Beat in almonds and zests until blended.

Divide dough into 6 greased and lightly floured 9x5-inch foil loaf pans. Bake at 350° for about 30 minutes or until tops are lightly browned. Remove from the oven and allow to cool until pans can be handled.

Ease loaves out of the pans and place on a cutting board. Use a very sharp knife and cut each loaf into 3/4-inch slices. Place slices on a cookie sheet and return to oven to lightly toast on both sides. Yields 6 dozen cookies.

Happy Birthday America
A Fourth of July Celebration

The Salads
Artichoke, Potato & Red Pepper Salad
Baby Red Potato Salad
Pasta Salad with Mushrooms, Sun-Dried Tomatoes
& Spinach Dressing
Green Pea, Pimiento & Onion Salad
Corn Salad with Red Peppers & Cilantro
Tomatoes Deborah
Cole Slaw with Horseradish Dressing
Mixed Bean Salad with Garlic Vinaigrette

Beans
Easiest & Best Barbecued Baked Beans

Breads
Hot Garlic Cheese Bread
Parmesan, Herb & Onion Cheese Bread

The Meats
Barbecued Brisket with Honey Barbecue Sauce
Golden Plum-Glazed Chicken Teriyaki
Honey Plum-Glazed Barbecued Spareribs
All-American Country Ribs with Honey Barbecue Sauce
Chicken Winglets with Red Hot Honey Glaze

Desserts
Best Apricot Walnut Squares
Butterscotch & Chocolate Chip Blondies

Easiest Apple Pie in a Crisp Cookie Crust
The Best Apple & Rhubarb Pie in a Flaky Pastry Crust

Brownie Sampler
Brownies
Fudge Brownies
Rocky Road Brownie Bars
Double Chocolate Fudge Brownies
Bittersweet Double Chocolate Brownies

Everybody, everywhere loves a backyard picnic...and the 4th of July is one of the best times to have one. The recipes include numerous salads, including artichokes, potatoes, pastas, vegetables; meats include barbecued brisket, chicken, spareribs; the best Barbecued Baked Beans; cookies and pies for dessert; and a Brownie Sampler for the children.

Depending on the number and tastes of your guests, choose any combination from the different categories. There are enough choices to please every taste.

Parmesan, Herb & Onion Cheese Bread

This is a nice "conversation" bread and truly delicious. Serve it on a large platter to accompany cheese or pate. Cut it into serving pieces or let everyone tear off a piece or two. Also, this is nice served warm with soup or salad.

- 3 cups flour
- 4 teaspoons baking powder
- 1/3 cup grated Parmesan cheese
- 2 tablespoons sugar
- 1 teaspoon Italian Herb Seasoning
- 2 tablespoons dried onion flakes
  pinch of salt

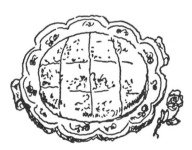

- 3/4 cup milk
- 1 cup sour cream
- 1/2 cup butter, melted

Beat together first group of ingredients until blended. Beat in remaining ingredients until blended, about 1 minute. Do not overbeat. Spread batter evenly into an oiled 12-inch round baking pan. Brush top with a little oil and sprinkle with additional grated Parmesan cheese.

Bake in a 350° oven for about 40 to 45 minutes, or until top is golden brown. Cut into wedges (squares or diamonds) to serve. Excellent with soups or salads. Yields about 12 servings.

Baby Red Potato Salad

You will love this salad on a buffet for its attractive and exciting colors. This is an adaptation of my Mom's potato salad so you will be enjoying the same delicious taste.

2 1/2   pounds baby red potatoes, scrubbed and cooked, unpeeled, in boiling water until fork tender. Do not overcook. Drain potatoes and refrigerate until chilled.

3   carrots, peeled and grated
6   green onions, finely chopped. Use the white and green parts.
2   tablespoons sugar
3   tablespoons cider vinegar
   salt and pepper to taste

3/4   cup mayonnaise

Cut potatoes into 1/4-inch wedges and place in a large bowl. Add the next 6 ingredients and toss potatoes to coat evenly. Allow mixture to rest for 10 minutes. Now add sufficient mayonnaise to coat potatoes and mix well. Cover bowl and refrigerate. To serve, decorate platter with green onion frills and carrot curls. Serves 8.

Corn Salad with Red Peppers & Cilantro

Corn salads are becoming more and more popular lately. This colorful salad is lovely to serve on a buffet.

3   packages (10 ounces, each) frozen corn
1   marinated red pepper, cut into small dice
1/4   cup chopped chives
2   tablespoons finely chopped cilantro
1   tablespoon chopped parsley leaves
3   tablespoons seasoned rice vinegar
1   tablespoon lemon juice
   pepper to taste

Cook the corn for 2 minutes in a saucepan. In a large bowl, place the corn with the remaining ingredients and toss to blend. Refrigerate until serving time. Serves 8 to 10.

Pasta Salad with Mushrooms, Sun-Dried Tomatoes & Spinach Dressing

This is a rather assertive dressing, as the pasta soaks up so much taste. You might even need a little more lemon juice. The addition of 2 cups diced, cooked, white chicken meat will transform this salad into a main course for a luncheon.

Spinach Dressing:
- 1/2 cup mayonnaise
- 1/2 cup low-fat sour cream
- 2 medium green onions, cut up. Use white and green parts.
- 4 tablespoons lemon juice
  salt and freshly ground pepper to taste

- 1 package (10 ounces) frozen chopped spinach, defrosted and drained. (Place spinach in a strainer and press out liquid.)

Salad:
- 1 pound penne pasta, cooked al dente (tender but firm), and drained
- 1/2 pound mushrooms, cleaned and sliced
- 4 sun-dried tomatoes, packed in oil, drained and chopped

To make the Spinach Dressing: In a food processor, blend together first 6 ingredients until onions are very finely chopped. Place mixture in a large bowl and stir in the spinach.

To Assemble the Salad: In a large bowl, toss together pasta, mushrooms and tomatoes until nicely mixed. Toss with dressing to taste. Serve in a large bowl and decorate with lemon slices and green onion frills. Serves 8.

Green Pea, Pimiento & Onion Salad

- 2 packages (10 ounces, each) frozen petite sweet peas
- 1/3 cup chopped green onions
- 1 tablespoon oil
- 4 tablespoons seasoned rice vinegar or red wine vinegar
- 1 jar (2 ounces) slivered pimiento
- 1 tablespoon grated Parmesan cheese
  salt and pepper to taste

Defrost peas and cook in boiling water for 2 minutes and drain. In a bowl, stir together all the ingredients until nicely blended. Cover and refrigerate until serving time. This is delicious served warm or cold. Serves 8.

Cole Slaw with Horseradish Dressing

        1   small head cabbage (about 1 pound), shredded
        1   cup chopped green onions

Dressing:
        3   tablespoons vinegar
        2   tablespoons sugar
      1/3   cup low-fat sour cream
      1/3   cup mayonaisse
        2   tablespoons prepared horseradish
        1   tablespoon celery seed
             salt to taste

Place cabbage and green onions in a large bowl. Stir together dressing
ingredients. About 1 hour before serving, toss dressing with the cabbage.
Cover bowl and refrigerate salad until ready to serve. Serves 8.

Mixed Bean Salad with Garlic Vinaigrette

*Using the canned beans saves you hours of preparation time, and the results are
very good, indeed. This is a good choice for a dinner in a Mexican or Spanish
mood. Italian is good, too. Can be prepared 1 day earlier and stored in the
refrigerator.*

        1   can (1 pound) red kidney beans, rinsed and drained
        1   can (1 pound) garbanzos (chick peas), rinsed and drained
      1/3   cup chopped green onions
        2   cloves garlic, minced
        2   tablespoons chopped parsley
        3   tablespoons oil
        6   tablespoons red wine vinegar
        1   tablespoon Parmesan cheese
             salt and pepper to taste

In a bowl, stir together all the ingredients, until blended. Cover bowl and
refrigerate until serving time. Serves 8.

Easiest & Best Barbecued Baked Beans

I have prepared this so many times for backyard picnics and barbecues and the response is always so great. It is amazingly easy to assemble and it can be prepared a day in advance and stored in the refrigerator. Make certain you have a pan with a tight-fitting lid that will safely go into the oven. Aluminum foil can be used as a cover, but it is a bit of a bother to remove and reseal when you check that the sauce doesn't run low. The following recipe works perfectly for me, without the need to add any more broth. I do not add salt or pepper. I have added the names of the national products I use so that you can duplicate this recipe exactly. I hope you enjoy this dish as much as so many of our friends have.

2	cans (15 ounces, each) Navy Beans packed in water, rinsed and drained
1	small onion, minced
3/4	cup barbecue sauce (Chris' & Pitt's Original BBQ Sauce)
3/4	cup dark brown sugar
1/4	cup dark molasses (Brer Rabbit Dark Molasses)
1	tablespoon Bovril (concentrated Beef-flavored Bouillon)
1/2	cup canned beef broth (Campbell's). Do not dilute.

In an oven-proof Dutch oven or lidded pan, add all the ingredients and stir until nicely mixed. Cover pan and bake in a 325° oven for 1 1/2 hours or until the sauce has thickened. Check after 1 hour and if sauce looks dry, add a little broth. (Normally, this is not necessary.) This should serve 8, but allow for extras. Enjoy.

Artichoke, Potato & Red Pepper Salad

If you find yourself in need of a great, colorful salad for a buffet or antipasto, this one is made from cupboard ingredients and is assembled in, literally, minutes. This salad can be made from scratch, but not worth the extra work. It is exceedingly attractive, white and red and shades of green. Can be prepared 1 day earlier and stored in the refrigerator.

1	jar (6 to 7 ounces) marinated artichoke hearts, cut into chunks. Do not drain.
1	can (1 pound) sliced potatoes, rinsed and drained
2	marinated red peppers, cut into slivers
1/4	cup chopped green onions
4	tablespoons lemon juice
	salt and pepper to taste

In a bowl, stir together all the ingredients until nicely blended. Cover and refrigerate until serving time. Serves 8.

Barbecued Brisket
with Honey Barbecue Sauce

Brisket is a very flavorful, cut of meat. It is especially good braised in this very tasty barbecue sauce. Use the sauce on chicken or pork or other barbecued meats.

1   brisket of beef, about 4 pounds, trimmed of fat. Sprinkle
       with salt, pepper, paprika and lots of garlic powder.

Barbecue Sauce:
   1   large onion, minced
  3/4   cup good quality barbecue sauce
  1/4   cup honey
  1/2   cup dark brown sugar
   1   can (10 1/2 ounces) beef broth
   2   tablespoons dark molasses

Place brisket in a 9x13-inch baking pan. Stir together Barbecue Sauce ingredients and pour over the brisket. Cover pan tightly with foil and bake in a 350° oven for about 2 1/2 to 3 hours or until meat is tender. Allow meat to cool and then refrigerate for several hours.

Remove meat from pan and cut into thin slices. Place meat in a porcelain baker. Remove, from the gravy, any fat that has solidified and drizzle gravy over the meat. Cover pan with foil. Can be held at this point in the refrigerator. To serve, heat in a 350° oven for about 30 minutes, or until heated through. Serves 8.

Hot Garlic Cheese Bread

12   slices thinly sliced French bread (about 1/4-inch thick)
  1   egg, beaten
  6   tablespoons grated Parmesan cheese
1/4   teaspoon garlic powder

Place bread in 1 layer on cookie sheet. Beat together egg, cheese, and garlic powder until blended. Brush mixture on top of bread slices. Bake in a 350° oven for 10 minutes or until topping is starting to bubble. Broil for a few seconds to brown tops. Serve at once. Yields 12 slices.

Golden Plum-Glazed Chicken Teriyaki

2   fryer chickens (about 2 1/2 pounds, each) cut into serving pieces. Baste with a Teriyaki Marinade. Sprinkle chicken with pepper and garlic powder.

Place chicken in one layer in a 12x16-inch baking pan and bake at 325° for 40 minutes. Baste with Hot Plum Glaze 2 or 3 times during the remainder of the baking, about 40 minutes or until chicken is tender and a deep, dark color. Serves 8.

Teriyaki Marinade:
1/2   cup soy sauce
2   tablespoons brown sugar

Stir together all the ingredients until mixture is blended and sugar is dissolved.

Hot Plum Glaze:

1   cup plum jam
2   tablespoons vinegar
2   tablespoons soy sauce
1/2   cup chili sauce
1   tablespoon brown sugar
    pinch of cayenne pepper

In a saucepan, heat together all the ingredients until blended.

Honey Plum-Glazed Barbecued Spareribs

4   pounds pork spareribs, cut into 2-rib pieces and sprinkled with salt and garlic powder to taste

In a covered Dutch oven casserole, cook ribs in 2-inches of simmering water for 30 minutes. Drain and discard water.

Place partially cooked ribs in a roasting pan and baste on all sides with Honey Plum Barbecue Glaze. Bake in a 350° oven for 30 minutes, basting 3 or 4 times with the barbecue sauce until the ribs are nicely glazed and tender. Serves 6.

Honey Plum Barbecue Glaze:
1   cup plum jam
1/4   cup honey
3/4   cup ketchup
1/4   cup vinegar
2   tablespoons lemon juice
    pinch of cayenne pepper
    salt and pepper to taste

In a saucepan, heat together all the ingredients until blended.

All-American Country Ribs with Honey Barbecue Sauce

Ribs can be prepared earlier in the day, but reduce cooking time by 15 minutes. Continue baking and basting before serving.

3 to 4   pounds country-style pork ribs, sprinkle with salt, pepper and garlic powder.

Honey Barbecue Sauce:
- 1   cup ketchup
- 1   cup chili sauce
- 1/2   cup honey
- 1/2   cup brown sugar
- 2   teaspoons dry mustard
- 1/4   cup vinegar
- 1/4   teaspoon cayenne pepper
- 1/4   cup (1/2 stick) butter
- salt and freshly ground pepper to taste

Lay ribs in a 12x16-inch roasting pan and bake in a 350° oven for about 45 minutes. Remove ribs from pan and drain off all fat that has been rendered. Return ribs to cleaned pan.

Stir together the Barbecue Sauce ingredients until blended, and baste ribs with sauce. Return ribs to 350° oven and continue baking and basting until ribs are tender and highly glazed. (Turn ribs now and again so they are sauced on all sides.) Unused sauce can be stored in the refrigerator for several weeks. Serves 6 to 8.

Alternate Preparation:
Now, there is an alternate way of making ribs that I thought you should know about. This method removes much of the excess fat. Place ribs in a stock pot with enough water to cover them. Bring to a boil, lower heat, and simmer ribs for about 45 minutes or until ribs are almost tender. Drain thoroughly. Now place ribs in a 12x16-inch baking pan, brush on all sides with Honey Barbecue Sauce and continue baking and basting until tender and glazed. Ribs made in this fashion can be completed on the barbecue, but make certain that the heat is low or the honey will burn.

Chicken Winglets
with Red Hot Honey Glaze

This is a nice addition to a backyard picnic. The Honey Glaze is hot but not unbearably fiery. Reduce the amount of cayenne pepper for a milder glaze. Leftover glaze can be stored in the refrigerator for several weeks.

    3   pounds chicken wings, tips removed and split at the joint.
        Sprinkle with salt, pepper and garlic powder. Brush lightly
        with a little melted margarine.

Red Hot Honey Glaze:
    1   cup good quality barbecue sauce
    1/2 cup honey
    2   tablespoons vinegar
    1   tablespoon soy sauce
    1/8 teaspoon cayenne pepper

    3   tablespoons sesame seeds

In a 12x16-inch baking pan, place wings in one layer. Bake at 350° for 40 minutes, basting now and again with the juices in the pan. Stir together glaze ingredients and baste wings on all sides. Sprinkle with sesame seeds. Continue baking and basting for 30 minutes, or until chicken is tender and a deep, dark color. Depending on appetites, serves 8 to 10.

Tomatoes Deborah

Years and years ago, this was a favorite salad with our friends. And yet, to this day, whenever I serve it, everyone still loves it. Recipe can be doubled or tripled.

    3   large tomatoes, cut into 1/2-inch slices
    2   tablespoons dried toasted onion flakes
    1   tablespoon chopped parsley leaves
    6   tablespoons salad oil
    3   tablespoons white wine vinegar
    3/4 teaspoon salt
    1   clove garlic, minced
    4   tablespoons grated Parmesan cheese

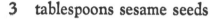

Place the tomatoes in a lovely glass serving bowl. Combine the remaining ingredients and mix well. Pour dressing over the tomatoes and marinate for at least 4 to 6 hours. Serves 4.

The Best Apple & Rhubarb Pie in a Flaky Pastry Crust

Apples and rhubarb are paired in this ultra-delicious pie. Very fruity and tart, it also serves beautifully, with large petals of flaky pastry allowing the apples and rhubarb to show through. It is further simplified with the use of a softer dough that can be pressed into the pan, avoiding the need to refrigerate or roll the pastry. This can be made in a 10-inch tart pan with a removable bottom.

Flaky Pastry:

1	cup butter (2 sticks)
2	cups flour
1/4	cup sugar
1	egg
2	tablespoons water (plus a few drops, if necessary, to hold dough together)
1	teaspoon cinnamon sugar

In a food processor, blend butter, flour and sugar until butter particles are the size of small peas. (Do not overprocess or the flakiness will be lost.) Lightly beat together the egg and water until blended. Add to the butter mixture and pulsate 4 or 5 times, or just until dough clumps together (adding a few drops of water, if necessary.) Place dough on floured wax paper and shape into a disc.

Pat 2/3 of the dough onto the bottom and up the sides of a greased 10-inch heart-shaped pan with a removable bottom. Bake in a 375° oven for 20 minutes, or until crust is lightly browned. Place Apple & Rhubarb Filling evenly over the crust. Divide remaining dough into three parts. With floured hands, pat each part into a 5-inch circle and place on top of pie. Sprinkle top with 1 teaspoon cinnamon sugar. Continue baking for about 30 minutes, or until top is golden brown. Serves 10.

Apple & Rhubarb Filling:

1 1/2	cups frozen rhubarb
1/4	cup orange juice
1/4	cup sugar
1	tablespoon lemon juice
3	large apples, peeled, cored and thinly sliced
1/3	cup sugar
3	tablespoons flour

In a saucepan, simmer together first 4 ingredients for 5 minutes. Place mixture in a large bowl. Add the remaining ingredients to the bowl and toss and stir until all the ingredients are nicely mixed.

Easiest Apple Pie in a Crisp Cookie Crust

This is one of the simplest of apple pies in the fullest sense of the word, and to my mind and taste, one of the best. A delicious crisp cookie crust filled with a tart fruity filling is a pure pleasure.

Crisp Cookie Crust:
- 1 cup butter
- 2 cups flour
- 1/3 cup sugar

- 1/4 cup water
- 1 teaspoon cinnamon sugar

In a food processor, blend butter, flour and sugar until butter particles are the size of small peas. (Do not overprocess or the flakiness will be lost.) Add water and pulsate 4 or 5 times, or until dough clumps together. Place dough on floured wax paper and shape into a ball.

Pat 2/3 of the dough onto the bottom and up the sides of a greased 10-inch heart-shaped pan with a removable bottom. Bake in a 375-degree oven for 20 minutes, or until crust is lightly browned. Place Apple Pie Filling evenly over the crust. Divide remaining dough into thirds, pat each into a 6-inch circle and place on top of pie. Sprinkle top with 1 teaspoon cinnamon sugar. Continue baking for about 30 minutes, or until top is golden brown. Serves 8.

Apple Pie Filling:
- 6 large apples, peeled, cored and thinly sliced
- 1/2 cup sugar
- 1/3 cup yellow raisins
- 1 teaspoon grated lemon peel
- 1 tablespoon flour

In a bowl, toss together all the ingredients until nicely mixed.

Note: -The crust can be prepared in a mixer using the instructions described above. Simply beat the butter with the flour and sugar until butter is the size of small peas. Then add the water and beat until dough clumps together.

Best Apricot Walnut Squares

> 1 package (6 ounces) dried apricots
> 1/2 cup sugar
>
> 1 cup butter, softened
> 1 cup sugar
> 1/2 cup brown sugar
> 2 teaspoons vanilla
>
> 2 eggs
>
> 2 1/4 cups flour
> 1/2 teaspoon baking powder
> 1/2 teaspoon baking soda
> 1/4 teaspoon salt (optional)
> 1 cup chopped walnuts

In a food processor, finely chop apricots with sugar. In the large bowl of an electric mixer, cream butter with sugars and vanilla. Beat in eggs until nicely blended. Beat in apricot mixture and remaining ingredients until blended.

Spread batter (it will be thick) into a greased 10x15-inch jelly-roll pan and bake at 375° for about 20 to 22 minutes, or until top is lightly browned. Do not overbake. Allow to cool in pan. When cool, cut into 1 1/2-inch squares and please use a sharp knife. Sprinkle with a little sifted powdered sugar or for a more festive appearance, brush tops with a little Apricot Glaze. Yields about 60 cookies.

Apricot Glaze:
> 3 tablespoons minced dried apricots
> 3 tablespoons orange juice
> 1 cup sifted powdered sugar

Stir together all the ingredients until blended. Brush cookies with glaze and allow glaze to dry.

Bittersweet Double Chocolate Brownies

4   ounces semi-sweet chocolate
1/4   cup butter, (1/2 stick)

1   cup brown sugar
1   cup sugar
4   eggs
     pinch of salt

3/4   cup flour
1/4   cup cocoa
1   cup chopped walnuts
1   cup semi-sweet chocolate chips

In the top of a double boiler, over hot, not boiling water, melt together the chocolate and butter. Beat together sugars, eggs and salt until mixture is very thick. Beat in chocolate mixture. Beat in flour and cocoa until blended. Stir in walnuts and chocolate chips.

Spread batter evenly in a lightly greased 9x13-inch baking pan and bake at 350° for 25 to 30 minutes, or until batter is just set and looks a little dry around the edges. (My perfect time is exactly 28 minutes for my oven. But oven temperatures vary and you will have to experiment to find your perfect time.) Allow brownies to cool in pan. Refrigerating them for 30 minutes will make cutting easier. Cut into 1 1/2-inch squares. Yields 48 brownies.

Butterscotch & Chocolate Chip Blondies

These crisp and crunchy bars are great with milk. Notice that they do not contain any eggs. A non-stick baker is important as these can stick to the pan.

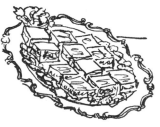

1   cup butter, softened
2   cups brown sugar
1/2   cup sour cream
2   teaspoons vanilla

2   cups flour
1   teaspoon baking powder
3/4   cup chopped walnuts
1   cup butterscotch chips
1/2   cup semi-sweet chocolate chips

In the large bowl of an electric mixer, beat together first 4 ingredients until blended. Mix together the remaining ingredients and stir into the butter mixture until blended. Do not overmix.

Spread batter evenly into a greased 10x15-inch non-stick baking pan and bake at 325° for about 30 minutes, or until top is browned. Allow to cool in pan. When cool, cut into 1 1/2-inch squares to serve. A sprinkling of sifted powdered sugar is nice if you want to dress them up a bit. Yields 60 cookies.

Rocky Road Brownie Bars

1	cup butter, softened
2	cups sugar
4	eggs
1/2	cup sour cream
2	teaspoons vanilla
1 1/2	cups flour
1/2	cup cocoa
1	teaspoon baking powder
3/4	cup chopped walnuts
3/4	cup semi-sweet chocolate chips
3/4	cup miniature marshmallows

In the large bowl of an electric mixer, beat together first 5 ingredients until blended. Stir together the remaining ingredients, add to butter mixture all at once, and stir until blended. Do not overmix.

Spread batter evenly into a greased 10x15-inch baking pan and bake at 350° for about 30 minutes or until top looks dry and a cake tester, inserted in center, comes out clean. Do not overbake. Allow to cool in pan. When cool, cut into squares to serve. Yields 48 cookies.

Double Chocolate Fudge Brownies

And yet another decadent brownie that will please the most exacting chocolate lover. These are very dense, deep, dark and delicious.

3/4	cup butter (1 1/2 sticks)
3	ounces unsweetened chocolate
3	ounces semi-sweet chocolate chips (1/2 cup)
6	eggs
2 1/2	cups sugar
3	teaspoons vanilla
1 1/2	cups sifted flour
1	cup coarsely chopped walnuts
1	cup semi-sweet chocolate chips

In the top of a double boiler, over hot, not simmering water, melt chocolates with butter. Allow to cool slightly. In the large bowl of an electric mixer, beat eggs with sugar and vanilla until mixture is nicely blended. Beat in chocolate mixture, just until blended. Beat in flour until blended. Stir in walnuts and chocolate chips. Do not overmix.

Grease bottom of a 9x13-inch baking pan and spread batter evenly. Bake at 350° for 30 to 35 minutes. Do not overbake. Allow to cool in pan and then refrigerate. (This will make cutting easier.) To serve, sprinkle with a little powdered sugar and cut into 1 1/2-inch squares. Yields 48 cookies.

Brownies

To make the perfect brownie for your taste, will require a few trials. In my oven, I bake brownies for 28 minutes. It is hard to test with a cake tester, but if you do use one, it should come out with a few moist crumbs clinging to it. It is a less than satisfactory test, but as each oven bakes with a slightly different character, please keep in mind that the longer you bake brownies, the crisper they become. Alternatively, the less you bake brownies, the more moist they are.

1	package (6 ounces) semi-sweet chocolate chips
2	ounces unsweetened chocolate, cut into small pieces
3/4	cup (1 1/2 sticks) butter
1	cup sugar
1	cup brown sugar
1	tablespoon vanilla
4	eggs
1	cup flour

In the top of a double boiler, over hot water, melt chocolate and butter. Allow to cool for about 5 minutes and place in the large bowl of an electric mixer. Beat in the sugars and vanilla. Beat in the eggs until blended. Beat in the flour until blended. Spread batter evenly in a greased 9x13-inch baking pan and bake at 350° for 26 to 30 minutes, or until top appears dry. Allow to cool in pan. When cool, cut into small squares. Yields 35 brownies.

Fudge Brownies

I know I have given you my version of brownies using only 1 stick of butter. But maybe, for a holiday or some special occasion, you may want to prepare the decadent one. Keep the portions small, so your conscience will be happy. The addition of walnuts and/or chocolate chips, I leave to your discretion. These are delicious plain or with either addition. These can be made with 1 stick of butter.

4	ounces unsweetened chocolate
1	cup butter, (2 sticks)
2	cups sugar
4	eggs
1	cup flour
1	tablespoon vanilla
1	cup chopped walnuts (optional)
1	cup semi-sweet chocolate chips (optional)

In the top of a double boiler, over hot water, melt chocolate with butter. Allow to cool slightly. Beat sugar with eggs for 2 minutes. Beat in chocolate mixture. Beat in remaining ingredients until blended. Spread mixture in a greased 9x13-inch baking pan and bake at 350° for 30 minutes or until top appears dry, and a cake tester, inserted in center, comes out with a few moist crumbs clinging to it. Allow to cool in pan. (Refrigerating makes it easier to cut.) When cool, cut into small squares. Yields 35 cookies.

Part Two

Great

Celebrations

One of the happiest thoughts to cross my mind is how far Americans have come in the love and appreciation and knowledge of good food. In the past, Americans have taken a lot of ribbing about our cooking and expertise in food. That was a long time ago and if that were true at any time, it could not be less true today.

Americans are extremely knowledgeable and creative about food. I do believe there are more excellent cooks in our nation today than you will find anywhere else in the world. When you consider...the number of cooking schools teaching every national cuisine...the food sections of newspapers and magazines featuring every imaginable cuisine...the number of magazines devoted entirely to the pleasure of good food...the number of cookbooks that are being published today, covering every pleasure of the table...and the number of restaurants, specializing in national and cross-national cuisines...it is truly staggering.

Americans buy more cookbooks, attend more cooking classes, and are familiar with international cuisines from their many travels to every part of the world. Americans read cookbooks like novels...read the ingredients like characters in a play...and a good cookbook is often their companion at bedtime.

The menus that follow reflect the broad range of how Americans cook and dine today. If you look through the menus you will see some of the great cuisines represented...Chinese, Mexican, Basque, French, English, Greek, Russian, Indian, Cajun. There simply wasn't room for more. And these celebration dinners, ranging from the formal Dinner at the Taj to the informal Country French Dinner, offer a variety of richness and interest.

The classic dishes have been modified to conform to American tastes and palates and time in the kitchen. And true to my original belief, most of the dishes have been created to be quick and easy to prepare. Most can be prepared ahead and heated before serving.

The amounts of fat and calories have been trimmed as much as possible without losing sublime taste. Low-calorie sour cream, cream cheese and non-fat yogurts and cottage cheese have been used wherever possible. But, dear friends, holidays and celebrations are not every day and do call for more than steamed chicken and vegetables. So keep the portions small and enjoy the pleasure of taste on those special occasions. You have the rest of the year to exercise discipline.

And now, it is my wish, that you will derive pure pleasure and enjoyment from the menus that follow. It is also my wish that, whenever possible, you share your table with family and friends. For when you think of it, cooking is the most loving art. It is truly the basis for bringing happiness and pleasure to others.

East of the Sun & West of the Moon
A Chinese New Year Banquet

Starters
Pork Dumplings & Apricot Peanut Sauce
Chinese Cucumber Salad

Main Courses
Kung Pao Chicken with Peanuts
Eggplant with Ground Pork
Chicken with Tangerine Sauce
Chinese Steamed Whole Red Snapper

Vegetable Fried Rice

Dessert
Vanilla Ice Cream with Apricot or Peach Puree
Butter Almond Cookies
Tea

Did you know that according to tradition, all good things will be bestowed upon you, if you serve a whole fish at the New Year Feast. The whole fish signifies success, long life and good fortune.

This is a Sample Menu with several options. Depending on your time frame and the number of guests you are inviting, you have many dishes to choose from. The dishes all go well together so choose one, two or three as the spirit moves you.

The Pork Dumplings served with the Cucumber Salad is an excellent starter. If you can find the Chinese cucumbers, they are sweet and delicious. If you cannot, then very thinly slice salad cucumbers.

Each of the dishes have "Notes for Advance Preparation." I feel it is a popular misconception that all Chinese dishes must be prepared at the last minute. If that were the case, then no one who prepares a Chinese meal would ever be with his/her guests during a dinner party. I do believe that with good planning, and having all the ingredients and sauces ready and measured, one can execute a complicated meal without any trouble.

So, toast to good health in the New Year with long life, good fortune and good happenings for all. This dinner is a perfect beginning.

Pork Dumplings & Apricot Peanut Sauce

Both the Pork Dumplings and the Apricot Peanut Sauce can be prepared in advance, making this a great dish to serve for an Asian dinner. Dumplings can be frozen in double thicknesses of plastic wrap and foil. To serve, defrost and heat in a 350° oven until heated through. Apricot Peanut Sauce can be prepared 1 week in advance. Pork can be substituted with ground beef or ground turkey.

Pork Dumplings:
- 1 pound lean ground pork
- 4 cloves finely minced garlic
- 1/3 cup finely minced green onions
- 2 tablespoons soy sauce (or teriyaki marinade)
- 1 egg, beaten
- 2 slices fresh bread, sprinkled with water and squeezed dry
- 1/4 teaspoon ground ginger
  salt and pepper to taste

  flaked coconut for coating dumplings

In a large bowl, mix together first group of ingredients until blended. Shape meat mixture into 1/2-inch balls, roll lightly in coconut flakes and flatten slightly. Place dumplings in a non-stick skillet and cook until bottoms are browned, about 2 minutes. Turn and brown other side. Serve with Apricot Peanut Sauce on the side for dipping. Yields 36 dumplings.

Apricot Peanut Sauce:
- 1/2 cup apricot jam
- 1 tablespoon brown sugar
- 2 tablespoons lemon juice
- 1 teaspoon soy sauce
- 2 tablespoons very finely chopped peanuts

In a small saucepan, heat together all the ingredients until sugar is dissolved. Serve sauce warm, not hot. Yields about 3/4 cup sauce.

Notes for Advance Preparation:
-Pork Dumplings can be made 1 day earlier and refrigerated or 1 week earlier and stored in the freezer.
-Apricot Peanut Sauce can be prepared 1 week earlier and stored in the refrigerator.

Chinese Cucumber Salad

Chinese cucumbers are thin, long and have very small seeds. Their flavor is intense and they truly are wonderful. Serve them in a small bowl on the side. They are a refreshing balance to the palate.

5   Chinese cucumbers, peeled and thinly sliced
1   clove garlic, minced
2   green onions, thinly sliced
1   small onion, peeled, cut into fourths and very thinly sliced
1   shallot, minced

1/2   cup seasoned rice vinegar

Combine all the ingredients in a bowl and refrigerate until serving time. Drain cucumbers when serving and add a few drops of additional rice vinegar. Serves 6.

Notes for Advance Preparation:
    -Cucumber salad can be prepared earlier in the day and stored in the refrigerator.

————————————

Vegetable Fried Rice

This is not the traditional fried rice, but it is very good, indeed. It is a gorgeous array of colors and presents beautifully. Everybody loves it because it is light and very flavorful. This can be made in advance and heated at serving time.

To Make Rice:
1 1/2   cups rice
    3   cups chicken broth
    1   teaspoon sesame oil
    1   tablespoon soy sauce
        salt to taste

To Make Vegetables:
    1   package (10 ounces) frozen corn, defrosted
    1   package (10 ounces) frozen petit peas, defrosted
    1   red pepper, seeded and cut into small dice
    1   tablespoon peanut oil

In a covered saucepan, stir together first 5 ingredients and simmer mixture for 30 minutes or until rice is tender and liquid is absorbed. In a wok or skillet, saute vegetables for 5 minutes or until tender. Add rice, stir and heat through. Serves 6 generously.

Notes for Advance Preparation:
    -Entire dish can be prepared 1 day earlier and stored in the refrigerator. Add a few drops of water when reheating.

Kung Pao Chicken with Peanuts

Kung Pao Chicken is one of my favorite Asian dishes. Restaurants usually prepare this dish very hot and spicy. I always order it "mild". Dried red chili peppers is the spice most often used. But Chinese Chili Sauce is a good substitute.

Chicken Mixture:

4	chicken breast halves (4 ounces, each) skinned, boned and cut into 1/2-inch cubes
3/4	cup peanuts
3/4	cup green onions, cut on the diagonal into 1/2-inch slices
3	cloves garlic minced
1/4	teaspoon Chinese Chili Sauce

Sauce:

3/4	cup rich chicken broth
1	tablespoon soy sauce
1	tablespoon hoisin sauce
1	tablespoon sesame oil
2	teaspoons rice vinegar
1	tablespoon cornstarch
2	tablespoons peanut oil

In a bowl, toss together Chicken Mixture. In another bowl, stir together Sauce ingredients.

In a wok or skillet, heat oil over high heat until sizzling hot. Add chicken mixture and toss and turn until chicken becomes opaque, about 1 to 2 minutes. Add the Sauce ingredients and continue stir frying, over high heat, until sauce thickens slightly, about 2 minutes. Serve over steamed rice. Serves 6.

Notes for Advance Preparation:
 -Chicken can be cut 1 day earlier and stored in the refrigerator.
 -Sauce can be assembled earlier in the day (omitting the cornstarch) and stored in the refrigerator. Stir in the cornstarch before using.

Eggplant with Ground Pork

This is one of the most delicious eggplant dishes. Chinese eggplants are sweet and do not need to be peeled. Broiling the eggplant in the delicious marinade can be done in advance. Pork can also be prepared in advance. Assembling the dish at the last minute makes it an ideal choice for a Chinese feast where work abounds.

Prepare Eggplant:

5	Chinese eggplants, stemmed and cut on the diagonal into 1/4-inch slices.
1	tablespoon lemon juice
1	tablespoon soy sauce
1	tablespoon sesame oil
1/4	teaspoon pepper

Place eggplant in one layer in a 10x15-inch baking pan. Stir together the next 4 ingredients and brush over the eggplant. Broil eggplant 4-inches from the heat, turning once, till firm tender, about 8 to 10 minutes. Set aside.

Prepare Pork:

1	tablespoon peanut oil
8	cloves garlic, minced
1	onion, chopped
	pinch of ground ginger
1/2	pound lean ground pork
3	tablespoons soy sauce

In a wok or skillet, heat oil until sizzling hot. Add the garlic and onion and stir fry for 2 minutes. Mix the meat with the ginger and soy, add it to the wok and stir fry over high heat, until meat is finely crumbled and loses its pinkness. Add the Sauce ingredients and stir fry, over high heat, until sauce thickens. Add the eggplant and toss to heat through. Serve with steamed rice or fried rice. Serves 6.

Sauce:

1/2	cup beef broth
1	tablespoon cornstarch
3	tablespoons oyster sauce
1	tablespoon soy sauce
1 1/2	tablespoons sesame oil
1	teaspoon sugar

Stir together all the ingredients until blended.

Notes for Advance Preparation:
-Eggplant can be cooked 1 day earlier and stored in the refrigerator.
-Pork can be cooked 1 day earlier and stored in the refrigerator.
-Sauce can be assembled earlier in the day (omitting the cornstarch) and stored in the refrigerator. Stir in the cornstarch before using.

Chicken with Tangerine Sauce

Tangerine Chicken is another one of my favorite Asian dishes. Succulent bites of chicken in a sweet and tangy Tangerine Sauce is a sheer delight. If tangerines are out of season, orange peel can be substituted.

Chicken Mixture:

4	chicken breast halves (4 ounces, each) skinned, boned and cut into 3/4-inch squares
3	tablespoons cornstarch

Vegetable/Tangerine Mixture:

3	tablespoons minced tangerine peel
3/4	cup green onions, cut on the diagonal into 1/2-inch slices
3	cloves garlic, minced
8	canned, peeled water chestnuts, thinly sliced
1/4	teaspoon Chinese Chili Sauce

Sauce:

3/4	cup rich chicken broth
3	tablespoons sherry
1	tablespoon soy sauce
1	tablespoon hoisin sauce
1 1/2	tablespoons sesame oil
2	teaspoons sugar
1	tablespoon cornstarch
2	tablespoons peanut oil

In separate bowls, stir together each group of ingredients.

In a wok or skillet, heat peanut oil over high heat until sizzling hot. Add chicken mixture and toss and turn until chicken becomes opaque, about 2 to 3 minutes. Remove with a slotted spoon. Add the Vegetable/Tangerine Mixture and stir fry until onions are firm tender, about 2 minutes. Add the chicken and the Sauce ingredients and continue stir frying, over high heat, until sauce thickens slightly, about 2 minutes. Serve with Fried Rice. Serves 6.

Notes for Advance Preparation:
- Chicken can be cut 1 day earlier and stored in the refrigerator.
- Vegetable/Tangerine Mixture can be prepared earlier in the day and stored in the refrigerator.
- Sauce can be assembled earlier in the day (omitting the cornstarch) and stored in the refrigerator. Stir in the cornstarch before using.

Chinese Steamed Whole Red Snapper

If you do not own a steamer, it is good to know that fish, wrapped in foil, steams nicely in the oven. This looks beautiful on a platter, decorated with green onion frills. If you choose not to fuss with the bones, ask the butcher to filet the fish, but keep the fillets whole.

Prepare Fish:
- 1 whole red snapper or sea bass, (3 pounds) thoroughly cleaned and scaled. Rinse in cold water and pat dry.
- 2 tablespoons dark soy sauce
- 1 teaspoon sesame oil
- 2 cloves garlic, minced

Dipping Sauce:
- 1/4 cup chicken broth
- 3 tablespoons oyster sauce
- 1/4 cup minced green onions
- 1 tablespoon dark soy sauce
- 1 tablespoon sesame oil
- 2 tablespoons lime juice
  pinch of ground ginger

Cut a piece of heavy-duty foil, large enough to completely seal the fish and lay it on a baking sheet. Place fish on foil. Mix together soy, sesame oil and garlic and brush it on the fish. Wrap fish in foil, folding the edges, 2 or 3 times, to thoroughly seal. Bake at 350° for 15 to 20 minutes, or for about 10 minutes for each inch of thickness.

Meanwhile, in a bowl, stir together Sauce ingredients. To serve, remove fish from foil and discard juices. Place fish on a serving platter and brush with Sauce. To cut, run a knife along the upper side of the backbone, releasing the top fillet. Remove the bone. Brush again with a little sauce. Serve with the remaining sauce on the side. Serves 6.

Notes for Advance Preparation:
-Fish can be wrapped earlier in the day and stored in the refrigerator.
-Dipping sauce can be prepared 3 days earlier and stored in the refrigerator.

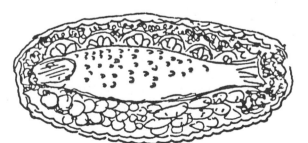

Butter Almond Cookies

Chinese almond cookies are traditionally made with lard. These flaky Butter Almond Cookies are a delicious substitute.

- 1/2   cup butter (1 stick), melted and cooled
- 1   cup flour
- 1/4   cup sifted powdered sugar
- 1/4   cup almond meal (finely grated almonds.) Use a nut grater to finely grate or purchase almond meal in health food stores.
- 1   teaspoon almond extract

    whole blanched almonds

In a bowl, stir together first 5 ingredients until mixture is blended. With floured hands, roll 1 heaping tablespoon of dough into a ball and flatten it slightly. Place on a greased cookie sheet and press an almond into the center. Bake at 350° for 13 to 15 minutes or until cookies are set and lightly browned. Yields about 16 cookies.

Vanilla Ice Cream with Fresh Apricot or Peach Puree

If you plan to serve this when apricots or peaches are not in season, then use frozen peaches as a good alternative. Frozen peaches are sold peeled and pitted.

- 8   scoops vanilla ice cream. These can be shaped earlier in the week, wrapped in double thicknesses of plastic wrap, and stored in the freezer.
- 8   teaspoons chopped, toasted almonds

Apricot or Peach Puree:
- 1   pound peaches or apricots, peeled and pitted
- 1   tablespoon concentrated frozen orange juice
- 1   tablespoon lemon juice
- 1   tablespoon sugar

In a food processor, blend together all the ingredients until fruit is pureed. Place a little fruit puree on a plate, top with a scoop of ice cream and sprinkle with a few chopped toasted almonds.

A Special Family Dinner with Old Favorites

Mushroom & Barley Soup
Petite Knishes with Potatoes & Onions (see Index), or
No-Knead Flatbread with Onions & Cheese

Roast Chicken with
Old-Fashioned Cracker Stuffing
Kasha Varnishkes (Kasha & Bow-Tie Noodles with Mushrooms & Onions)
Spiced Peaches or Apricots (see Index)
Maple-Glazed Carrots with Currants & Cinnamon

Dark Chocolate Fudge Sour Cream Cake with Chocolate Buttercream
Viennese Walnut & Apricot Bars
Velvet Brownies with Walnuts & Chocolate Buttercream

While this dinner is informal, it is by no means plain, and can be served to family and friends for some special occasion. A birthday, anniversary or a homecoming will become memorable with this menu.

The vegetables are safely tucked in the soup, so no wrinkled noses in that department. The little knishes are wonderful and will certainly start a tradition in your home. They are exceedingly easy to prepare and freeze beautifully. Alternatively, the Flatbread is excellent with the soup.

This menu is made up of old favorites. Roast Chicken with Cracker Stuffing, Kasha & Noodles with Mushrooms & Onions, Maple Glazed Carrots, Spiced Peaches or Apricots.

Desserts are wonderful. The Dark Chocolate Fudge Sour Cream Cake is one of my favorites; as are the Hungarian Apricot Walnut Bars. And who doesn't love Brownies topped with a little Buttercream? If you like your Brownies plain, omit the Buttercream and decorate with a faint sprinkle of sifted powdered sugar.

No-Knead Flatbread with Onions & Cheese

This is a very popular bread in many Italian restaurants. It is a Focaccia which can be made with any number of flavors. It is very simple to prepare at home, for a few ingredients are simply beaten together and then the rising takes place at room temperature while you are free to do other things. There are many alternatives to onions and cheese. Rosemary and garlic, olives, raisins are all good.

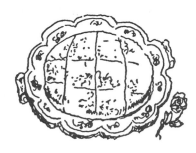

5 1/2	cups flour
1	teaspoon salt
2	cups warm water (110°)
1	package active dry yeast
1/4	cup olive oil
1	cup chopped green onions
1/2	cup grated Parmesan cheese

In the large bowl of an electric mixer, mix flour and salt. In a glass measuring cup, soften yeast in warm water. Beat yeast mixture into the flour until blended. Beat in the olive oil. Continue beating for 5 minutes. Drizzle a little oil over the dough, cover the bowl and allow to rise at room temperature for 1 hour. Punch dough down and beat in the onions and cheese.

Spread dough evenly into a 10x15x1-inch oiled baking pan, cover with a towel and allow to rise at room temperature for 1 1/2 hours. Place pan on a baking sheet (to prevent bottom from overbrowning) and bake at 400° for 30 to 35 minutes, or until top is golden brown. Cut into squares to serve. Yields 15 3-inch squares.

Mushroom & Barley Soup with Petite Knishes with Potatoes & Onions

You would have to go far and wide to find a more "comforting" soup. This is a great soup and a joy to serve. The Petite Knishes is one of my favorites and I hope you enjoy them as much as my family and friends do. Please boil the egg barley separately so as to remove the starch.

1 1/2	pounds mushrooms, cleaned and very thinly sliced
1/2	pound baby carrots, sliced
2	large onions, finely chopped
6	shallots, minced
4	cloves garlic, minced
6	tablespoons butter
1	package (7 ounces) egg barley (barley-shaped egg noodles)
1	quart boiling water
6	cups rich chicken broth
1	teaspoon dried dill weed
	salt and pepper to taste

In a Dutch oven casserole, saute together first group of ingredients until onions are soft and all the liquid rendered is evaporated. In a separate pot, boil the egg barley in simmering water until almost tender and drain in a large strainer. (Don't use a collander or your barley will run down the drain.) Add the barley and the remaining ingredients to the Dutch oven and simmer soup for 10 minutes, stirring now and again. Serves 10.

Roast Chicken with
Old-Fashioned Cracker Stuffing

This is a highly-seasoned Basting Mixture that will give a rich and succulent flavor to the chicken and will also add the most beautiful color. I prefer to bake the stuffing separately, so I prepare the stuffing with rich chicken broth to make up for the drippings from the bird.

> 2 whole chickens, (about 3 to 4 pounds, each). Brush inside and
> out with Basting Mixture.

In a 12 x 16-inch place chickens and bake at 350° for 1 hour 15 minutes, basting now and again with Basting Mixture. Chickens will be a gorgeous golden color and very, very delicious. Serves 8.

Basting Mixture:
- 1/2 cup margarine or butter
- 1 teaspoon garlic powder
- 1 teaspoon onion powder
- 2 teaspoons paprika
- salt to taste

In a saucepan, heat together all the ingredients until margarine or butter is melted.

Old-Fashioned Cracker Stuffing:
- 3 onions, chopped
- 2 stalks celery, finely chopped
- 4 shallots, minced
- 1 carrot, grated
- 2 teaspoons poultry seasoning flakes (or 1/2 teaspoon ground
    poultry seasoning)
- 4 tablespoons butter (can double this amount, if desired)

- 9 cups soda cracker crumbs (about 12 ounces)
- 2 eggs, beaten
- salt and pepper to taste

- 3 cans (10 1/2 ounces, each) chicken broth (use only enough to
    make a soft stuffing)

In a Dutch oven casserole, saute together first 6 ingredients until onions are soft. Place mixture in a large bowl and toss in crumbs, eggs and seasonings. Add enough chicken broth to make a soft stuffing (not too dry, but not soggy, either.)

Place stuffing in a 9x13-inch porcelain baker, and bake at 350° for 30 minutes or until heated through and top is crusty. Serves 8.

Kasha Varnishkes

(Kasha & Bow-Tie Noodles with Mushrooms & Onions)

1   cup medium-grain kasha
1   egg, beaten

2   cups chicken or vegetable broth
2   tablespoons butter or margarine
    salt and pepper to taste

4   ounces bow-tie egg noodles, cooked until tender and drained

2   onions, chopped
1/2   pound mushrooms, sliced
2   tablespoons butter or margarine

In a Dutch oven casserole, stir together kasha and beaten egg until blended. Cook, over medium heat, stirring and turning until the egg has dried, and grains are separated, about 2 minutes. Stir in the broth, butter and seasonings, cover pan and cook, over low heat, until liquid is absorbed, about 20 minutes. Fluff with a fork.

Cook bow-tie noodles in briskly boiling water until tender and drain. Set aside. In a skillet, saute onions and mushrooms in butter until onions are tender and beginning to brown. Add the cooked noodles and onion mixture to the kasha, and fluff everything nicely with a fork. Heat through.   Serves 8.

Maple-Glazed Carrots with Currants & Cinnamon

1 1/2   pounds baby carrots, cooked in boiling water for 8 minutes or
        until tender and drained. Salt to taste.

2   tablespoons butter
1/4   cup maple syrup
1/4   cup dried currants

Prepare whole baby carrots, and set aside. In a large skillet, heat together butter and maple syrup. Add carrots and cook, turning with a spatula for 5 minutes or until carrots are shiny and glazed. Add the currants and continue cooking for about 3 minutes   Serves 8.

Dark Chocolate Fudge Sour Cream Cake with Chocolate Buttercream

1/2	cup butter
1/2	cup brown sugar
3/4	cup sugar
2	teaspoons vanilla
2	eggs

2/3	cup semi-sweet chocolate chips, melted
1	cup sour cream

1 1/4	cups flour
2	tablespoons sifted cocoa
1	teaspoon baking powder
1/2	teaspoon baking soda

In the large bowl of an electric mixer, beat together butter and sugars until mixture is light and fluffy. Beat in vanilla. Beat in eggs, chocolate and sour cream, beating well after each addition. Stir together the remaining ingredients and add, all at once, beating until blended.

Divide batter between 2 greased 10-inch springform pans and bake at 350° for about 30 to 35 minutes or until a cake tester, inserted in center, comes out clean. Allow to cool in pans.

When cool, remove from pans and fill and frost with Chocolate Buttercream. Serve on a lovely footed platter. Serves 12.

Chocolate Buttercream:
1/2	cup butter, softened
1	package (6 ounces) semi-sweet chocolate chips, melted
1	teaspoon vanilla

Beat butter until light and creamy. Beat in the chocolate until blended. Beat in vanilla. Will lightly fill and frost 1 10-inch layer cake.

Viennese Walnut & Apricot Bars

If you love apricot jam with walnuts, make these cookies at your first opportunity. They are a marvelous blend of flavors and textures. All together...a butter cookie crust with a hint of lemon, a tart apricot layer and crunchy nut topping...delicious.

Lemon Cookie Crust:
- 1/2 cup butter or margarine
- 1/2 cup sugar
- 1 egg, beaten
- 2 tablespoons grated lemon peel

- 1 1/4 cups flour

- 1/2 cup apricot jam, heated

Walnut Filling:
- 2 cups walnuts, finely ground in a food processor with 1/4 cup sugar
- 2 eggs, beaten
- 1/2 cup sugar
- 1/4 cup flour
- 1/4 teaspoon baking powder
- 1 teaspoon vanilla

To Make Lemon Cookie Crust: In the large bowl of an electric mixer, beat together butter and sugar until blended. Beat in eggs until blended. Beat in lemon until blended. Beat in flour until blended and a soft dough forms. Do not overbeat. Dust dough lightly with flour and with floured fingers, pat dough on the bottom and 1/2-inch up the sides of a greased 9x13-inch baking pan. Bake at 350° for 15 minutes or until dough is just beginning to take on color. Spread apricot jam on crust to 1/2-inch from edge.

To Make Walnut Filling: Beat together filling ingredients until blended and spread it evenly over the jam. Continue baking at 350° for 25 minutes or until filling is set and golden brown. Cut into squares or bars to serve. A faint sprinkle of sifted powdered sugar is a nice touch. Yields 48 cookies.

Velvet Brownies with Walnuts
& Chocolate Buttercream

This is a super velvety brownie, that I know you will love. The only addition is chopped walnuts. Chocolate chips, dates, raisins, or even grated white chocolate can be added. The brownie base is truly delicious. Notice the large amount of vanilla.

3/4	cup butter (1 1/2 sticks)
4	ounces unsweetened chocolate
1	teaspoon instant coffee
4	eggs
2	cups sugar
1	tablespoon vanilla
1	cup flour
1/4	teaspoon salt
1	cup chopped walnuts

In the top of a double boiler, over hot, not simmering water, stir together butter, chocolate and instant coffee until mixture is blended. Beat eggs with sugar and vanilla until mixture is creamy, about 5 minutes. Beat in the chocolate mixture until blended. Stir in the flour, salt and walnuts until blended.

Spread batter in a greased 9x13-inch baking pan and bake at 400° for 22 minutes, or until a cake tester, inserted in center, comes out with a few moist crumbs and top looks dry. Allow to cool in pan. When cool, spread top with Chocolate Buttercream which is optional. Keep the portions small. Yields 48 brownies.

Chocolate Buttercream:
2/3	cup melted semi-sweet chocolate chips
1/3	cup melted butter
1	teaspoon vanilla
	pinch of salt

Stir together all the ingredients until blended.

Note: -Do not overbake or brownies will be dry. On the other hand, do not underbake, or brownies will be pasty.

A New Orleans Sampler at Mardi Gras

Oysters Royale with Garlic, Herbs & Cheese
or
Hot & Spicy Cajun Cornmeal Beef Pie

Etouffée with Shrimp
Corn & Crabcakes with Red Pepper & Tomato Sauce
or
New Orleans Spicy Hot Fried Chicken
New Orleans Corn & Red Pepper Saute
Cajun Tomato Rice

Cajun Orange Date Nut Muffins
Cajun Honey Corn Muffins with Currants

New Orleans Bread Pudding with Apricots & Pecans &
Bourbon Street Sauce
Pecan Bars on Cookie Crust

Here is a sampling of some of the wonderful dishes we enjoyed on our many visits to New Orleans. It was difficult to choose which dishes to include, so at best, consider this a nicely rounded out menu.

The Oysters Royale when served as an hors d'oeuvre and spooned from the casserole, will need some small plates and forks close by. When served in individual ramekins, it can be served as an hors d'oeuvre or as a first course. The Cajun Cornmeal Beef Pie can be cut into squares or wedges. The Etouffée is one of the best-tasting and lovely served with Corn & Crabcakes. Alternatively, the Spicy Fried Chicken with the classic Corn & Red Pepper Saute and Cajun Rice is a great main course.

Two delicious muffins, Orange Date Nut and Cajun Honey Corn are a nice addition to the table. For dessert the classic bread pudding with Bourbon Street Sauce and Pecan Bars as an optional cookie.

Oysters Royale with Garlic, Herbs & Cheese Crumbs

If you are serving this as a casserole, it is best served as a small entree with hors d'oeuvres and drinks. Simply have a large serving spoon and a few small plates close by. To serve as a first course at dinner, I suggest you make individual servings. This can be prepared in individual ramekins. Simply layer crumb mixture, oysters, crumb mixture and a generous sprinkling of grated Parmesan cheese on top. Heat for about 20 minutes at 350° until heated through. Casserole, or individual ramekins, can be prepared earlier in the day, stored in the refrigerator and heated before serving.

   6   cloves garlic, minced
   2   onions, finely chopped
   6   shallots, minced
1/2 cup butter (1 stick)

1/4 cup dry white wine
1/2 teaspoon paprika
1/2 teaspoon thyme flakes
1/4 teaspoon sage
     salt and pepper to taste

   6   cups fresh egg bread crumbs, about 12 slices of bread, crusts removed and made into crumbs in food processor
3/4 cup grated Parmesan cheese
1/8 teaspoon cayenne pepper

   1   can (8 ounces) whole oysters packed in water, drained. Reserve juice.
   3   tablespoons grated Parmesan cheese

In a Dutch oven casserole, saute garlic, onion and shallots in butter until onion is soft, but not browned. Add the next 6 ingredients and simmer mixture until wine is almost evaporated. Toss in the crumbs, cheese and cayenne pepper until blended. Now add enough of the drained oyster juice until crumbs hold together.

In a 9-inch round porcelain baker, layer half the crumb mixture, the drained oysters and then the remaining crumbs on top. Sprinkle top with the 3 tablespoons grated Parmesan. Bake in a 350° oven for about 20 to 25 minutes, or until piping hot. Spoon directly from the porcelain baker onto individual small plates. Serves 8.

Hot & Spicy Cajun Cornmeal Beef Pie with Chiles and Cheese

Everybody loves this pie. Basically, it is two crusty layers of cornmeal with a spicy layer of beef and chiles sandwiched in-between. It is hot and spicy, but you can reduce the amount of red pepper, if you like it less hot. Cut into squares, this can also be served as an accompaniment to soup.

3/4	pound ground beef
1	medium onion, grated
4	cloves garlic, minced
3	whole green chiles (canned) coarsely chopped (4 ounces)
1	cup grated Cheddar cheese
1/8	teaspoon cayenne pepper, or more to taste
1	cup yellow cornmeal
2	eggs
1	cup milk
1 1/2	teaspoons baking soda
1/4	cup melted butter (1/2 stick)
	salt and pepper to taste

In a skillet, saute together beef, onion and garlic until meat is crumbly and loses its pinkness. Drain beef mixture and toss with chiles, cheese, and cayenne pepper. In another bowl, beat together the remaining ingredients until blended.

In a greased 10-inch quiche pan, pour 1/2 the cornmeal batter. Sprinkle meat mixture evenly on top, and pour remaining batter over all. Bake in a 350° oven for about 25 minutes or until top is golden brown and batter is set. Serve warm. Serves 8.

Etouffée with Shrimp

A shrimp etouffée is not a stew or a chowder, but basically a dish served in a small amount of sauce. This dish entails a few steps, but they can be prepared earlier in the day up to the point of sauteing the shrimp. Shrimp can be sauteed 1 hour before serving. When ready to serve, reheat the sauce, then add the shrimp and heat through. Do not overcook at this point.

For the Roux:
- 2 1/2 tablespoons oil
- 1/4 cup flour

In a skillet, heat the oil. Stir in the flour and and continue cooking, stirring constantly, until flour is golden brown. Be careful not to burn the roux. If it burns, it must be discarded.

- 1 onion, chopped
- 1 stalk celery, peeled and chopped
- 1 red bell pepper, seeded and chopped
- 4 tablespoons butter

- 1 cup clam broth
- 1 cup water
- 1/4 teaspoon each, white pepper, black pepper, sweet basil & thyme flakes
- 1/8 teaspoon cayenne pepper
  salt to taste

- 2 pounds medium shrimp
- 1 cup chopped green onions
- 4 tablespoons butter

In saucepan, saute vegetables in butter until onions are soft. Stir in the clam broth, water and seasonings and bring mixture to a simmer. Stir in the roux and continue cooking and stirring until mixture thickens slightly, about 4 minutes.

In a large skillet, saute shrimp and onions in butter until shrimp become opaque. Do not overcook. Add shrimp to the saucepan and cook until heated through. Serves 8.

Corn & Crabcakes
with Red Pepper & Tomato Sauce

While this is a great hors d'oeuvre, it can also be served for a light dinner. In that case, make the patties twice the size and figure 2 for each serving. Crabcakes can be prepared earlier in the day and reheated at time of serving. Reheat in a 350° oven for about 10 minutes or until heated through.

Corn & Crabcakes:

1	medium onion, chopped
1	small red pepper, seeded and diced
1	tablespoon butter
1	egg, beaten
1/4	cup chopped chives
1/2	teaspoon dried dill weed
1/2	cup fresh bread crumbs mixed with 1/4 cup cream
1	pound cooked crabmeat, flaked
1/2	cup frozen corn kernels, defrosted and lightly mashed
	pinch cayenne pepper
	salt and pepper to taste

In a skillet, saute onion and pepper in butter until onion is transparent. Place mixture in a large bowl. Add the remaining ingredients to the bowl and stir until everything is nicely mixed. Shape mixture into 1-inch balls and flatten into patties. Saute crabcakes in butter until browned on both sides. Serve with Red Pepper & Tomato Sauce on the side for dipping. Yields 24 patties.

Red Pepper & Tomato Sauce:

1	small red pepper, seeded and diced
1	medium tomato, peeled, seeded and diced
1	onion, finely chopped
3	cloves garlic, minced
1/4	teaspoon dried dill weed
2	tablespoons butter
1/4	cup dry white wine
1/2	cup cream
2	tablespoons lemon juice
	salt and pepper to taste

In a skillet, saute together first 6 ingredients until vegetables are soft. Add the wine and continue cooking until wine has evaporated. Add the cream and heat through. Stir in the lemon juice and seasonings. Puree mixture in a food processor. Serve warm or place sauce into a bowl and refrigerate. Heat lightly before serving. Serve warm not hot.

New Orleans Spicy-Hot Fried Chicken

As you probably know, I do not have a special fondness for peppery dishes that make your eyes tear and your breath come short. This chicken is "hot" but your palate will not get overpowered.

> 2   fryer chickens, (about 2 1/2 pounds, each). Ask the butcher to cut each chicken into 10 pieces, (2 legs, 2 thighs, 2 wings and 4 breast pieces.) Save the backs and necks for another use.
>
>   Pepper Seasoned Coating
>
> 2   eggs
> 2   tablespoons water

Roll the chicken pieces in the Pepper Seasoned Coating until they are nicely coated. Beat together the eggs with the water until blended.

Dip the coated chicken pieces in the egg mixture and saute them in a little hot oil until they are golden brown on all sides. Place chicken pieces in a 12x16-inch roasting pan and bake for 25 to 30 minutes or until tender. Serves 8.

Pepper Seasoned Coating:
      1/2   cup flour
      1/2   cup grated Parmesan cheese
    1 1/2   teaspoons garlic powder
        1   teaspoon onion powder
        1   tablespoon paprika
      1/2   teaspoon cayenne pepper
            salt to taste (I used 1/2 teaspoon)

In a plastic container with a tight-fitting lid, combine all the ingredients and shake to blend. Unused coating mix can be stored in the freezer.

New Orleans Corn & Red Pepper Saute
(Maque Choux)

Corn, combined with red pepper, green onions and tomatoes is one of the most beautiful dishes to serve. The colors excite the palate. It promises and delivers good taste and enjoyment.

1	large red bell pepper, seeded and chopped
3/4	cup chopped green onions
2	tablespoons butter or margarine
2	tomatoes, peeled, seeded and chopped
2	packages (10 ounces, each) frozen corn
1/3	cup chicken broth
1/3	cup half and half
1/4	teaspoon each, sweet basil and thyme flakes
	salt and pepper to taste
	pinch of cayenne pepper

In an uncovered saucepan, saute together first 3 ingredients until pepper is softened. Add the next 3 ingredients and simmer mixture until most of the liquid is absorbed, about 10 minutes. Add the remaining ingredients and simmer mixture for an additional 10 minutes or until thickened. Serves 8.

Cajun Tomato Rice

Rice with tomato, pepper, onion and garlic is a great accompaniment to the etouffée. The cayenne pepper adds a little bite. You can add a little more pepper if you like it hotter.

2	shallots, minced
2	cloves garlic, minced
1/2	medium red bell pepper, seeded and chopped
1	tomato, peeled, seeded and finely chopped
2	tablespoons butter
	salt and pepper to taste
2	shakes cayenne pepper
2	cups rice
4	cups chicken broth
1/3	cup chopped chives

In a saucepan, saute together first group of ingredients until vegetables are soft. Stir in the rice and broth. Lower heat, cover pan and simmer mixture until rice is tender and liquid is absorbed, about 30 minutes. Stir in the chopped chives before serving. Serves 8.

Cajun Orange Date Nut Muffins

When you serve one of the hot peppery Cajun dishes, this is a nice accompaniment to consider. It is a perfect taste balance. It is deeply flavored with orange and sparkled with raisins, dates and walnuts.

- 1 egg
- 1 cup buttermilk
- 1/3 cup melted butter
- 3/4 cup sugar
- 1 medium orange, grated (about 6 tablespoons)

- 1 1/4 cups flour
- 1 cup whole wheat flour
- 2 teaspoons baking powder
- 1 teaspoon baking soda
- 1 teaspoon cinnamon
- 1 cup chopped, pitted dates
- 1/2 cup yellow raisins
- 3/4 cup chopped walnuts

In a large bowl, beat together first 5 ingredients until blended. In another bowl, combine the remaining ingredients and add them, all at once, to the buttermilk mixture. Stir until dry ingredients are just moistened. Do not overmix.

Divide batter between 12 paper-lined muffin cups and bake in a 400° oven for 22 to 25 minutes, or until muffins are lightly browned and a cake tester, inserted in center, comes out clean. Allow to cool for 10 minutes, and then remove from pan and continue cooling on a rack. Serve these warm with whipped creamy butter. Yields 12 generous muffins.

Cajun Honey Corn Muffins with Currants

- 1 cup yellow cornmeal
- 1 cup milk
- 1/4 cup sour cream
- 1 egg
- 1/4 cup honey
- 1/3 cup butter, melted
- 1/3 cup sugar

- 1 1/4 cups flour
- 1 tablespoon baking powder
- 1 cup dried currants

Beat together first 7 ingredients until blended. Stir together next 3 ingredients and add, all at once, stirring until blended. Do not overmix. Divide batter between 12 paper-lined cups and bake in a 400° oven for 22 minutes, or until a cake tester, inserted in center, comes out clean. Allow to cool for 10 minutes, and then remove from pan and continue cooling on a rack. Yields 12 muffins.

New Orleans Bread Pudding with Apricots & Pecans & Bourbon St. Sauce

    3   eggs
1 1/2   cups sugar
    4   teaspoons vanilla
    4   tablespoons melted butter
    3   cups milk

   12   slices stale (or toasted) raisin bread, crusts removed and cubed,
            about 12 ounces
    4   ounces chopped dried apricots (1 cup)
  1/2   cup chopped pecans
    1   tablespoon cinnamon sugar

In a large bowl, beat together first 5 ingredients until blended. Toss in bread and allow to stand until liquid is evenly absorbed. Stir in apricots. Place mixture into a buttered 9x13-inch baking pan and sprinkle top with pecans and cinnamon sugar. Press pecans gently into the top to avoid burning. Bake at 350° for about 1 hour or until pudding is set and golden brown. To serve, cut into squares and serve with a spoonful of Bourbon Street Sauce on top. Whipped Creme Fraiche Vanilla is also delicious. Serves 10.

Bourbon Street Sauce:
    1   cup sugar
  1/2   cup butter
    2   tablespoons water

    1   egg, well beaten
  1/4   cup Bourbon whiskey

In the top of a double boiler, over hot water, heat together first 3 ingredients until sugar is melted. Stir in beaten egg and Bourbon and cook and stir until sauce is slightly thickened and mixture reaches 170° on a candy thermometer. Do not overcook. Yields about 1 1/4 cups sauce.

Whipped Creme Fraiche Vanilla:
  3/4   cup cream, whipped
    1   tablespoon sugar
    1   teaspoon vanilla
  1/4   cup sour cream
    2   teaspoons Bourbon

Beat cream with sugar and vanilla until stiff. Beat in sour cream and Bourbon until blended.

Pecan Bars on Cookie Crust

Cookie Crust:
  - 1 1/2   cups flour
  - 1/3   cup sugar
  - 1/2   cup butter or margarine (1 stick)

In the large bowl of an electric mixer, beat together all the ingredients until mixture resembles coarse meal. Pat mixture evenly into a lightly greased 9x13-inch pan and bake at 350° for 15 minutes, or until crust is just beginning to take on color.

Pecan Filling:
  - 6   tablespoons butter or margarine, melted
  - 1 1/2   cups brown sugar
  - 2   eggs
  - 2   teaspoons vanilla

  - 3/4   cup flour
  - 1   teaspoon baking powder
  - 1   teaspoon cinnamon
  - 1/4   teaspoon salt
  - 2   cups chopped pecans

In the large bowl of an electric mixer, beat together first 4 ingredients until blended. Beat in remaining ingredients until blended. Pour mixture into prepared crust and continue baking at 350° for about 20 to 25 minutes or until top is set. Allow to cool in pan. When cool, drizzle with Vanilla Glaze. Cut into squares or bars. Yields about 40 cookies.

Vanilla Glaze:
  - 1/2   cup sifted powdered sugar
  - 2   tablespoons cream
  - 1/4   teaspoon vanilla

Stir together all the ingredients until blended. Add a little sugar or cream to make glaze a loose drizzling consistency.

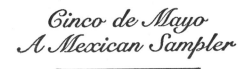

Cinco de Mayo
A Mexican Sampler

Strawberry Margueritas

Starters
Fresh Tomato Salsa with Corn & Chiles
Layered Mexican Dip with Chiles & Cheddar
Guacamole Mold with Tomatoes, Onions & Chiles
Easiest & Best Guacamole with Tomatoes, Onions & Chiles

Mexican Corn & Chile Soup
Tortillas with Tomatoes & Cheese

Old West Tamale Casserole
Red Beans, Pink Rice & Green Onions
or
Chili con Carne
Golden Mexican Rice with Tomato & Chiles
or
Red Hot Lentil Chili
Mexican Cornbread with Chiles & Cheese

Brownie Cake with Chocolate Buttercream
Giant Oatmeal, Chocolate & Walnut Crisp

Hot Cocoa for a Crowd
Hot Chocolate for Special Occasions

The popularity of Mexican food has spread from coast to coast. This menu contains some of the popular dishes and, at best, it is the tip of the iceberg. All of the dishes are spicy, but none are very hot.

Margueritas are delicious with the different Starters. Most restaurants serve Fresh Tomato Salsa with corn chips at the beginning of the meal, but the layered Mexican Dip or one of the guacamole recipes would be a good choice for home entertaining. Mexican Corn & Chile Soup with Tortillas with Tomatoes & Cheese is a great soup course. Two exciting colorful rice recipes; the Tamale Casserole pairs well with the Red Beans & Pink Rice, as does Chili con Carne with Golden Mexican Rice. The Red Hot Lentil Chili with Mexican Cornbread is a nice change from chili beans.

For dessert, a few chocolates to choose from...a Brownie Cake, or a Giant Oatmeal Chocolate Crisp and two wonderful chocolate beverages.

Fresh Tomato Salsa with Corn & Chiles

Adding corn to fresh salsa is a nice touch. Serve this with scrambled eggs, roast chicken, raw vegetables or corn chips.

3	medium tomatoes (about 1 pound), finely chopped
1/3	cup finely chopped green onions
4	tablespoons finely chopped red onion
2	tablespoons chopped cilantro
1/2	cup frozen corn kernels
1	can (4 ounces) diced green chiles
1	tablespoon oil
2	tablespoons red wine vinegar
2	tablespoons lemon juice
1/8	teaspoon hot pepper flakes
	salt and white pepper to taste

In a large bowl, stir together all the ingredients, cover bowl and refrigerate for several hours. Yields about 3 1/2 cups.

Layered Mexican Dip with Chiles & Cheddar

1	onion, chopped
2	cloves garlic, minced
1	tablespoon oil
1	pound lean ground beef or turkey
1	envelope prepared Taco Mix (about 1.25 ounces)
	salt and pepper to taste
1	can (1 pound) refried beans
1	cup sharp Cheddar cheese, grated
1	can (4 ounces) diced green chiles
1	cup low-fat sour cream
2	tomatoes, peeled, seeded and chopped
1/2	cup chopped green onions

Saute together first 3 ingredients until onion is transparent. Add the next 4 ingredients and saute until meat loses its pinkness. Drain beef and place in a 9x9-inch baking pan. Spread refried beans over the top and sprinkle cheese and chiles evenly over all. Bake at 350° for 15 to 20 minutes, or until heated through and cheese is melted. Stir together the remaining ingredients and spoon on top of casserole. Serve at once with tortilla chips for dipping. Delicious. Serves 8 as a hefty hors d'oeuvre.

Guacamole Mold with Tomatoes, Onions & Chiles

1	package unflavored gelatin
1/2	cup water
4	avocados, mashed
4	tablespoons lemon juice, or more to taste
1	cup sour cream
1	can (4 ounces) chopped green chiles
1	small onion, grated
1	tomato, peeled, seeded and chopped
2	tabasco peppers, finely minced

In a metal measuring cup, soften gelatin in water. Place cup in a pan of simmering water and stir until gelatin is dissolved.

In a large bowl, stir together the remaining ingredients until well mixed. Stir in the dissolved gelatin. Spread mixture evenly into a 6-cup mold and refrigerate until firm.

Unmold onto a lovely platter and decorate with green leaves and scored lemon slices. Serve with toasted flour tortillas for spreading.

To toast flour tortillas:
Cut flour tortillas into wedges and toast in a 350° oven until crisped. Or place whole tortillas in a toaster oven for about 1 or 2 minutes, or until tortillas are crisped. Bubbles will form. This is normal. Guests will have to break off a piece of the crisped tortilla to enjoy with the mold.

Easiest & Best Guacamole with Tomatoes, Onions & Chiles

2	large avocados, mashed
1	small onion, finely chopped
1	can (4 ounces) diced green chiles
1	tomato, seeded and chopped
4	tablespoons lemon juice
1/2	cup low-fat sour cream

Combine all the ingredients in a large bowl and stir until blended. Serve with crisp tortilla chips for dipping. Yields about 2 cups.

Mexican Corn & Chile Soup

Please note that in the following recipe, "corn" appears twice. In the first group of ingredients, it is coarsely chopped. In the second group of ingredients, it is left whole.

2	tablespoons butter
2	large onions, chopped
6	shallots, minced
2	carrots, grated
2	cloves garlic, minced
1	package (10 ounces) frozen corn kernels
6	cups chicken broth
	salt and white pepper to taste

1	package (10 ounces) frozen corn kernels
1	can (7 ounces) diced green chiles
1	can (15 ounces) garbanzos, rinsed and drained
2	teaspoons turmeric
2	teaspoons ground cumin
1	tablespoon chopped cilantro

In a large covered stockpot, bring first group of ingredients to a boil, lower heat and simmer mixture for 30 to 40 minutes, or until vegetables are very tender. Blend the vegetables in a food processor until mixture is finely chopped and return them to the soup. Stir in the remaining ingredients and simmer soup for 15 minutes. Serve with Tortillas with Tomatoes & Cheese. Serves 8.

Tortillas with Tomatoes & Cheese:

8	corn tortillas, cut into fourths. These will be reassembled.
1	cup chopped tomatoes
1	cup grated Jack cheese
8	teaspoons grated Parmesan cheese

In a 12x16-inch pan, reassemble the corn tortillas. Sprinkle each with 2 tablespoons tomato, 2 tablespoons cheese and 1 teaspoon Parmesan. Broil for 1 or 2 minutes, or until cheese is melted and top is lightly browned. With a spatula, remove from pan and place on serving platter. Serves 8.

Old West Tamale Casserole
with Sour Cream, Chili & Cheese

There is probably no dish that you can make that is easier than this one or more fun to eat. Everybody loves it. Serve it with some hot corn tortillas, spread with a little sweet butter.

8	prepared tamales (about 3 ounces, each) from the refrigerated section in your market. Cut tamales into 1-inch slices.
1	chili brick (1 pound) from the refrigerated section in your market
1	can (1 pound) stewed tomatoes, chopped. Do not drain.
1	cup sour cream
2	cups medium sharp Cheddar cheese, grated (4 ounces)
1/2	cup chopped green onions

In a 12-inch porcelain baker, place tamale slices evenly. Heat together the chili brick and stewed tomatoes until mixture is blended. (If chili is very thick, dilute with 1/2 cup beef broth.)

Spread chili mixture over the tamale slices. Spread sour cream on top and sprinkle with grated cheese and green onions. Heat in a 350° oven for about 30 to 40 minutes or until casserole is heated through and cheese is melted. Serve with pink rice   Serves 8.

Red Beans, Pink Rice & Green Onions

This casserole is beautiful and delicious too. Pink rice, red beans, green onions add color and excitement to this dish.

2	tablespoons oil
1 1/2	cups long-grain rice
3	cups chicken broth
2	small tomatoes, peeled, seeded and chopped
1	can (1 pound) red kidney beans, rinsed and drained
	salt and pepper to taste
3	green onions, finely chopped. (Use the green part of the onion.)

In a saucepan, stir together first 7 ingredients. Cover pan and simmer mixture for 30 minutes, or until rice is tender and liquid is absorbed. When rice is cooked, stir in the green onions. Serve as an accompaniment to dinner in a Mexican mood. Serves 8.

Chili con Carne

This is our family's favorite chili. The flavor is wonderful. Joey doesn't like it with beans, so when he visits, I omit them.

- 3   onions, chopped
- 6   cloves garlic, minced
- 2   tablespoons oil
- 3   pounds boneless chuck steak, coarsely ground ("chili grind")

- 2   cans (10 1/2 ounces, each) beef broth
- 3   tablespoons Masa Harina (finely ground corn meal)

- 4   tablespoons chili powder (or more to taste)
- 1   tablespoon cumin powder
- 1   tablespoon paprika
- 1   tablespoon dried oregano flakes
- 1   can (16 ounces) tomato sauce
- 2   teaspoons sugar
- 1/4 teaspoon red pepper flakes, (or more to taste)
- 1   can (1 pound) red kidney beans, rinsed and drained (optional)
- 1   can (7 ounces) diced green chiles

In a Dutch oven casserole, saute onions and garlic in oil until onions are softened. Add the beef and cook until the meat loses its pinkness. Stir beef broth with Masa Harina and add to casserole. Stir in the remaining ingredients and simmer mixture, partially uncovered, for 45 minutes, or until meat is tender and mixture is thickened. Serves 8.

Golden Mexican Rice with Tomato & Chiles

- 1   medium tomato, chopped
- 1   can (4 ounces) diced green chiles
- 1   tablespoon oil

- 1 1/2 cups rice
- 3   cups chicken broth
- 1   teaspoon turmeric
- 1/2 teaspoon ground cumin
       salt and pepper to taste

In a saucepan, cook tomato and chiles in oil for 2 minutes, stirring. Stir in the remaining ingredients, cover pan, and simmer mixture for 30 minutes, or until rice is tender and liquid is absorbed. This is excellent to serve with Chili con Carne or Red Hot Lentil Chili. Serves 8.

Red Hot Lentil Chili

Lentils are becoming more and more popular in recipes other than soup. Here, I spice them with chili, cumin and cayenne pepper. An interesting dish and simple to prepare.

1   package (1 pound) lentils, rinsed and picked over for particles
2   large onions, chopped
6   cloves garlic, minced
3   carrots, grated
1   can (28 ounces) crushed tomatoes in puree
8   cups chicken broth
4   tablespoons chili powder
2   teaspoons ground cumin
2   teaspoons sugar
1   teaspoon oregano flakes
1/8   teaspoon cayenne pepper
    salt and pepper to taste

In a Dutch oven casserole, stir together all the ingredients and bring to a boil. Lower heat, cover pan and simmer mixture for about 1 hour or until lentils are tender. Serve in deep bowls with cornbread. Serves 8.

Mexican Cornbread with Chiles & Cheese

To the basic bread you can add 3/4 cup of coarsely mashed corn kernels, fresh or frozen. This adds a little texture to the bread. Chiles and cheese can also be omitted, if you are looking for a simple, basic corn bread.

2   eggs
1   cup low-fat sour cream
1 3/4   cups milk
1/4   cup sugar
6   tablespoons melted butter

2   cups yellow cornmeal
3/4   cup flour
1   tablespoon baking powder

1   can (4 ounces) diced green chiles
1   cup grated Jack cheese

Beat together first 5 ingredients until blended. Combine next 3 ingredients and add, all at once, beating until blended. Stir in the chiles and cheese. Pour batter into a greased 9x13-inch baking pan and bake at 350° for 45 minutes or until top is golden brown. Serves 12.

Brownie Cake
with Chocolate Buttercream

This very simple cake is extremely moist and chocolaty. You will enjoy the fact that it assembles easily and can be frozen. This is a cake-like brownie, not the dense chocolate fudge kind. Cake can be prepared 1 day earlier and stored in the refrigerator.

2	cups flour
2	cups sugar
1	teaspoon baking soda
1/2	cup butter (1 stick)
1	cup water
1/3	cup unsweetened cocoa
1/2	cup sour cream
2	eggs
2	teaspoons vanilla
1	cup chopped walnuts

Place flour, sugar and baking soda in large bowl of mixer. In a saucepan, heat together butter, water and cocoa to boiling point. Pour butter mixture into bowl with flour mixture and beat for 1 minute or until blended. Beat in sour cream, eggs and vanilla until blended. Stir in nuts.

Pour batter into a lightly greased 10x15-inch jelly-roll pan. Bake in a 350° oven for 20 minutes or until a cake tester, inserted in center, comes out clean. Do not overbake. Frost with Chocolate Buttercream Frosting when cool and cut into 2-inch squares.. Yields 35 2-inch cookies.

Chocolate Buttercream Frosting:

1	cup butter (2 sticks), softened
4	tablespoons unsweetened sifted cocoa
3/4	cup sifted powdered sugar
1	teaspoon vanilla

Beat butter until creamy. Beat in remaining ingredients until blended.

Hot Cocoa for a Crowd

2 quarts milk (can use part half and half for a richer taste)
2/3 cup cocoa, sifted
2/3 cup sugar
1 teaspoon vanilla

In a 4-quart enamel saucepan, stir together all the ingredients until blended. Bring mixture to a simmer, stirring now and again, until cocoa comes just to the point of boiling. Serve in mugs with a cinnamon stick, a splash of chocolate liqueur for the grown-ups, or mini-marshmallows for the kids. Yields 8 cups or 12 servings.

Hot Chocolate for Special Occasions

6 cups milk
1 1/2 teaspoons vanilla
1 1/4 cups semi-sweet chocolate chips

In the top of a large double boiler over simmering water, or in a heavy duty saucepan, over low heat, heat milk and vanilla. Add chocolate and continue stirring until chocolate is dissolved. Pour into mugs and serve. Yields about 12 servings.

Strawberry Margueritas

1/4 cup white Tequila
1/4 cup freshly squeezed lime juice
1 ounce Triple Sec
2 to 3 strawberries, hulled
1/2 cup ice cubes

This will yield 2 servings. In a blender, place all the ingredients and blend until ice is very finely chopped and strawberries are pureed.

Giant Oatmeal, Chocolate & Walnut Crisp

Not quite a tart nor a cake, this little gem is actually a giant walnut and oatmeal cookie that is topped with a fudgy chocolate frosting. It is very thin, so don't think anything went wrong.

Cookie Crust:

1/4	cup quick oats (not instant oats)
1/4	cup chopped walnuts
3/4	cup flour
1/3	cup sugar
6	tablespoons (3/4 stick) butter cut into 6 pieces

Filling:

2	eggs
1/3	cup cocoa
1/2	cup sugar
2	tablespoons butter
1/3	cup water
2	teaspoons vanilla
1/2	cup walnuts

For the Crust: In a food processor, place all the ingredients, and pulse mixture until mixture is nicely blended, about 30 seconds. Mixture will be crumbly. Pat mixture on the bottom of a greased 9-inch springform pan and bake at 350° for 20 minutes, or until crust is lightly browned.

For the Filling: In the small bowl of an electric mixer, beat the eggs, just until blended. In a saucepan, heat together next 5 ingredients, until butter is melted. Remove from heat, and slowly beat chocolate mixture into the eggs, until blended. Do not overbeat.

Sprinkle walnuts into prepared crust and pour chocolate filling evenly over nuts. Return to oven and bake at 350° for an additional 20 minutes, or until frosting is just set. Remove from oven and allow to cool in pan. Cut into small wedges to serve. Serves 8.

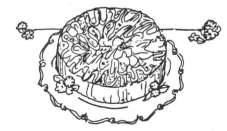

Spring Bacchanal! a la Basque
The Rites of Spring

Tapas de Champiñon Piraness
(Mushrooms Stuffed with Goat Cheese & Pine Nuts)

Ensalada de Provincia
(Provincial Salad with Marinated Tomatoes, Onions & Olives)

Assorted Country-Style Breads

Pasta de Basile e Tomate
(Fresh Linguini with Basil & Sun-Dried Tomato Sauce)

Cordero a la Francesca con Papas Roastizadas
(Rack of Lamb with Garlic & Mustard Sauce & Roasted Potatoes)
or
Pollo a la Basque con Papas Roastizadas
(Chicken in Lemon Saffron Sauce with Roasted Potatoes)

Papa Roastizadas
(Roasted Potatoes)

Veregena, Anillos, Calabazitas
(Roasted Vegetable Platter with Eggplant, Onion Rings, Zucchini)

Fantasia Lemon Cheesecake with
White Chocolate & Fresh Raspberries

This is a grand dining experience and one of the best dinners ever. It is a long dinner, but not heavy. From the very beginning, delicious stuffed mushrooms herald the good things to come. The salad is small, but is an attractive blaze of color (and flavor.) The linguini course can be omitted, but I hope you don't.

Timing is important for the lamb. Place it in the oven 50 minutes before you are planning to serve it and remove it from the oven when it registers 140° (rare). By the time it is carved at the table, it will be medium rare. The chicken requires less attention, can be prepared earlier in the day and reheated at serving time (but please don't overheat it or it will toughen up.)

The potatoes and vegetables are gorgeous when served attractively on a large platter with their beautiful colors and fragrance. Roasted potatoes are enjoyed by all. The Lemon Cheesecake accented with raspberries and white chocolate is the perfect ending to this meal.

Tapas de Champiñon Piraness
(Mushrooms Stuffed with Goat Cheese & Pine Nuts)

Goat Cheese & Pine Nut Filling:
- 1/4 pound log chevre goat cheese, softened
- 1/4 pound low-fat cream cheese, softened
- 3/4 cup garlic croutons, crushed into crumbs
- 1/4 cup minced chives
- 1/4 cup finely chopped pine nuts

- 1 pound medium-sized mushrooms, cleaned and stems removed
  grated Parmesan cheese to sprinkle on top
  minced chives to sprinkle on top

Mix together filling ingredients until blended. Mound mixture into mushroom caps and sprinkle tops lightly with grated Parmesan and chives. Place mushrooms on a cookie sheet and broil for a few minutes until tops are browned. Yields about 20 to 24 stuffed mushrooms and serves 6 to 8.

Note: -Mushrooms can be assembled earlier in the day and broiled before serving.

Ensalada de Provincia
(Provincial Salad with Marinated Tomatoes, Onions & Olives)

- 1 pound tomatoes, cut into 1/4-inch slices
- 1/2 medium red onion, very thinly sliced and separated into rings
- 1 can (2 ounces) sliced black olives
- 2 tablespoons chopped parsley leaves
- 4 ounces crumbled feta cheese

Dressing:
- 1/4 cup olive oil
- 1/4 cup white wine vinegar
- 1/4 cup grated Parmesan cheese
- 1 clove garlic, minced
  salt and pepper to taste

- 1/2 cup garlic croutons. (Use the croutons that resemble pennies.)

In a bowl, toss together salad ingredients. In a glass jar with a tight-fitting lid, shake together dressing ingredients and pour over the salad. Cover bowl and refrigerate for several hours. Just before serving, toss garlic croutons into the salad. Serves 6.

Cordero a la Francesca con
Papas Roastizadas
(Rack of Lamb with Garlic & Mustard Sauce & Roasted Potatoes)

This will be baked before serving, so timing is important. It is also important to undercook the lamb slightly. If you remove it from the oven at 140° or "rare", it will be medium-rare by the time it is carved at the table.

- 2 racks of lamb, (14 chops total; about 3 1/2 pounds trimmed weight, i.e. fat trimmed, rib bones trimmed, chine bone removed). Place a meat thermometer in the thickest part of center rib eye without touching the bone.
- 2 tablespoons Dijon mustard
- 6 cloves garlic, minced

Stir together mustard and garlic and spread thinly over the lamb. Place lamb in a 9x13-inch baking pan. Cover loosely with plastic wrap and refrigerate for several hours. Preheat oven to 350°. Roast lamb for about 1 hour, or until meat thermometer registers 140° for rare. Cover bones with decorative frills. With a flourish, carve roast at the table. Serve with Roasted Potatoes and Garlic Mustard Sauce on the side. Serves 6.

Garlic Mustard Sauce:
- 1/2 pound mushrooms, chopped. (This can be done in a food processor.)
- 6 cloves garlic, finely minced
- 2 shallots, finely minced
- 2 tablespoons butter

- 1/4 cup dry white wine

- 1 can (10 1/2 ounces) beef broth
- 1 teaspoon Bovril, beef-seasoned stock base
- 2 teaspoons Dijon mustard
- 3 tablespoons chopped chives
- 1 tablespoon chopped parsley
  salt and pepper to taste

Saute together mushrooms, garlic and shallots in butter until mushrooms are tender and liquid rendered is evaporated. Add wine and simmer mixture until wine has almost evaporated. Add the remaining ingredients and simmer sauce for 5 minutes.

Note: -Sauce can be prepared 1 day earlier and stored in the refrigerator. Heat before serving.

Pollo a la Basque con Papas Roastizadas
(Chicken Cutlets in Lemon Saffron Sauce with Roasted Potatoes)

This is a subtle sauce that is light and flavorful. The Roasted Potatoes are a great accompaniment. Sauce can be prepared earlier in the day and stored in the refrigerator. Chicken can be prepared earlier in the day, and reheated in a 350° oven until just heated through. Do not overheat.

8   chicken breast halves, sprinkled with garlic powder and flour.
     Brush lightly with 3 tablespoons melted butter.

Bake chicken at 350° for 20 minutes or until just cooked through. Do not overbake.

Lemon Saffron Sauce:
1/2   pound mushrooms, thinly sliced
6   shallots, minced
2   garlic cloves, minced
2   tablespoons butter

1/4   cup dry white wine

1/2   cup rich chicken broth
3 to 4   saffron threads
1   tablespoon lemon juice
1/2   cup cream or half and half
     salt to taste

In a saucepan, saute together first 4 ingredients until mushrooms are tender and liquid is evaporated. Add the wine and continue cooking until wine has evaporated. Soften the saffron in the chicken broth and add to the sauce with the remaining ingredients. Simmer sauce, uncovered, for 10 minutes or until slightly thickened. Place the chicken on a serving platter, surround with Roasted Potatoes and spoon a little sauce on top. Pass the remaining sauce at the table. Serves 8.

Papas Roastizadas
(Roasted Potatoes)

8   medium potatoes, peeled and cut into 1-inch slices
6   tablespoons melted butter
1/4   cup rich chicken broth
     salt and pepper to taste

In a bowl, toss potatoes in butter, broth and seasonings until nicely coated. Spread potatoes in 1 layer in a 10x15-inch non-stick baking pan. Bake at 350°, turning now and again, until potatoes are tender and nicely browned, about 50 minutes.

Veregena, Anillos, Calabazitas

(Roasted Vegetable Platter with Eggplant, Onion Rings, Mixed Zucchini)

This an attractive and exciting vegetable presentation. Vegetables should be served al dente...not too raw, nor mushy, either. Serve on a large platter. Green and yellow zucchini are nice; mushrooms can be added; and keep the onions in rings.

2	Japanese eggplants, cut into 1/2-inch slices. Do not peel.
3	onions, cut into 1/4-inch slices and separated into rings
4	zucchini, cut on a sharp diagonal into 1/4-inch slices. Do not peel.
1/2	cup rich chicken broth
2	tablespoons olive oil
2	tablespoons lemon juice
	salt and freshly ground pepper to taste

In a 9x13-inch pan, toss together all the ingredients. Cover pan with foil and bake at 350° for 20 minutes. Remove foil and continue baking for about 20 minutes, turning now and again until vegetables are tender. Place pan under the broiler for 1 to 2 minutes to brown the tops. Serve warm. Add a splash of lemon juice to taste. Serves 6 to 8.

Pasta de Basile e Tomate

(Fresh Linguini with Basil & Sun-Dried Tomato Sauce)

1	pound fresh linguini, cooked in 4 quarts boiling water until al dente and drained. Fresh linguini cooks in minutes, so watch the time carefully.

Basil & Sun-Dried Tomato Sauce:

8	shallots, minced
8	cloves garlic, minced
2	tablespoons olive oil
4	sun-dried tomatoes (packed in oil) drained and chopped
2	cans (1 pound, each) stewed tomatoes, chopped. Do not drain.
6	tablespoons tomato paste (1/2 of a 6-ounce can)
1/3	cup chopped fresh basil
	pinch of cayenne pepper

Saute shallots and garlic in olive oil until shallots are transparent. Add the remaining ingredients and simmer sauce for 10 minutes. Serve sauce over linguini. A teaspoon of grated cheese is nice, but optional. Serves 6 to 8.

Note: -Sauce can be prepared earlier in the day and stored in the refrigerator. Heat before serving.

Fantasia Lemon Cheesecake with White Chocolate & Fresh Raspberries

You must use the old-fashioned cream cheese for this recipe. It can be purchased at most cheese shops. Some of the cream cheese makers now add gums and fillers to make cream cheese more spreadable. However, this does often create a problem with cheesecakes. If you do use the more modern cream cheese, then reduce the sour cream to 1/4 cup. Otherwise, the cream cheese could become runny and not firm up. This is the easiest and best pie...and does not need to be baked.

Lemon Cheese Filling:

2	packages (8 ounces, each) cream cheese, softened
1/2	cup sour cream
1 1/4	cups sifted powdered sugar
2	tablespoons lemon juice
2	teaspoons grated lemon zest (the yellow part of the peel)

Beat together all the ingredients until blended. Spread mixture evenly into prepared crust and refrigerate until firm. Place raspberries along the edge forming a 1-inch border and sprinkle grated white chocolate in the center. Serves 8.

Vanilla Lemon Cookie Crust:

1 1/2	cups vanilla wafer crumbs
1/4	cup finely chopped walnuts
2	teaspoons grated lemon zest (the yellow part of the peel)
3	tablespoons sugar
1/3	cup butter melted

Line a 10-inch springform pan with parchment paper and lightly grease the paper. In a bowl, stir together all the ingredients and press mixture on the bottom and 1-inch up the sides of the prepared pan. Bake at 350° for 8 minutes, or until top is just beginning to take on color. Set aside to cool.

Topping:

1	pint fresh raspberries
4	tablespoons grated white chocolate

Country French Dinner

Baked Brie with Strawberries & Almonds, or
Baked Brie with Currants & Pine Nuts

French Mushroom Salad Darling

French Flatbread with Cheese & Chives

Cassoulet of Lamb Shanks and Beans

Nut Lovers' Greatest Walnut Cake with
Raspberries & Lemon Drizzle

French Flatbread with Cheese & Chives

This is a great bread in the French mood and so nice for dipping into soups or stews. Bread can be prepared a day earlier, carefully wrapped in double thicknesses of plastic wrap, and heated before serving.

3	cups self-rising flour
3	tablespoons sugar
1	can (12 ounces) beer, cold or at room temperature

1/2	cup chopped chives
1/2	cup grated Swiss cheese
1	teaspoon thyme flakes

4	teaspoons oil
1/4	cup grated Parmesan cheese
1	tablespoon sesame seeds

In the large bowl of an electric mixer, beat together first 3 ingredients until blended. Beat in the next 3 ingredients until blended, about 1 minute. Do not overbeat.

Place oil on the bottom of a 12-inch round baker and spread batter evenly in pan. Brush top with oil that collects on the sides. Sprinkle top with grated Parmesan and sesame seeds.

Bake at 350° for about 45 minutes or until top is golden brown. Allow to cool in pan. To serve, cut into wedges...or serve whole and allow guest to tear off a piece or two.

French Mushroom Salad Darling

This is a most delectable salad and very suitable for a formal or informal dinner. It is a beautiful salad with white mushrooms, flecked with chives and parsley, served on a cradle of lettuce. Unused dressing can be stored in the refrigerator for 1 week.

- 1 egg yolk
- 1/4 cup red wine vinegar
- 2 tablespoons red wine
- 2 tablespoons Dijon-style mustard
- 3 tablespoons chopped chives
- 1 tablespoon chopped parsley
- 1 teaspoon sugar
  salt and pepper to taste

- 3/4 cup peanut oil

- 1 pound mushrooms, cleaned, stems removed and thinly sliced

In a food processor container, place egg yolk, vinegar, wine, mustard, chives, parsley, sugar, salt and pepper. Blend for 30 seconds.

Now add oil in a steady trickle, with the motor running, until dressing is creamy and oil is thoroughly incorporated. Pour dressing to taste over the mushrooms and toss until mushrooms are completely coated. Sprinkle with some chopped chives and serve at once. Yields 1 1/2 cups.

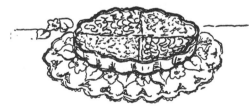

Baked Brie with Strawberries & Almonds

- 1 wheel of brie (8-inch circle) weighing about 2 pounds. Remove the outer rind of mold from the top. Place brie in an 8-inch round quiche dish or porcelain baker.
- 1/2 cup chopped almonds

- 1 cup sliced fresh strawberries

Mark the top of the brie into 4 wedges. Fill alternate wedges with almonds and leave alternate wedges unfilled. Place brie in a 350° oven and bake for about 20 minutes, or until brie is soft. Fill unfilled wedges with sliced strawberries. Serve at once with small toast points or pale soda crackers.

Cassoulet of Lamb Shanks and Beans

Though very country and heady with garlic, this is still a very exciting dish and very satisfying. Purchase small lamb shanks as they are tender and less fat. They also are good as an individual portion. Serve it with some crusty French bread.

1   pound Great Northern dried white beans, washed
       and picked over for any foreign particles
2   quarts water

6   small lamb shanks (about 12 ounces, each) trimmed of visible fat
2   onions, chopped
6   cloves garlic, minced
2   tablespoons olive oil

1   can (1 pound) stewed tomatoes, chopped. Do not drain.
1   can (10 1/2 ounces beef broth)
2   tablespoons tomato paste
1   teaspoon sugar
1/2   cup dry red wine
1   teaspoon thyme flakes
       salt and pepper to taste

In a Dutch oven casserole, bring beans and water to a boil. Boil vigorously for 5 minutes, remove from heat and allow to stand for 1 hour. Drain beans in a collander and discard liquid.

In the same Dutch oven casserole, brown lamb shanks, onions and garlic in oil for about 10 minutes, tossing and turning. Add the beans and the remaining ingredients, cover casserole and simmer mixture for about 1 1/2 to 2 hours or until beans and meat are tender. Serve with a crusty French bread and a green salad. Serves 6.

Baked Brie with Currants & Pine Nuts

1   wheel of brie (8-inch circle) weighing about 2 pounds. Remove
       the outer rind of mold from the top. Place brie in an 8-inch
       round quiche dish or porcelain baker.
3/4   cup currants
3/4   cup pine nuts

Mark the top of the brie into 4 wedges. Fill alternate wedges with currants and pine nuts. Place brie in a 350° oven and bake for 20 minutes, or until brie is soft. Serve at once with small toast points or pale soda crackers.

Nut Lovers' Greatest Walnut Cake
with Raspberries & Lemon Drizzle

If nut cakes are your fancy, this is a little "treasure" you will enjoy often. The nut crust is like an old-fashioned cookie crust, topped with raspberry jam and covered with a tender nut layer. The Lemon Drizzle adds the perfect tartness.

Nut Cookie Crust:

3	ounces butter (3/4 stick), softened
1/2	cup sugar
1	egg
1	cup flour
1	teaspoon vanilla
1	cup chopped walnuts
1/2	cup seedless red raspberry jam, heated

Cream butter and sugar until butter is light. Beat in egg, flour and vanilla until mixture is blended. Beat in chopped walnuts. Spread mixture on the bottom and 1/2-inch up the sides of a buttered 10-inch springform pan and bake at 350° for 20 to 25 minutes or until crust is set. Spread heated raspberry jam on top.

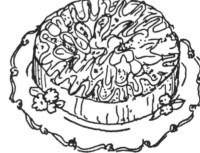

Nut Cake:

3	eggs
1/2	cup sugar
1 1/2	cups walnuts, finely chopped
2	tablespoons flour
1/4	teaspoon baking powder
1	teaspoon vanilla

Beat eggs with sugar for about 3 minutes or until eggs are light and fluffy. Stir in the walnuts, flour, baking powder and vanilla until blended.

Pour mixture into a prepared Nut Cookie Crust and bake in a 350° oven for 40 minutes, or until top is browned and a cake tester, inserted in center, comes out clean. Allow to cool in pan.

When cool, swirl Lemon Drizzle on top in a circular and decorative fashion. To serve, cut into small wedges.. Serves 12.

Lemon Drizzle:
Stir together 1/2 cup sifted powdered sugar with 2 teaspoons lemon juice until blended. Add a little sugar or lemon juice until glaze is a drizzling consistency.

Dining al Fresco
A Star"light" Dinner

Potage of Zucchini & Tomatoes with
Batonettes of Cheese

Chicken in a Delicate Mushroom & Lemon Dill Sauce
Toasted Orzo with Mushrooms & Onions
Peas with Mushrooms & Lemon Sauce

Royal Rhubarb & Strawberry Compote or
Spiced Peaches with Walnuts

Frozen Chocolate Yogurt & Chocolate Sauce in Meringue Shells
Petite Butter Crescents or

Frozen Strawberry Yogurt in Meringue Shells
Lemon Butter Wafers or

Frozen Peach Yogurt & Raspberry Sauce in Meringue Shells
Apricot Walnut Chewies

If you are looking for a menu that is extravagant and exciting, yet on the light side, this is a good one to consider. I have served this simple menu and given it to friends so many times and the reports are that it has always been a terrific success. I have included several options which have a good deal of variety and interest. While I call this a Light Menu, it does not compare to steamed vegetables with a twist of lemon. This menu is positively delicious and interesting and merely on the light side.

From the very beginning, this is a splash of brilliant colors and interesting shapes, not to mention the rich variety of tastes. This is also very easy on the hostess, for every dish can be prepared one day earlier and heated before serving...except for the chicken which I would prepare slightly undercooked earlier in the day.

The desserts are truly simple to prepare and quite beautiful to serve. Meringue shells, filled with frozen yogurt and a colorful sauce is reasonably low in calories, yet looks extravagant and enticing. Cookies, to serve with the frozen yogurt, are chosen to balance tastes.

Potage of Zucchini & Tomatoes
with Batonettes of Cheese

What a sublime soup, marvelously flavored with onions and garlic and herbs. The Batonettes are incredibly good, and exceptionally easy to prepare, starting, as they do, with frozen puff pastry. This soup can be served either warm or chilled.

6   medium zucchini, scrubbed, but do not peel. Cut into thin slices.
2   large onions, chopped
4   cloves garlic, minced
2   shallots, chopped
2   tablespoons butter

1   can (1 pound) stewed tomatoes, finely chopped. Do not drain.
2   cans (10 1/2 ounces, each) chicken broth
2   teaspoons lemon juice
1/2 teaspoon sugar
1   tablespoon chopped parsley
1/2 teaspoon dried dill weed or more to taste
    salt to taste

1/2 cup half and half

In a Dutch oven casserole, saute first 5 ingredients together, until vegetables are soft and liquids rendered are evaporated. Do this over medium-low heat, stirring from time to time. Place mixture in food processor and blend until mixture is coarsely chopped.

Spoon vegetables back into Dutch oven and add the next 7 ingredients. Simmer soup for 20 minutes, with cover slightly ajar. Just before serving, add cream and heat through. Serve with Batonettes of Cheese as the loveliest accompaniment. Yields 8 servings.

Batonettes of Cheese:
1   sheet frozen puff pastry, about 12x12-inches
1   egg, beaten
1/2 cup grated Parmesan cheese
1/4 teaspoon dill weed

Cut puff pastry into thirds, yielding 3 strips 4x12-inches. Cut each strip into 1-inch batonettes (little batons), yielding 36 slices, measuring 4x1-inches. Place on a cookie sheet and baste with beaten egg. Sprinkle with combination of cheese and dill. Bake in a 350° oven until puffed and brown. Store unused batonettes in an air-tight container. Yields 36 batonettes.

Chicken in a Delicate Mushroom & Lemon Dill Sauce

This is one of the simplest, most elegant dishes you can serve for the most discriminating dinner party. Yet it is simple enough to prepare for family and friends some Sunday night, too. The sauce is subtle and delicate with a good deal of depth and character. And it can be prepared, from the beginning to end, in 30 minutes.

4   chicken breasts, boned and cut in halves. Sprinkle lightly with salt and garlic powder. Dust lightly with flour and brush lightly with 3 tablespoons melted butter.

Mushroom & Lemon Sauce:

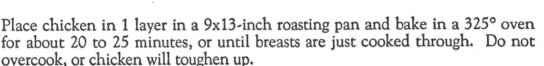

1/2	pound mushrooms, sliced
2	cloves garlic, minced
2	shallots, minced
2	tablespoons butter
1/4	cup dry white wine
1/2	cup rich chicken broth
1	tablespoon chopped parsley
1/2	teaspoon dried dill weed
	salt to taste
1/2	cup cream
1	tablespoon lemon juice

Place chicken in 1 layer in a 9x13-inch roasting pan and bake in a 325° oven for about 20 to 25 minutes, or until breasts are just cooked through. Do not overcook, or chicken will toughen up.

Meanwhile, saute together, mushrooms, garlic, shallots in butter until mushrooms are tender, but not browned, and all the liquid rendered is absorbed. Add the wine and cook until the wine is evaporated. Add the remaining ingredients and simmer sauce for about 10 minutes, uncovered, or until it is slightly thickened.

Place the warm chicken on a lovely platter and spoon a little sauce on the top. Pass the remaining sauce at the table. Serves 8.

Note: -*Sauce can be prepared earlier in the day and heated before serving.*
      -*Chicken can be sprinkled with seasoning and flour earlier in the day, but bake before serving.*

Toasted Orzo with Mushrooms & Onions

Orzo comes in 3 sizes, small, medium or large. I prefer the large size for it's dramatic appearance. Serving it with mushrooms and onions is truly wonderful.

2	cups large-size orzo (rice-shaped pasta)
1 1/2	tablespoons oil
4	cups chicken broth
	salt and pepper to taste
1	onion, chopped
1/2	pound mushrooms, sliced
1	tablespoon oil

In a Dutch oven casserole, saute orzo in oil until the first sign of color. Add broth and seasonings, cover pan and simmer orzo for 35 minutes, or until orzo is tender and liquid is absorbed.

Meanwhile, in a large skillet, saute together onion and mushrooms in oil until onion is tender and liquid rendered is evaporated. Stir mushroom mixture into cooked orzo and heat through. Serves 8 to 10.

Peas with Mushroom & Lemon Sauce

1/2	pound mushrooms, sliced
1	small onion, minced
1	clove garlic
2	tablespoons butter
1/2	cup chicken broth
3	tablespoons lemon juice
1/8	teaspoon ground poultry seasoning
	salt and pepper to taste
2	packages (10 ounces, each) frozen peas

In an uncovered saucepan, saute together first 4 ingredients until onion is soft. Add the next 5 ingredients and simmer sauce for 2 minutes. Add the peas and simmer peas for 3 minutes or until they are tender. Serves 8.

Spiced Peaches with Walnuts

This very versatile, tart and spicy fruit is nice to serve with chicken or veal. It is also great to serve as a topping for ice cream or non-fat yogurt. It is attractive and colorful on a buffet. Can be prepared earlier in the day and heated before serving. Apples or apricots can be substituted for the peaches. Can be served warm or cold.

8   peaches, (about 2 pounds) peeled, pitted and cut in half
1/2   cup orange juice

2   tablespoons sugar
1/2   teaspoon cinnamon
3   sprinkles, each, ground nutmeg and ground cloves
1/2   cup coarsely cut walnuts

Place peaches in one layer in a shallow baker and pour orange juice on top. Stir together sugar, cinnamon, nutmeg and cloves and sprinkle evenly over the fruit.

Bake peaches in a 350° oven, basting every now and again, about 20 minutes. Sprinkle top with walnuts and bake another 10 minutes. Serve warm or at room temperature. Serves 8.

To make Spiced Apples with Walnuts:
Substitute 2 pounds apples, peeled, cored and sliced, for the peaches. Total baking time is 45 minutes. Sprinkle with walnuts after 35 minutes and then bake 10 minutes longer.

To make Spiced Apricots with Walnuts:
Substitute 2 pounds apricots, peeled, halved and stoned, for the peaches. Baking time is the same as for the peaches.

Royal Rhubarb & Strawberry Compote

This simple but very delicious compote is always a pleasure to serve. It is tart, fruity and refreshing. Make extras as almost everyone takes seconds. Recipe that follows is doubled...as any leftover compote can be stored in the refrigerator

1   bag (20 ounces) frozen rhubarb
1/2   cup orange juice
1/2   cup sugar
2   tablespoons lemon juice

1   package (12 ounces) frozen strawberries

In a saucepan, simmer together first 4 ingredients until rhubarb is tender, but not mushy, about 10 minutes. Add the strawberries, and simmer compote for 2 minutes. Serves 8 to 10.

Frozen Strawberry Yogurt in Meringue Shells

This is one of the easiest desserts to prepare, as the shells and frozen yogurt can be purchased. It is, also, a beautiful choice for a formal or informal summer dinner. It looks spectacular with its white base, a mountain of frozen pink yogurt and red strawberries, sparkled with liqueur, on the top and sides. The meringue shells can be purchased in most bakeries. They can be filled with the yogurt earlier in the afternoon and stored in the freezer. Remove from the freezer 10 minutes before serving, if yogurt is frozen solid. Spoon the fresh strawberries on the top and sides just before serving. Recipe for Meringue Shells follow, if you choose to prepare your own.

8	meringue shells, about 4-inches in diameter
4	cups frozen non-fat strawberry yogurt
1 1/2	pints fresh strawberries, sliced (reserve 8 large strawberries for decorating the tops)
3	tablespoons Grand Marnier liqueur
4	teaspoons chopped toasted almonds (optional)

Pile yogurt into meringue shells in a high swirl, (4 ounces in each), cover with plastic wrap and freeze until serving time. Mix together sliced strawberries and Grand Marnier about 1 hour before serving and store in the refrigerator. To serve, spoon the strawberries over the yogurt and place one whole strawberry on top. A sprinkling of chopped toasted almonds is a nice addition. Serves 8.

Frozen Peach Yogurt & Raspberry Sauce in Meringue Shells:
-Substitute non-fat peach yogurt and top with defrosted raspberries in syrup.

Frozen Chocolate Yogurt & Chocolate Sauce in Meringue Shells:
-Substitute non-fat chocolate yogurt and top with a drizzle of chocolate syrup or chocolate sauce.

Meringue Shells

While these are available at most bakeries, the recipe is included in the event your bakery does not sell them. The shells are attractive filled with frozen strawberry yogurt and drizzled with sliced strawberries. Chocolate frozen yogurt, a drizzle of chocolate sauce and a sprinkle of toasted sliced almonds is also beautiful. Meringue shells are basically not baked but dried in the oven. Don't allow them to brown. Meringue kisses can be crushed and served as a base for the yogurt.

> 3   egg whites, at room temperature
> 3/4   cup sugar

In the large bowl of an electric mixer, at medium speed, beat whites until they are foamy. Start adding the sugar, a tablespoon at a time and increase speed to high. Keep beating while adding the sugar slowly, until meringue is stiff and shiny. Line a cookie sheet with parchment paper and drop meringue by the heaping tablespoon onto the paper. With the back of a spoon, indent the center and build up the sides. Bake at 225° for 1 hour, turn oven off and allow meringues to dry for several hours in the oven. Shells should not brown. This will yields 12 meringue shells.

To Make Meringue Kisses:
These are low-calorie, non-fat little kisses that you may want to serve with non-fat yogurt on another occasion. They can be crushed and served as a base or they can be served whole on the side. Follow instructions as above, but drop meringue by the heaping teaspoonful onto a parchment-lined pan. Yields about 48 small kisses.

Petite Butter Crescents

These are very small, petite morsels of deliciousness that are nice to serve with frozen yogurt or ice cream. These can be shaped into crescents, into flat little wafers or small rings.

> 1/2   cup butter (1 stick), softened
> 1/4   cup sifted powdered sugar
> 1/2   teaspoon vanilla
> 1   cup flour, sifted
> 1/3   cup very finely chopped walnuts or pecans

Cream together butter, sugar and vanilla. Beat in flour until blended. Beat in nuts until blended. Shape 1 teaspoon of dough into tiny crescents. Place on a lightly greased cookie sheet and bake at 350° until dough is set and just beginning to take on color. Do not allow cookies to get brown. Allow to cool and sprinkle with sifted powdered sugar. Yields about 40 cookies.

Lemon Butter Wafers

These are intensely lemon-flavored, so cut down on the lemon zest if you like it milder. Make certain the lemon zest is very finely grated.

- 1/2 cup butter (1 stick), softened
- 1/4 cup sugar
- 1 teaspoon vanilla
- 1 cup flour
- 1 tablespoon finely grated lemon zest (yellow part of the peel)

Cream together butter, sugar and vanilla. Beat in flour until blended. Beat in lemon zest until blended. Shape 1 teaspoon of dough into 1-inch wafers. Place on a lightly greased cookie sheet and bake at 325° until dough is set and just beginning to take on color. Do not allow cookies to get brown. Allow to cool and sprinkle with sifted powdered sugar. Yields about 30 cookies.

Apricot Walnut Chewies

- 2 cups yellow cake mix, without pudding
- 1/2 cup butter (1 stick)

- 1 package (6 ounces) dried apricots, finely chopped
- 1 1/2 cups coarsely chopped walnuts

- 1 can (14 ounces) condensed milk

Beat together cake mix and butter until blended. Pat mixture on the bottom of a 9x13-inch pan. Sprinkle top with apricots and walnuts. Drizzle condensed milk evenly over all.

Bake cookies in a 350° oven for about 30 or 35 minutes or until topping is golden brown. Allow to cool in pan. Cut into squares and sprinkle lightly with sifted powdered sugar. Yields about 48 chewies.

A Midsummer Night's Celebration

Mushroom Duxelles with Toast Points, or
Royal Crown Mousse of Salmon

Coulibiac of Dilled Chicken & Mushrooms with
Cucumbers in Sour Cream
or
Oven-Grilled Vegetable Salad

Butterflied Roast Leg of Lamb with Lemon, Garlic & Yogurt
Bulgur with Lemon & Chives
Honey Carrots with Onions, Yogurt & Dill

Lemon & Almond Tart with Raspberry Jam & Meringue Topping
White Chocolate Cheesecake with Almond Macaroon Crust

This is a semi-formal dinner, very special, and perfect for a birthday or anniversary celebration. From beginning to end, it creates an air of originality and creativity. Mushroom Duxelles, very delicate and delicious on dainty toast points, is a nice starter. The Royal Crown Mousse of Salmon is loved by all.

As a first course, the Coulibiac of Dilled Chicken is fit for a King. This is the recipe I gave the chef to prepare as the first course at my daughter's wedding...so you know it is a favorite. A little Cucumber Salad goes well with it. Or you may wish to serve a Grilled Vegetable Salad, which is so popular nowadays.

The Butterflied Leg of Lamb, served with Bulgur and Honeyed Carrots has everyone asking for more.

And for dessert, choose from 3 very incredible summer desserts...a White Chocolate Mousse, a White Chocolate Cheesecake or a very special Lemon & Almond Tart.

Every dish can be prepared earlier and heated before serving.

Mushroom Duxelles with Toast Points

You will enjoy serving this incredible mushroom delicacy with simple toast points as a light introduction to dinner. This can be served warm (not hot) or cool (not cold). It is light and delicate and very flavorful.

1 onion, minced
1 tablespoon butter

1 pound mushrooms, thinly sliced
3 tablespoons lemon juice
salt and pepper to taste

1/4 cup sour cream
1/4 cup chopped chives

In a large skillet, saute onion in oil until onion is soft. Add the mushrooms, lemon juice and seasonings and saute mushrooms until mushrooms are tender and liquid rendered is evaporated. Place mushroom mixture in a bowl and stir in sour cream and chives. Serve with Toast Points. Yields 6 small servings.

To make Toast Points:
4 slices thin-sliced white bread, crusts removed
butter

Spread each slice of bread with a thin coating of butter. Cut bread slices on the diagonal. Cut each diagonal into 2 triangles. You will have 16 toast points. Place on a cookie sheet and bake at 350° for just a few minutes, or until toast points are dry but not browned. Time will vary depending on the freshness of the bread, so keep an eye on the bread as it bakes. Place on a serving platter covered with plastic wrap until ready to serve.

Cucumbers in Sour Cream

3 large cucumbers, peeled and thinly sliced. Place in a bowl and refrigerate until serving time. Drain thoroughly.

Sour Cream Dressing:
1 teaspoon sugar
1/8 teaspoon pepper
1 tablespoon lemon juice
2 tablespoons vinegar
3/4 cup low-fat sour cream
4 tablespoons chopped chives

Mix the cucumbers with the dressing ingredients and serve at once. Do not allow to stand too long or cucumbers will render their liquid and dressing will become watery. Serves 6 to 8.

Royal Crown Mousse of Salmon

1	package (1 tablespoon) unflavored gelatin
1/4	cup cold water

1 1/2	cups low-fat sour cream
4	tablespoons lemon juice
1/3	cup finely chopped chives
1	tablespoon finely chopped parsley
1/2	teaspoon dried dill weed
1/2	pound sliced smoked salmon. Cut slices into 3/4-inch squares.

In a metal measuring cup, soften gelatin in water. Place cup in a pan with simmering water, and stir until gelatin is dissolved.

In a large bowl, stir the remaining ingredients until blended. Stir in the dissolved gelatin until blended.

Place mixture into a 4-cup ring mold and refrigerate until firm. Unmold onto a lovely footed platter and decorate with green onion frills, cherry tomatoes and lemon slices sprinkled with parsley.

Oven-Grilled Vegetable Salad

2	large onions, peeled and cut into 8 wedges
2	zucchini, (do not peel), ends removed, and cut into 1/2-inch slices
2	Japanese eggplants, (do not peel), stems removed, and cut into 1/4-inch slices
2	red, yellow or green bell peppers, cored and cut into 8 wedges
4	cloves garlic, minced
2	tablespoons olive oil
1/4	cup red wine vinegar or lemon juice
1	teaspoon sugar
	salt and pepper to taste

In a 9x13-inch roasting pan, place all the ingredients and toss and turn until vegetables are evenly coated. Settle the vegetables evenly in the pan, cover pan with foil and bake at 350° for 30 minutes. Remove the foil and continue baking for about 30 minutes, or until vegetables are tender and flecked with brown. Serve warm as a salad, or as a vegetable accompaniment to roast chicken or veal. Serves 8.

Coulibiac of Dilled Chicken & Mushrooms

This heavenly first course is rather simple to prepare when using the prepared puff pastry. Puff pastry can be cut into rounds or triangles. After baking, the puff is cut in half, and the succulent chicken mixture is sandwiched in between. Some of the chicken and sauce can cascade around the pastry and the plate can be sprinkled with a little dill This is a small portion. Puff pastry portions can be made larger by stacking 3 patty shells and yielding 8 triangles.

2	tablespoons butter
1	small onion, minced
1/4	cup minced shallots
1/2	pound mushrooms, sliced and tossed with 1 tablespoon lemon juice
1/3	cup dry white wine
3	teaspoons flour
1/2	pound chicken breast, sauteed quickly in 2 teaspoons of butter, and cut into 1/2-inch pieces
1	cup sour cream
1/2	teaspoon dried dill weed
	salt to taste

In a large skillet, saute together first 3 ingredients until onions are transparent and not browned. Add the mushrooms with the lemon juice and saute until all the liquid rendered is evaporated. Add the wine and cook until wine has evaporated. Add the flour and cook and stir for 2 minutes. Stir in the cooked chicken, sour cream, dill and salt and cook for 1 minute, stirring.

Cut a triangle of puff pastry in half, crosswise. Spoon some of the chicken on the bottom half and top it with the remaining half. Garnish plate lavishly with sprays of dill and lemon flowers sprinkled with parsley. Fills 6 pastry triangles.

To Prepare Triangles of Puff Pastry:

1	package puff pastry patty shells (6)
1	beaten egg
12	sprinkles grated Parmesan cheese

Stack 2 patty shells and roll out to measure a 5-inch circle. Cut circle into 4 wedges. Repeat with remaining patty shells. You will have 12 triangles. Brush tops lightly with beaten egg and sprinkle generously with grated Parmesan cheese. Bake at 350° for 20 to 25 minutes or until puffed and golden. Yields 12. Remaining triangles can be frozen and served with soup or salad.

Butterflied Roast Leg of Lamb with Lemon, Garlic & Yogurt

1   leg of lamb, about 5 pounds, boned and butterflied,
      sprinkled with salt and pepper

1   cup unflavored yogurt
1   onion, finely chopped
1/4 cup oil
4   tablespoons lemon juice
3   cloves garlic, minced
1/2 teaspoon dried dill weed

In a ceramic or plastic bowl, place the leg of lamb. Combine the remaining ingredients and spread it on all sides of the lamb. Cover the bowl with plastic wrap and refrigerate it for several hours or overnight.

Lay the boned lamb in a 9x13-inch roasting pan, and spread some of the yogurt marinade on the cut side of the lamb. Roast the lamb, skin side down, in a 350° oven for about 1 1/2 hours or until a meat thermometer, inserted in the fleshiest part of the lamb, registers 150° for medium-rare and 160° for medium.

Remove any trace of fat from the juices, slice the lamb and drizzle the natural juices over the lamb. Serve with rice seasoned with lemon and dill. Cucumber salad is a nice accompaniment. Serves 6 to 8.

Note: *-When I last made the lamb, I roasted it in the following manner. It was a bit unconventional, but the results were so excellent, that I will share them with you. To avoid last minute reheating, I started the lamb about 3 hours before serving. I roasted it at 350° for 1 hour, reduced the oven temperature to 150° and continued roasting for 2 hours. Somewhere, in between, I defatted the natural juices, and at serving time, the lamb was pink and juicy and perfect for serving. Carve it at the table and serve with pride.*
     -Whichever method you choose, be certain to check your meat thermometer for the degree of doneness.

Bulgur with Lemon & Chives

This is a basic recipe for bulgur. You can add to it any number of minced cooked vegetables...onions, carrots, cauliflowerets, baby peas and the like.

2	shallots, minced
2	teaspoons margarine

1 1/2	cups bulgur (cracked wheat)
2	tablespoons margarine
3	cups vegetable broth
2	tablespoons lemon juice
	salt and pepper to taste

1/2	cup chopped chives

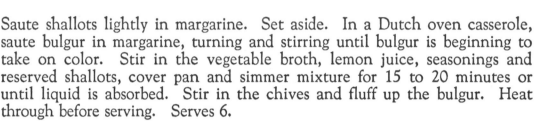

Saute shallots lightly in margarine. Set aside. In a Dutch oven casserole, saute bulgur in margarine, turning and stirring until bulgur is beginning to take on color. Stir in the vegetable broth, lemon juice, seasonings and reserved shallots, cover pan and simmer mixture for 15 to 20 minutes or until liquid is absorbed. Stir in the chives and fluff up the bulgur. Heat through before serving. Serves 6.

Honey Carrots with Onions, Yogurt & Dill

1	onion, chopped
3	shallots, minced
2	tablespoons butter

1	package (1 pound) frozen baby carrots
2	teaspoons honey
1	tablespoon chopped parsley
1/4	cup chicken broth
	salt and pepper to taste

1/2	cup yogurt
1/2	teaspoon dill weed

In a skillet, saute onion and shallots in butter until onion is transparent. Add the carrots, honey, parsley, broth and seasonings. Cover pan and cook over low heat, until carrots are tender. Stir in the yogurt and dill and heat through. Do not allow to boil. Serves 6.

White Chocolate Cheesecake
with Almond Macaroon Crust

When you prepare this glorious dessert, you will wonder how anything so extravagantly delicious could be so easy. A further bonus, this mousselike cheesecake does not have to be baked and can be assembled in very little time.

Almond Macaroon Crust:

1/3	cup butter, melted
3	tablespoons cinnamon sugar
1 1/2	cups macaroon cookie crumbs
1/2	cup chopped almonds

Stir together all the ingredients until blended. Pat mixture on the bottom of a 10-inch glass pie plate and bake in a 350° oven for 8 minutes. Allow to cool.

White Chocolate Cheesecake Filling:

1	package (8 ounces) cream cheese, at room temperature
3/4	cup sifted powdered sugar
6	ounces white chocolate, melted
1	cup cream
1	teaspoon vanilla
1	tablespoon rum

Beat cream cheese and sugar until cream cheese is light and fluffy. Beat in the melted white chocolate. (Place bowl in a larger bowl with warm water to keep chocolate from firming up too rapidly while you whip the cream.)

Beat cream with vanilla and rum until stiff. Remove bowl from water bath and beat in the whipped cream until blended. Pour mixture into prepared crust and refrigerate until firm.

Top can be decorated with grated semi-sweet chocolate and chocolate leaves. Or you may prefer to spoon a little raspberries in syrup, on the top, at serving time. Either are delicious accompaniments.

*Note: -This dessert can be prepared a day ahead and stored in the refrigerator.
-White chocolate can be melted in the top of a double boiler over hot, not boiling water.*

Lemon & Almond Tart with Raspberry Jam & Meringue Topping

This superb tart is a bit more work, but for a holiday or special occasion it is a grand choice. It is basically a thin cake flavored with lemon and almonds, a thin layer of seedless raspberry jam and an almond meringue topping. If you do not own a nut grater, don't make this recipe. The food processor will not grate the almonds to a flour-like consistency. You will need 6 ounces of blanched almonds to produce the 2 cups needed in this recipe. Some health food stores sell "Almond Meal for Macaroons" and if you are able to find it, I would recommend it as a first choice.

For the Cake Layer:

3	egg whites
1/4	cup sugar
1	cup grated blanched almonds (almond meal)
3	egg yolks
3/4	cup sugar
1	teaspoon almond extract
2	tablespoons grated lemon (use fruit, juice and peel)
1	cup grated blanched almonds
2	tablespoons flour
3/4	cup seedless raspberry jam, heated

Beat egg whites until foamy. Gradually beat in the sugar until whites are stiff, but not dry. Fold in the almonds until blended.

In another bowl (you can use the same beaters), beat egg yolks with sugar until light and creamy, about 3 minutes. Beat in the next 4 ingredients until blended. Gradually fold the whites into the yolk mixture until just blended.

Spread batter evenly into a 10-inch wax-paper lined springform pan and bake at 350° for 30 minutes, or until top is golden brown. Allow to cool for 10 minutes and then, brush raspberry jam on the top, leaving a 1/2-inch border.

Spread Almond Meringue on the top, making certain to cover the border. Bake at 350° for 30 minutes or until top is golden brown. Allow to cool in pan. To serve, decorate top with sifted powdered sugar. Serves 10.

Almond Meringue:

3	egg whites
1/4	cup sugar
1	cup grated blanched almonds (almond meal)

Beat egg whites until foamy. Gradually beat in the sugar until whites are stiff, but not dry. Fold in the almonds until blended.

Ladies of the Club Luncheon

Mimosas

Cous Cous Chicken Salad with Artichokes,
Red Peppers, Garbanzos & Raisins

Spiced Apple & Orange Compote

Light & Lovely Lemon Butter Muffins

Easiest & Best Almond & Raspberry Tart, or
Queen Antoinette Peach Tart with Royale Lemon Cream
Coffee and Tea

Cous Cous Chicken Salad with Artichokes, Red Peppers, Garbanzos & Raisins

This salad is gorgeous and so easy to prepare. It is a great dish to serve a large group, as it can be prepared a day before serving and stored in the refrigerator. As an added touch, before serving, sprinkle top with whole cashews and a few additional raisins. Do not add the cashew nuts earlier as they can become too soggy for my taste. Chopped dried apricots can be substituted for the raisins.

3	cups water
2	cups pre-cooked cous cous
2	jars (7 ounces) marinated artichoke hearts, chopped. Do not drain.
4	marinated red peppers, cut into 1/4-inch strips
1	can (1 pound) garbanzos, rinsed and drained
1/2	cup dark raisins, (plumped in orange juice and drained)
1/2	cup chopped green onions
1/4	cup lemon juice, or more to taste
2	cups cooked and chopped boneless chicken breasts

Sprinkle on Top:
1   cup cashew nuts
    additional raisins or chopped dried apricots

In a saucepan, bring water to a boil. Sprinkle in the cous cous, cover pan and cook for 1 minute. Remove pan from the heat. After another minute, fluff the cous cous several times, to separate the grains. Allow to cool. In a large bowl, toss the cous cous with the remaining ingredients, cover bowl and refrigerate. Serve with spiced apples, peaches or apricots. Serves 6.

Queen Antoinette Peach Tart with Royale Lemon Cream Filling

This little gem is a delicious dessert to consider for a Sunday night dinner with family and friends. It is truly delicious and using the frozen peaches you can make it at any time of the year. Of course, fresh peaches are preferred. In this case, you will need 1 1/2 pounds of peaches, peeled, stoned and thinly sliced.

Butter Cookie Crust:

2	cups flour
1/4	cup sugar
1	cup butter (2 sticks), softened
1	egg
3	tablespoons cream

Beat together flour, sugar and butter until mixture resembles fine meal. Beat together egg and cream and add, beating until just blended. Do not overbeat. Pat dough on the bottom and 1-inch up the sides of a greased and parchment-lined 10-inch springform pan and bake at 350° for 15 minutes, or until top looks dry and is just beginning to take on color.

Royale Lemon Cream Filling:

1	pound frozen peaches, thinly sliced
1 1/2	cups sour cream
1	egg
6	tablespoons sugar
2	tablespoons grated lemon
1	teaspoon almond extract

Layer peaches into prepared crust, in a decorative manner. Beat together the remaining ingredients and pour evenly over the peaches. Bake at 350° for about 35 minutes, or until custard is set and just beginning to brown. Allow to cool in pan. When cool, remove from pan and cut into wedges to serve.

Mimosas

Depending on the number of guests, allow 2 ounces of chilled champagne or white wine and 2 ounces of chilled orange juice for each serving. Add a strawberry or a thin slice of orange for color. Freeze orange juice in an ice cube tray if you want to chill the drink further. Serve in stemmed glasses.

Spiced Apple & Orange Compote

Using apples, peaches or apricots, this tart and mouth-watering compote is a great fruit accompaniment. It can be prepared 1 day earlier and stored in the refrigerator. It is exceedingly delicious served warm or cold.

3	large apples, peeled, cored and sliced
1/2	orange, grated. Use fruit, juice and peel, about 3 tablespoons.
1/2	cup orange juice
6	tablespoons cinnamon sugar
	pinch of nutmeg and ground cloves

In a 9x13-inch baking pan, place the first 3 ingredients and sprinkle top with cinnamon sugar and spices. Bake at 350° for 30 minutes. Serve warm or cold. Serves 6.

Light & Lovely Lemon Butter Muffins

1/2	cup butter, softened
2	eggs
2/3	cup sugar
1/2	cup lemon juice
1	tablespoon grated lemon zest (the yellow part of the peel)
2	cups flour
3	teaspoons baking powder
12	sprinkles sugar for topping

Beat together first 5 ingredients until blended. Beat in flour and baking powder until blended. Do not overbeat. Divide batter between 12 paper-lined muffin cups and sprinkle top with a little sugar. Bake at 400° for 20 minutes, or until a cake tester, inserted in center, comes out clean. Allow to cool in pan for 10 minutes, and then remove from pan and continue cooling on a rack. Remove paper linings before serving. Yields 12 muffins.

Easiest & Best Almond & Raspberry Tart

The flavors of almond and raspberry are a great pair. It is one of my preferred combinations...as this is one of my preferred tarts. It is on the order of a Linzer Tart, but different, in that the dough is not crusty, but fine, delicate and fragrant with almonds. This can be prepared 1 day earlier and stored at room temperature, covered with plastic wrap.

1	package (8 ounces) almond paste, crumbled
3/4	cup butter (1 1/2 sticks), softened
1/2	cup sifted powdered sugar
1	teaspoon almond extract
2	eggs, at room temperature
1	cup flour
1/2	teaspoon baking powder
1	teaspoon grated lemon zest (lemon part of the peel)
1	cup raspberry jam, heated

In the bowl of an electric mixer, beat together first 4 ingredients until mixture is thoroughly blended, and light and fluffy. Beat in the eggs until blended. Beat in the flour, baking powder and lemon zest just until blended.

Spread 3/4 of the batter on the bottom of a greased and parchment-lined 10-inch springform pan and spread the jam evenly over the top. Drop rounded teaspoons of the remaining batter along the edge and in the center, dotting them in a decorative fashion, resembling a flower. Allow some of the jam to show through. Bake at 350° for 45 minutes, or until top is golden brown. Allow to cool in pan.

When cool, brush top with Lemon Glaze. Cut into wedges to serve. Serves 10 to 12.

Lemon Glaze:
Stir together 1/2 cup sifted powdered sugar and 1 tablespoon lemon juice until blended. Brush glaze on the petals of dough on top.

A Sedate and Proper Victorian Tea

Petite Sandwiches
Cucumber & Chives
Smoked Salmon & Dill
Goat Cheese & Sun-Dried Tomatoes
Turkey & Cranberry Sauce
Ham with Honey Mustard

Scones
Victorian Scones with Apricots & Pecans
Basic Scones with Currants & Walnuts
or Cranberries & Almonds or
Chocolate Chips & Hazelnuts

Spreads
Lemon Cream Cheese
Clotted Vanilla Cream
Devonshire Vanilla Cream
Jam Butters or Butter and Jam

Cookies & Pies
Delicate Lemon Shortbread with Lemon Curd
Victorian Pretty Maids of Honor Bars
Red Raspberry Butter Cookies with Coconut Meringue
World's Best Apricot Walnut Dainties
Bonnie Apple Pie in Apricot Cookie Crust

Tea

Everyone enjoys the friendship and the warmth of a Tea Party. As everything can be prepared in advance, it is also a delight for the hostess. Little sandwiches, on their serving platter, can be tightly wrapped in plastic wrap and stored in the refrigerator. Scones, spreads, cookies, can all be on their serving platters. When guests arrive, off come the plastic wraps and everything is ready.

The key words for a successful tea, are "keep the portions very small". Use the thinnest-sliced white bread you can find. Cut the cookies into small squares. It is important that you keep everything petite and delicate. This is not dinner, but a lovely afternoon repast.

I prefer to use tea bags when serving tea. It allows you to offer a variety of teas and your guests can choose their favorite flavor. Have plenty of hot water ready in a silver urn or in a kettle on the stove, to pour into attractive tea pots. Allow 1 tea bag for each cup of tea.

Petite Sandwiches

GENERAL RULES

1. Keep portions very small. It is important that you keep portions petite and delicate.

2. Use the thinnest-sliced bread you can find. Cut off the crusts and cover one side of each slice with a film of butter.

3. Spread a thin coating of filling on top of the butter and top with another slice of bread, buttered-side down.

4. Cut each slice into 4 small squares or 4 small triangles. Each slice of bread will produce 2 small sandwiches.

5. Figure 6 small sandwiches per person.

6. If you prefer to use small cookie cutters in attractive or seasonal shapes, that is fine.

SPREADS

Cucumber & Chives:
Peel cucumber, cut in half lengthwise and scoop out the seeds. Slice cucumber on the slicing side of a 4-sided grater. (This will produce the thinnest shaved slices.) Place a thin layer of cucumber on the bread and sprinkle with chives.

Smoked Salmon & Dill:
Spread bread with a thin slice of salmon and sprinkle with a pinch of dill.

Goat Cheese & Sun-Dried Tomato:
Mash goat cheese with a little sour cream and spread on bread. Place a thin sliver of sun-dried tomato on top.

Turkey & Cranberry Sauce:
Place a thin slice of turkey on the bread and spread a thin coating of cranberry sauce.

Ham with Honey Mustard:
Spread each slice of bread with Honey Mustard. Cover with a thin slice of baked ham.

Victorian Scones with Apricots & Pecans

- 2 cups flour
- 1 tablespoon baking powder
- 1/2 cup sugar
  pinch of salt
- 1/2 cup cold butter (1 stick), cut into 8 pieces

- 1/2 cup chopped dried apricots
- 1/2 cup chopped pecans

- 2 eggs
- 1/3 cup cream
- 1 teaspoon vanilla

In the large bowl of an electric mixer, beat together first 5 ingredients, until mixture resembles coarse meal. Stir in apricots and pecans. Beat together eggs, cream and vanilla and add, all at once, stirring until blended. Do not overmix.

Spread batter evenly into a greased 10-inch springform pan and bake at 400° for about 20 to 25 minutes or until top is golden brown. Allow to cool in pan and cut into wedges to serve. Serve with Lemon Cream Cheese or butter and jam. Serves 8 to 10.

Lemon Cream Cheese

This lovely spread tastes very much like a cheesecake filling and is great with scones.

- 1 package (8 ounces) cream cheese
- 1/4 cup sifted powdered sugar
- 2 tablespoons lemon juice
- 1/2 teaspoon grated lemon zest (yellow part of the peel)
- 1/4 teaspoon vanilla

Beat cream cheese until light and fluffy. Beat in remaining ingredients until blended. Place in a lovely crock or bowl, cover and refrigerate until serving time. Yields about 1 cup.

Basic Scones with Currants & Walnuts

2	cups flour
1	tablespoon baking powder
1/2	cup sugar
	pinch of salt
1/2	cup cold butter (1 stick), cut into 8 pieces
1/2	cup dried currants
1/2	cup chopped walnuts
2	eggs
1/3	cup cream
1	teaspoon vanilla

In the large bowl of an electric mixer, beat together first 5 ingredients, until mixture resembles coarse meal. Stir in currants and walnuts. Beat together eggs, cream and vanilla and add, all at once, stirring until blended. Do not overmix.

Spread batter evenly into a greased 10-inch springform pan and bake at 400° for about 20 to 25 minutes or until top is golden brown. Allow to cool in pan and cut into wedges to serve. Serve with Clotted Cream, Devonshire Cream, or butter and jam. Serves 10.

Chocolate Chip & Hazelnut Scones:
Delete currants and walnuts and add 1/2 cup semi-sweet chocolate chips and 1/2 cup chopped hazelnuts.

Cranberry & Almond Scones:
Delete currants and walnuts. Stir in 1/2 cup cranberries and 1/2 cup chopped almonds, at the end, after adding the eggs and cream.

Clotted Vanilla Cream

This is my Creme Fraiche Vanilla with an English accent. To keep the cream stiff, prepare this 4 hours earlier. Cream will settle somewhat after that, but it will still be a delicious spread.

- 1   cup cream
- 1/2   cup sour cream
- 2   tablespoons sugar
- 1/4   teaspoon vanilla

Beat cream until stiff. Beat in remaining ingredients until blended. Spoon the mixture in a serving bowl, cover and refrigerate. Yields 2 cups.

Devonshire Vanilla Cream

This is an alternative spread for the scones. You may want to serve both.

- 1   package (8 ounces) cream cheese, at room temperature
- 3   tablespoons sour cream
- 3   tablespoons cream
- 2   tablespoons sugar
- 1/2   teaspoon vanilla

Beat cream cheese until light and fluffy. Beat in the remaining ingredients until blended. Spoon the mixture in a serving bowl, cover and refrigerate until serving time. Yields about 2 cups.

Jam Butters

- 1/2   cup (1 stick) butter, softened
- 1/4   cup fruity jam or preserves

Beat butter until light and fluffy. Beat in jam or preserves until blended. Yields 1 cup.

Delicate Lemon Shortbread with Lemon Curd

1   cup butter
1/2 cup sugar

2   cups flour
1   teaspoon baking powder

1   tablespoon grated lemon zest (yellow part of the peel)

Beat together butter and sugar until light and creamy. Combine flour and baking powder and add, all at once, beating until nicely blended. Do not overbeat.

Spread dough into a 10-inch greased tart pan with a removable bottom. Cut dough into 16 wedges and prick each wedge 2 or 3 times with a fork. Bake at 325° for 30 minutes, or until top is lightly browned. Cut through the wedges again, as they will run together. Serve with a spoonful of tart Lemon Curd. Yields 16 small servings.

Lemon Curd:
1/2 cup sugar
2   eggs
4   tablespoons lemon juice

1/4 cup butter (1/2 stick)
1   tablespoon finely grated lemon zest (yellow part of the peel)

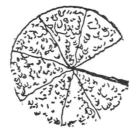

In the top of a double boiler, lightly beat together sugar and eggs until blended, about 1 minute. Beat in lemon juice until blended. Place pan over simmering water and cook, stirring constantly, until mixture thickens, about 5 minutes. Do not allow to boil or it will curdle.

Remove the top of the double boiler from the hot water, and stir in the butter, 1 tablespoon at a time, until blended.   Stir in the lemon zest. Allow to cool. When cool, lay a film of plastic wrap on the curd to prevent a skin from forming and refrigerate until serving time. Yields about 1 cup.

Victorian Pretty Maids of Honor Bars

This is my version of the delicate English classic. An almond cookie base topped with apricot jam and almond paste is truly wonderful.

Almond Cookie Crust:

1 1/2	cups flour
1/4	cup sugar
3/4	cup butter
1/2	cup finely chopped almonds
1	egg, beaten
3/4	cup apricot jam, sieved

In the large bowl of an electric mixer, beat together flour, sugar and butter until mixture resembles coarse meal. Beat in the almonds. Add the beaten egg and beat until a dough forms. Do not overbeat.

Pat mixture on the bottom and 1/2-inch up the sides of a greased 9x13-inch baking pan and bake in a 350° oven for 20 minutes or until top is very lightly browned. Spread apricot jam evenly over the top. Spread Almond Filling evenly over the jam.

Bake at 350° for about 25 minutes, or until the topping is set and top is browned. Allow to cool in pan. When cool, cut into squares and sprinkle top faintly with sifted powdered sugar. Yields 4 dozen cookies.

Almond Filling:

1	package (7 ounces) almond paste
1/2	cup sugar
1	tablespoon flour
2	eggs
2	tablespoons cream
1	teaspoon almond extract

Beat together all the ingredients until blended.

Red Raspberry Butter Cookies with Coconut Meringue Topping

There are several variations for this great cookie. It can be prepared with apricot jam which is wonderful and almonds or pecans can be substituted for the walnuts.

Butter Cookie Crust:
- 1 1/2 cups flour
- 1/2 cup sifted powdered sugar
- 3/4 cup butter, cut into 12 pieces
- 2 tablespoons grated lemon peel
- 2 egg yolks

Filling:
- 1 1/4 cups seedless red raspberry jam
- 1 cup chopped walnuts

Topping:
- 2 egg whites
- 1/2 cup sugar
- 1/2 cup coconut flakes

In the large bowl of an electric mixer, beat together all the crust ingredients until mixture resembles coarse meal. Pat mixture on the bottom and 1-inch up the sides of a buttered 9x13-inch baking pan and bake in a 350° oven for 15 minutes. Spread raspberry jam evenly over the crust and sprinkle walnuts on top.

Beat egg whites with sugar until stiff. Beat in the coconut flakes until blended. Spread mixture evenly over the nuts and bake at 350° for about 25 minutes or until meringue is golden brown. To serve, cut into 1 1/2-inch squares. Yields 4 dozen cookies.

World's Best Apricot Walnut Dainties

These dainty little chewies are tart, crunchy and delicious. Cut into small squares, they are perfect for afternoon tea.

1	cup butter (2 sticks), softened
1	cup sugar
1	cup brown sugar
2	eggs
1	teaspoon vanilla
2 1/4	cups flour
1/2	teaspoon baking powder
1/2	teaspoon baking soda
1	package (6 ounces) dried apricots, chopped
1	cup chopped walnuts

Beat together butter and sugars until creamy. Beat in eggs and vanilla until blended. Beat in remaining ingredients until blended.

Spread dough evenly into a 10x15-inch jelly roll pan and bake in a 375° oven for 20 to 25 minutes or until top is lightly browned. Allow to cool in pan and cut into squares to serve. Sprinkle top lightly with sifted powdered sugar or drizzle with Lemon Glaze. Yields about 5 dozen cookies.

Lemon Glaze:
Stir together 1 tablespoon lemon juice and 1/2 cup sifted powdered sugar until blended. Add a little sugar or lemon juice to make glaze a drizzling consistency.

Bonnie Apple Pie in Apricot Cookie Crust

This is a lovely pie to serve at tea. It is a low pie, very delicate and delicious. In absence of a heart-shaped pan, use a 10-inch springform pan, lined with parchment paper. Instructions remain the same. The Cream Glaze adds a very nice touch, but it can be omitted. Sprinkle top with a little sifted powdered sugar if omitting the glaze.

Butter Cookie Crust:

1	cup butter
2	cups flour
1/3	cup sugar
1	beaten egg
1	tablespoon water
1/2	cup apricot jam

In a food processor, blend butter, flour and sugar until butter particles are the size of small peas. (Do not overprocess or the flakiness will be lost.) Beat egg with water and add to the processor. Pulsate 4 or 5 times, or until dough clumps together. Place dough on floured wax paper and shape into a ball.

Pat 2/3 of the dough onto the bottom and up the sides of a greased 10-inch heart-shaped pan with a removable bottom. Bake in a 375° oven for 20 minutes, or until crust is lightly browned.

Spread apricot jam evenly over warm crust and top with Apple Pie Filling. Divide remaining dough into thirds, pat each into a 6-inch circle and place on top of pie. Continue baking for about 30 minutes, or until top is golden brown. Allow to cool in pan. When cool, brush circles of dough on top with Cream Glaze. Serves 8.

Apple Pie Filling:

3	large apples, peeled, cored and thinly sliced
1/3	cup sugar
1	teaspoon grated lemon peel
1	tablespoon flour

In a bowl, toss together all the ingredients until nicely mixed.

Cream Glaze:

1	tablespoon cream
1/2	cup sifted powdered sugar

Stir together cream and sugar until blended.

A Noisy & Boisterous Kaffee Klatch

Cookies
My Best Lemon Cookies
Butter Pecan Balls
Honey Butterscotch Oatmeal Chewies
Dried Fruit & Nut Bars
Little Chocolate Chip Goldies

Cakes
Date & Walnut Sherry Cake with Sherry Glaze
Holiday Cherry Walnut Cake with Orange Glaze

Tart
Almond Macaroon & Raspberry Tart

Candy
Creamy Soft Velvet Fudge

Coffee & Tea

Little Chocolate Chip Goldies

To make these into "Blondies", substitute butterscotch chips for the chocolate chips. Both versions are memorable.

1	cup butter, softened
2	cups brown sugar
2	eggs
2	teaspoons vanilla
2	cups flour
1/2	teaspoon baking powder
1 1/2	cups semi-sweet chocolate chips
1	cup chopped walnuts

Beat together butter and sugar until light and fluffy, about 3 minutes. Beat in eggs and vanilla until blended. Beat in remaining ingredients until blended.

Spread batter evenly into a greased 9x13-inch baking pan and bake in a 350° oven for about 30 minutes, or until top is golden brown. Do not overbake. Allow to cool in pan and cut into 1 1/2-inch squares. To serve, sprinkle lightly with sifted powdered sugar. Yields 48 squares.

Honey Butterscotch Oatmeal Chewies
with Raisins & Pecans

I love oatmeal cookies that are chewy, chunky and filled with all manners of good things. This marvelous bar cookie is one of my favorites. It is truly delicious, and I hope you enjoy it as much as I do.

1 1/4	cups sugar
1/2	cup butter, softened
2	eggs
1/2	cup honey
1	teaspoon vanilla
1 3/4	cups flour
2	cups quick-cooking oats
1	teaspoon baking soda
	pinch of salt
1	cup butterscotch chips
1	cup chopped pecans
1/2	cup raisins

Beat together first 5 ingredients until blended. Beat in the next 4 ingredients until blended. Stir in the remaining ingredients.

Spread batter evenly into a greased 10x15x1-inch jelly roll pan and bake in a 350° oven for 25 minutes or until top is browned and a cake tester, inserted in center, comes out clean. Allow to cool in pan and then cut into squares to serve. Yields 5 dozen 1 1/2-inch squares.

Note: -Make certain that your jelly roll pan is at least 1-inch deep or batter
           will overflow while baking. Some jelly roll pans are 1/2 or 3/4-inch
           deep and are not deep enough for this recipe.
         -Decorate with a faint sprinkling of sifted powdered sugar.

My Best Lemon Cookies

This is a variation of my Mom's Lemon Cookies which everybody adores. The crust is a magnificent lemon butter cookie. The lemon topping is tart and flavorful.

Lemon Butter Cookie Crust:
- 3/4 cup butter (1 1/2 sticks)
- 1 1/2 cups flour
- 1/3 cup sifted powdered sugar
- grated zest of 1 lemon (yellow part of the peel)

Lemon Curd Topping:
- 3 eggs
- 1 1/3 cups sugar
- 3 tablespoons flour
- 3/4 teaspoon baking powder
- 5 tablespoons lemon juice
- grated zest of 1 lemon

Beat together crust ingredients until mixture is blended. Pat mixture evenly into a 9x13-inch lightly greased baking pan. Bake at 350° for about 20 minutes, or until crust is set and just beginning to take on color.

Beat together topping ingredients until blended. Pour topping evenly on baked crust. Return to oven and continue baking for 30 minutes or until curd is set. Allow to cool in pan. To serve, cut into 1 1/2-inch squares and sprinkle with sifted powdered sugar. Yields about 48 cookies.

Butter Pecan Balls

To avoid breakage, small delicate baked goods are much easier to cool on brown paper, than on a rack. Brown paper is inexpensive and can be purchased in rolls.

- 1 cup butter (2 sticks)
- 1/2 cup sugar
- 2 teaspoons vanilla
- 2 cups cake flour
- 1 1/2 cups finely chopped pecans

  sifted powdered sugar for dusting

Cream together butter and sugar. Beat in vanilla. Beat in flour until blended. Beat in pecans until blended. Shape dough into 3/4-inch balls and place on a lightly greased cookie sheet. Bake at 350° for about 12 to 14 minutes, or until cookies are set and just beginning to take on color. Do not brown. Allow cookies to cool on brown paper and roll in sifted powdered sugar when cool. Yields about 5 dozen cookies.

Dried Fruit & Nut Bars

These soft, velvety bars with a cake-like texture and a tart lemon glaze are lovely to serve around the holidays. The Lemon Glaze is very light and syrupy and should be brushed on. Serve them with spiced apple juice or cider.

- 1 cup margarine
- 1 cup brown sugar
- 1 cup sugar
- 2 teaspoons vanilla

- 4 eggs

- 3 1/2 cups flour
- 2 teaspoons baking powder
- 2 cups minced fruit bits (chopped, mixed dried fruits) **or**
     1 1/2 cups minced dried apricots
- 1 cup chopped walnuts

Beat together first 4 ingredients until mixture is creamy. Beat in eggs until blended. Mix together flour and baking powder and beat in until blended. Stir in fruits and nuts. Spread batter into a greased 12x16-inch pan and bake at 350° for 20 to 23 minutes, or until top is lightly browned. Allow to cool in pan and cut into bars when cool. Brush with Lemon Glaze after bars are cut. Yields 96 bars 2x1-inch, or 48 squares 2x2-inch.

Lemon Glaze:
- 2 tablespoons lemon juice
- 1/2 cup sifted powdered sugar

Stir together lemon juice and sugar until blended. Mixture will not be a drizzling consistency. Brush onto cut bars and allow to set for about 1 hour before serving.

Almond Macaroon & Raspberry Tart with Lemon Cookie Crust

This divine dessert is one of the finest tasting tarts. The Lemon Cookie Crust is the perfect balance for the Almond Macaroon Topping and the raspberry jam adds the perfect blend of tartness.

Lemon Butter Cookie Crust:

1 1/4	cups flour
1/2	cup sugar
1	teaspoon baking powder
1/2	cup butter (1 stick), slightly softened
1	tablespoon lemon peel
1	egg, beaten
3/4	cup raspberry jam, heated

In the large bowl of an electric mixer, beat together first 5 ingredients until the mixture resembles coarse meal. Beat in the egg until a soft dough forms. Pat dough on the bottom and 1-inch up the sides of a greased 10-inch springform pan and bake in a 350° oven for 18 minutes, or until dough is set and just beginning to take on color.

Spread raspberry jam evenly on crust. Pipe a lattice on the top, with the Almond Macaroon Topping, allowing some of the jam to show. Bake in a 350° oven for 35 to 40 minutes, or until top is lightly browned. Allow to cool in pan. When cool, sprinkle top lightly with sifted powdered sugar and cut into wedges to serve. Delicious! Serves 8 to 10.

Almond Macaroon Topping:

1/2	cup butter (1 stick), softened
2/3	cup sugar
1	teaspoon almond extract
2	eggs
2	cups finely grated almonds (or almond meal from health food stores.) This is as fine as whole wheat flour..

Cream together butter and sugar. Beat in extract and eggs until blended. Beat in grated almonds. (Mixture will be very thick.) Transfer mixture to a pastry bag with a 1/2-inch star tip. (You will be piping a lattice on the tart.) If you do not own a pastry bag with a 1/2-inch star tip, then spoon the Almond Macaroon on the top to form a decorative petal or floral pattern.

Date & Walnut Sherry Cake with Sherry Cream Glaze

This is a delicious choice around the holidays. It is a rather large, dense cake, filled with dates and walnuts and wonderfully flavored with spices.

1	cup butter (2 sticks) softened
2	cups sugar
6	eggs
2	teaspoons vanilla
1/2	cup sherry
2	cups flour
1	teaspoon baking powder
1	teaspoon baking soda
2	teaspoons cinnamon
1/2	teaspoon powdered cloves
1/2	teaspoon ground nutmeg
2	cups chopped dates
2	cups chopped toasted walnuts
2	tablespoons flour

Beat together butter and sugar until mixture is creamy. Beat in eggs, one at a time, beating well after each addition. Beat in the sherry. Stir together the next 6 ingredients and add, all at once, beating until blended. Toss together dates, walnuts and flour and add, beating until blended.

Spread batter into a greased and floured 10-inch springform pan and bake in a 325° oven for 55 minutes or until a cake tester, inserted in center, comes out clean. Allow to cool in pan.

When cool, drizzle top with Sherry Cream Glaze and allow a little to run down the sides. This is a large cake and yields 12 generous servings.

Sherry Cream Glaze: Stir together 2 tablespoons sherry and 1 cup sifted powdered sugar until blended. Drizzle on the top and down the sides of cooled cake.

Holiday Cherry Walnut Cake with Orange Glaze

This is an interesting and densely filled fruit cake, very compact and definitely not the fluffy style. Slice the cherries into thirds, rather than chop them coarsely. This allows for a prettier slice. Wrap the cakes in pretty colored cellophane and tie them with bright red ribbons for a lovely gift from your kitchen.

1	cup butter
2	cups sugar
6	eggs
1	cup sour cream
1	teaspoon vanilla
3	cups flour
1	teaspoon baking powder
1/2	teaspoon baking soda
1	cup sliced maraschino cherries
1	cup yellow raisins
2	cups chopped toasted walnuts

In the large bowl of an electric mixer, beat together first 5 ingredients until blended. Stir in the flour, baking powder and soda until blended. Stir in the cherries, raisins and walnuts until blended. Do not overmix.

Divide batter between 8 greased and lightly floured mini-loaf pans (3x5-inches) and bake in a 325° oven for 40 to 50 minutes, or until a cake tester, inserted in center, comes out clean. Allow to cool in pans for 15 minutes and then remove from pans and continue cooling on a rack. When cool, brush tops with Orange Glaze. Yields 8 mini-loaves.

Orange Glaze:
Stir together 3 tablespoons orange juice and 1 cup sifted powdered sugar until blended. Brush glaze on cooled cakes.

Creamy Soft Velvet Fudge
(My very favorite.)

If you are an impassioned fudge lover, and if you prefer the soft, velvety fudge, this is a nice recipe to consider. Miniature marshmallows and toasted almonds can be used, instead of the walnuts, and you will have the best Rocky Road Fudge you have ever tasted. If you are planning to freeze this delicious confection, then freeze it in large pieces. Cut fudge into 6 pieces approximately 4x5-inches and wrap securely in double thicknesses of plastic wrap and then foil. Allow to defrost, and then cut into squares to serve. It is better to freeze this in large portions, or you will be eating the smaller pieces straight from the freezer.

4	cups sugar
1/2	cup butter
1	cup cream
1/2	teaspoon salt
2	jars (7 ounces, each) marshmallow cream
3	packages (6 ounces, each) semi-sweet chocolate chips
1	package (12 ounces) milk chocolate chips
2	cups chopped toasted walnuts
1	tablespoon vanilla

In a saucepan, cook together sugar, butter, cream and salt, stirring until sugar melts and mixture reaches 234° on a candy thermometer. Stir in the marshmallow cream until blended. Stir in the chocolate until blended. Stir in walnuts and vanilla until blended.

Pour mixture into a lightly oiled 12x16x1-inch baking pan and spread evenly. Allow to cool in pan. When cool, cut into 1-inch squares and place in bon bon wrappers. Yields about 5 pounds of fudge and 192 individual squares.

To Make Rocky Road Fudge:
Substitute chopped toasted almonds for the walnuts. Then add 2 cups miniature marshmallows.

To Make Fruit & Nut Fudge:
Add 1 cup raisins to make Fruit & Nut Fudge.

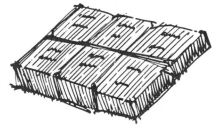

Columbus Day Dinner

The Best Rice-Stuffed Tomatoes with Garlic & Herbs or
Mushroom Salad with Lemon & Garlic Dressing or
Bean Salad with Italian Herb Dressing

Garlic Cheese Lemon Bread

Chicken Romano Stuffed with Sun-Dried Tomatoes, Basil & Mozzarella
in Garlic Lemon Sauce

Risotto with Mushrooms & Onions

Buttered Italian Green Beans with Onions or
Italian Green Beans with Tomato, Onions & Cheese

Tartufo alla Tre Scalini Caffe or
Italian Glacé Biscuit Tortoni with Macaroons & Cherries

Caffe Latte

An Italian dinner with something old and something new. The salads and bread are traditional, but served with a stuffed tomato it is "buonissimo."

The Stuffed Chicken Romano is a new combination of flavors. Risotto with your choice of Italian Green Beans is a lovely accompaniment.

All the dishes on this menu can be prepared in advance. If you prepare the chicken earlier in the day, undercook it slightly. Vegetables can be made earlier in the day and reheated at time of serving. Sauce can be made several days earlier and stored in the refrigerator.

Biscuit Tortoni is a classic. My version is light and creamy and yields a large number. As they keep in the freezer for one month, they are nice to have on hand. Recipe can be halved. Of course, everybody will love the Tartufo and keep the cherries in the center as a surprise. The Caffe Latte... half coffee, half milk...is one of my favorites.

The Best Rice-Stuffed Tomatoes
with Garlic & Herbs

I love stuffed tomatoes...as a first course or as an accompaniment to dinner. When we visited Italy, I ate one practically every day. These are very much like the ones we enjoyed, rather simple, pure flavors accented with a delicious sauce.

12   medium tomatoes (about 3 pounds). Cut a thin slice off the tops, scoop out the centers with a grapefruit knife and then a teaspoon. Reserve the tomato pulp.

Tomato & Rice Filling:
 2 1/2   cups cooked rice (see below)
           reserved tomato pulp
   1   tablespoon oil
   1   small onion, grated
   2   cloves garlic, minced
   1   teaspoon sweet basil flakes
   3   tablespoons minced parsley
        salt and freshly ground pepper to taste

Prepare tomatoes. Mix together all the filling ingredients until blended. Stuff the tomatoes loosely with filling and place any leftover rice mixture on the bottom of a 9x13-inch porcelain baker. Settle the tomatoes over the rice. Pour Tomato, Garlic & Herb Sauce over the tops.

Cover pan loosely with foil, and bake in a 350° oven for about 40 minutes or until tomatoes are tender, but not mushy. (Cooking time will vary, so check after 30 minutes.) Serve warm not hot. Yields 12 stuffed tomatoes.

Tomato, Garlic & Herb Sauce:
   1   tablespoon oil
   1   can (1 pound) stewed tomatoes, finely chopped
   4   tablespoons tomato paste
   1   small onion, grated
   2   cloves garlic, minced
   2   teaspoons sugar
   1   teaspoon sweet basil flakes
   1   teaspoon Italian Herb Seasoning flakes
        salt and pepper to taste

Stir together all the ingredients until blended.

To precook rice:
Cook 1 cup rice in 3 cups of rapidly boiling water until tender and drain.

Bean Salad with Italian Herb Dressing

This simple little dressing can be used over an antipasto or mixed green salad.

Bean Salad:
- 1   can (15 ounces) garbanzo beans, rinsed and drained
- 1   can (15 ounces) red kidney beans, rinsed and drained
- 1/3   cup chopped green onions
- 1/4   cup chopped red onions

Italian Herb Dressing:
- 1/4   cup oil
- 1/4   cup red wine vinegar
- 1   shallot, minced
- 1   teaspoon oregano flakes
- 1   teaspoon sweet basil flakes
- 1/4   teaspoon thyme flakes
- 2   cloves garlic, put through a press
  - salt and freshly ground pepper to taste

In a bowl, toss beans and onions. Combine dressing ingredients in a glass jar with a tight-fitting lid and shake vigorously until blended. Pour dressing to taste over the beans and toss to combine. Cover bowl and refrigerate until ready to use. Serves 6.

Note: -Unused dressing can be stored for 1 week in the refrigerator.
*   -Salad can be made 1 day earlier and stored in the refrigerator.*

Garlic Cheese Lemon Bread

In order to keep the calories low, the amount of topping, I must admit, is a little skimpy. You could use a little more of everything.

- 1   loaf Italian bread, cut in half lengthwise. To facilitate serving, cut serving-size slices 3/4 down into the bread.

- 1/4   cup olive oil
- 2   cloves garlic, put through a press
- 2   tablespoons lemon juice

- 1/2   cup grated Parmesan cheese or more to taste

Combine olive oil, garlic and lemon juice. Spread this mixture on the cut surface of bread. Sprinkle tops with grated cheese. Broil for a few minutes or until top is lightly browned.

Mushroom Salad with Lemon & Garlic Dressing

The Salad:
- 1 pound mushrooms, thinly sliced
- 1/2 cup chopped chives

Lemon & Garlic Dressing:
- 1/4 cup olive oil
- 1/4 cup lemon juice
- 2 tablespoons chopped chives
- 2 cloves garlic, minced
- 1 teaspoon Dijon-style mustard
- 2 tablespoons grated Parmesan cheese
- salt and pepper to taste

In a bowl, place mushrooms and chives. Combine dressing ingredients in a glass jar with a tight-fitting lid and shake vigorously until blended. Pour dressing to taste over the mushrooms, cover bowl and refrigerate until ready to use. Serves 6.

Note: -Unused dressing can be stored for 1 week in the refrigerator.

Buttered Italian Green Beans with Onions

- 2 packages (10 ounces, each) broad Italian Green Beans

- 1 medium onion, finely chopped
- 2 tablespoons butter
- 1/4 cup chicken broth
- salt and pepper to taste

Cook vegetables in boiling water for 4 minutes or until firm-tender. Drain and refresh under cold running water.

Meanwhile, saute onion in butter until onion is just beginning to brown. Add the broth, seasonings and green beans, and continue cooking and turning until beans are tender. Serves 6.

Note: -Entire dish can be made earlier in the day and refrigerated. Reheat before serving.

Chicken Romano with Sun-Dried Tomatoes, Basil & Mozzarella in Garlic Lemon Sauce

This is a new variation on an old theme. The flavors of sun-dried tomatoes and basil are very popular today and understandably so. This recipe is very easy to increase to serve 12.

- 8 chicken breast halves (about 4 ounces each), boned, skinned and gently pounded to flatten. Sprinkle with garlic powder and pepper to taste.
- 8 tablespoons minced basil leaves (1/2 cup)
- 8 tablespoons minced sun-dried tomatoes (1/2 cup)
- 4 ounces grated Mozzarella cheese

Divide basil, sun-dried tomatoes and Mozzarella on each chicken breast half. Tuck in the sides, roll up each breast and secure with toothpicks. Roll chicken in Seasoned Bread Crumbs and place in a 9x13-inch baking pan. Baste with Garlic Lemon Sauce.

Bake in a 325° oven for about 45 minutes, basting with Garlic Lemon Sauce every now and again. Do not overcook. Serves 8.

Seasoned Crumbs:
- 1/2 cup bread crumbs
- 1/2 cup flour
- 1/4 cup grated Parmesan cheese
- 1 teaspoon garlic powder
- 1 teaspoon onion powder
- 2 teaspoons paprika
- 1/2 teaspoon salt

Combine the ingredients in a plastic zip-lock bag and shake until blended. Unused crumbs can be stored in the freezer for several months.

Garlic Lemon Sauce:
- 1/2 cup butter (1 stick)
- 2 cloves garlic, put through a press
- 4 tablespoons lemon juice
- 1 teaspoon parsley flakes

Heat together all the ingredients until butter is melted. Use to baste chicken. Yields about 3/4 cup sauce.

Risotto with Mushrooms & Onions

Making risotto in the traditional manner, requires standing over the pot for 30 minutes, stirring in 1/2 cup chicken broth at a time, until about 6 cups of chicken broth are used. This makes the arborio rice creamy and soupy. This risotto is a little firmer, and a lot easier to execute. This recipe can be prepared in advance and heated before serving.

1	cup rice
2	cups chicken broth
1	tablespoon olive oil
	salt and pepper to taste

1/2	pound mushrooms, sliced
1	onion, chopped
1	tablespoon olive oil

In a covered saucepan, stir together first 5 ingredients and simmer mixture for 30 minutes, or until rice is tender and liquid is absorbed. Meanwhile, in a skillet, saute mushrooms and onion in oil, until onion is soft and liquid rendered is evaporated. When rice is cooked, stir in the mushroom mixture and heat through. Serves 6.

Italian Green Beans with Tomato, Onions & Cheese

2	packages (10 ounces, each) frozen Italian green beans
2	medium tomatoes, peeled, seeded and chopped
1	small onion, minced
1/2	cup rich chicken broth
1/2	cup tomato sauce
	salt and pepper to taste

2	tablespoons grated Parmesan cheese

In a saucepan, simmer together first 7 ingredients, until green beans are tender, about 15 minutes. Sprinkle top with grated cheese before serving. Serves 6.

Tartufo alla Tre Scalini Caffe

This delightful chocolate iced cream dessert is the famous specialty of the Caffe Tre Scalini in Rome. It holds so many fond memories for our family, as it was the first taste we sampled in Rome. It was 8 o'clock in the evening when our plane arrived and we raced by taxi to Tre Scalini. The Piazza was filled with barkers and vendors, fire eaters and jugglers. Young women walked around the edge of the Piazza and young men flirted and carried on. The evening was filled with unbelievable life and energy. And we sat and ate Tartufos and watched the gorgeous people of Rome pass by. We have been back to Tre Scalini many times since, and yes! you can go home again. The magic of our first visit has never diminished.

The original recipe for the chocolate ice cream is a zealously guarded secret, but using a very excellent quality chocolate ice cream produces a fine Tartufo. Keep the cherries in the center as a surprise.

- 24 glacéed cherries
- 2 tablespoons rum (optional). Omit the rum for the youngsters.

- 12 large scoops of chocolate ice cream

- 1 1/2 cups semi-sweet chocolate chips
- 1/3 cup butter

- 3/4 cup toasted slivered almonds

Soak cherries in rum. With a large ice cream scooper, scoop out 12 balls of ice cream and place on a wax paper-lined cookie sheet. Press 2 cherries into each center, working quickly, and place in freezer until very firm, about 1 hour.

In the top of a double boiler, over hot, not boiling water, melt chocolate and butter together. Allow to cool slightly. Remove 1 ball of ice cream at a time, spear it with a fork and quickly dip and roll it into the melted chocolate. Return it to the wax paper and sprinkle each ball with toasted almonds. Work quickly and return these to the freezer until firm. When frozen solid, store in double plastic bags. Serve in a lovely stemmed glass or glass dessert dish so that the chocolate and nuts show through. Yields 12.

Note: -This dessert can be made in stages. You can prepare the ice cream balls one day and store in the freezer covered securely with plastic wrap. The ice cream can be dipped into chocolate on another day.
-Entire dessert can be prepared 2 or 3 days earlier and stored in the freezer in double plastic bags.
-Remove from the freezer 5 minutes before serving.

Italian Glacé Biscuit Tortoni with Macaroons & Cherries

Biscuit Tortoni is a refreshing and satisfying dessert after a hefty Italian meal. Serve with Amaretti cookies or other plain cookies or macaroons. Recipe can be halved.

6	egg whites, at room temperature
1/2	cup sugar
2	cups cream
4	tablespoons sugar
1	teaspoon vanilla
1/2	teaspoon almond extract
1/2	cup chopped toasted almonds
1/2	cup macaroon cookie crumbs
1/2	cup chopped, drained maraschino cherries

Beat egg whites with sugar until stiff and glossy. Beat cream with sugar, vanilla and almond extract until stiff. Beat in almonds, macaroon crumbs and cherries. Fold in beaten whites. Divide mixture between 18 paper-lined cups and freeze until firm. When ready to serve, remove paper liner and place in a lovely stemmed glass or dessert dish. Sprinkle tops with finely ground almonds or additional macaroon crumbs. Yields 18 servings.

Caffé Latte

3	cups milk
3	cups double strength brewed hot coffee
	sugar to taste

Heat the milk in an enamel saucepan until it comes just to the point of boiling. In a coffee server, mix together the hot milk and hot coffee. Serve in glass mugs with sugar to taste. Serves 6.

An Italian Sampler

Breads
Stir & Bake Italian Bread Sticks
(Grissinis)
Toppings for Crostini
Olive & Garlic Spread
Tomato & Garlic Spread
Mushroom & Garlic Spread

Salad
Bruschetta with Tomato & Garlic

Main Courses
Cioppino Romano
Oven-Fried Eggplant Parmesan with 5-Minute Tomato Sauce
Baked Ziti with Ricotta & Mozzarella in Instant Tomato Sauce

Desserts
Lemon Gelati with Raspberry Sauce
Butter Cream Cookies
Cassata Romana with Chocolate & Raspberries
Italian Rum & Raisin Bread Pudding & Vanilla Raisin Sauce
Old-Fashioned Bread Pudding Cheesecake
Cappuccino Supreme

In this menu you will find some things old and some things new and many dishes to choose from. This menu works well for an informal celebration, a homecoming or a family birthday. More and more are the times when we celebrate or entertain in an informal manner. But when you serve great food, the excitement is always high.

The Bread Sticks (Grissinis) are the classic and very easily prepared. Crostini with the varied toppings for the bread (to replace butter) are very popular today. I have included several toppings that I know you will enjoy. Bruschetta is also served in most Italian restaurants. While the tomato salad is often served directly on the bread, I prefer to serve it separately, where each person spoons the salad to taste. This also prevents the bread from getting soggy.

Cioppino, Eggplant Parmesan and Baked Ziti are old and enjoyable favorites. And for dessert, a light Lemon Gelati with Raspberry Sauce accompanied with Butter Cookies. Or the classic Casata Romana which is memorable. Or you may prefer some interesting and very original Bread Puddings, created in the Italian mood. The soup base for the Cioppino can be prepared a day earlier and the fish cooked at the last minute when reheating. Other than that, this is another make-ahead menu.

Stir-&-Bake Italian Garlic Bread Sticks
(Grissinis)

This is another favorite that is delicious and satisfying and a great accompaniment to soup, salad or dinner in general. It is an adaptation of my chewy dough and very simple to prepare, as dough does not have to be kneaded nor does it have to rise...just stir and bake.

1	package dry yeast
1/2	cup lukewarm water (110°)
1	teaspoon sugar
1	cup lukewarm water (110°)
3	cups flour
1	tablespoon sugar
3/4	teaspoon salt
1	cup flour
1	egg, beaten
	coarse-grind garlic powder, grated Parmesan cheese and/or sesame seeds for sprinkling on top

Soften yeast in 1/2 cup water and sugar until yeast starts to foam. If yeast does not foam, it is inactive and should be discarded.

To the bowl, add the next 4 ingredients and beat, for about 3 minutes, or until dough is very smooth. (This takes the place of kneading.) Now, slowly beat in the remaining 1 cup flour until blended. Turn dough out onto a lightly floured board and shape into a smooth ball.

Divide dough into 24 pieces. Roll each piece of dough, between your palms, into a 1/4-inch thick rope and place on a lightly greased cookie sheet. Brush top with beaten egg and sprinkle with coarse-grind garlic powder, and/or grated Parmesan and/or sesame seeds.

Bake in a 400° oven for about 15 to 18 minutes, or until tops are lightly browned. Yields 24 bread sticks.

Bruschetta with Tomato & Garlic
(Tomato & Garlic Salad with Parmesan Bread)

This is a very popular salad featured in most Italian restaurants. Spooned on Parmesan Toast it is recklessly delicious. It is easy to prepare, can be made earlier in the day and stored in the refrigerator. Parmesan bread can be assembled earlier in the day, covered securely with plastic wrap and broiled before serving.

Tomato & Garlic Salad:
- 4   medium tomatoes, seeded and diced
- 3   cloves garlic, minced
- 3   tablespoons olive oil
- 2   tablespoons lemon juice
- 2   tablespoons chopped fresh basil (or 1 teaspoon sweet basil flakes)
     salt and pepper to taste

In a bowl, toss together all the ingredients until nicely mixed. Cover bowl and refrigerate until serving time. To serve, place tomatoes in a bowl and surround with Parmesan Bread. Allow guests to spoon the Bruschetta on the bread to taste. Serves 6.

Bruschetta (Parmesan Bread):
- 12   thin slices (1/4-inch thick) crusty Italian bread
- 6   teaspoons butter
- 12   teaspoons grated Parmesan cheese

Spread each slice of bread with 1/2 teaspoon butter and 1 teaspoon of grated cheese. Place slices on a cookie sheet and broil for 1 minute, or until cheese melts and just begins to color. Watch carefully for there are only seconds between brown and burnt.

Toppings for Crostini

Many Italian restaurants serve olive oil instead of butter for spreading on bread. A little puddle of olive oil is poured on the bread plate and the warm bread is dipped into it. Many serve more complex toppings that add a great deal of excitement to the meal. Here are a few to consider.

To Make Crostini:
Crostinis are thin slices of Italian bread that are lightly toasted. They should be brushed with olive oil, but if you are cutting down on oils, skip it. Fresh Italian Bread, warmed and not toasted, is a wonderful alternative.

Olive Oil:
A cruet of the best extra-virgin olive oil can be passed at the table. You must have a bread plate for the olive oil. Look for an olive oil with a beautiful bouquet and fragrance.

Olive Oil with a Splash of Balsamic Vinegar:
Place a little olive oil on the plate and a few drops of vinegar. Swirl the bread into the mixture.

Olive & Garlic Spread:
Mince together 1/2 cup pitted black Italian olives, 1/2 cup pitted green Italian olives, 2 cloves garlic, 1 tablespoon chopped parsley and black pepper to taste. Place in a bowl and stir in 2 tablespoons lemon juice and 2 tablespoons olive oil. Place mixture in a small bowl and serve with crusty Italian bread. Yields about 1 1/4 cups or 20 tablespoons. Figure about 1 tablespoon for each slice of bread.

Tomato & Garlic Spread:
Finely chop together 1/2 pound Italian plum tomatoes, 2 cloves garlic, 1 tablespoon chopped basil leaves, salt and pepper to taste. Place mixture in a bowl and stir in 2 tablespoons olive oil, 2 tablespoons lemon juice and salt and pepper to taste. Yields about 1 1/4 cups or 20 tablespoons. Figure about 1 tablespoon for each slice of bread.

Mushroom & Garlic Spread:
In a skillet, saute together 2 cloves minced garlic and 1/2 pound finely chopped mushrooms in 1 tablespoon olive oil until mushrooms are tender and liquid rendered is evaporated. Place mixture in a bowl and add 2 tablespoons minced Italian parsley leaves, 2 tablespoons lemon juice, 2 tablespoons olive oil and salt and pepper to taste. Yields about 1 1/4 cups or 20 tablespoons. Figure about 1 tablespoon for each slice of bread.

Cioppino Romano
(Italian Fishermen's Stew)

While this recipe seems lengthy, it is actually the essence of simplicity to prepare. All of the soup base ingredients are merely placed in the pan and simmered.

Soup Base:

1/4	cup oil (you can use part olive oil)
2	onions, chopped
4	cloves garlic, finely minced
1	cup green onions, chopped
1	can (16 ounces) stewed tomatoes, chopped. Do not drain.
1	can (8 ounces) tomato sauce
1	cup dry red wine
1	can (7 ounces) minced clams. Do not drain.
2	cups clam juice
1/4	cup minced parsley
1	teaspoon oregano
1/4	teaspoon each, thyme and basil
1	teaspoon sugar
1/2	teaspoon red pepper flakes
1/4	teaspoon turmeric
	salt and pepper to taste

In a Dutch oven, combine all the ingredients and simmer mixture for 30 minutes, uncovered. Bring soup to a rolling boil and add:

2 pounds of assorted fish or shellfish, including cod, snapper, halibut, snapper, halibut, flounder, sole or haddock. Fish should be filleted and cut into 1 or 2-inch slices. Scallops, clams, and lobster add a wonderful dimension to this dish. There are no rules.

Keep soup at a slow boil for about 10 minutes or until the fish become opaque. Do not overcook. Serve in deep soup bowls with some Crusty Italian bread. Serves 6.

Note: -*If you use shrimp, make certain that the black veins are removed. Crab and lobster should be carefully scrubbed and cut into pieces. All clams that do not open should be discarded.*
-*Soup base can be prepared earlier in the day and refrigerated. At serving time, bring soup to a rolling boil and then add the fish before serving.*

Oven-Fried Eggplant Parmesan with Lemon & Chives

This is a delicious vegetable dish or a great first course. It can be prepared earlier in the day and heated before serving. The sauce is one of the best...very fresh, pure and flavorful. Sauce is wonderful over pasta, too.

1	cup unflavored low-fat yogurt
2	tablespoons lemon juice
1/4	cup chopped chives
1/2	cup savory cracker crumbs
1/2	cup grated Parmesan cheese
1	eggplant (about 1 pound) peeled and cut into 3/8-inch slices. Sprinkle with salt and pepper.
4	ounces Mozarella cheese, grated
1/4	cup grated Parmesan cheese

In a bowl, stir together yogurt, lemon juice and chives until blended. In a rimmed plate, stir together crumbs and grated Parmesan cheese.

Brush eggplant slices on both sides with yogurt mixture and coat on both sides in crumb mixture. Place eggplant slices, in one layer, on a greased jelly roll pan and bake at 400° until golden brown, about 20 minutes. Carefully, turn and brown other side.

In a 9x13-inch baking pan, spread 1/3 the sauce, top with 1/2 the eggplant, the grated Mozarella, 1/3 sauce, remaining eggplant and then remaining sauce. Sprinkle top with grated Parmesan cheese. Place casserole in a 350° oven until heated through and cheese is melted. Serves 6.

Five-Minute Tomato Sauce:

6	cloves garlic, thinly sliced
2	tablespoons olive oil
1	can (1 pound) stewed tomatoes, chopped. Do not drain.
1/4	teaspoon sweet basil flakes
2	teaspoons onion flakes
1/4	teaspoon Italian Herb Seasoning
1	teaspoon sugar
1	shake red pepper flakes
	salt and pepper to taste

Saute garlic in oil for 30 seconds. Add the remaining ingredients, cover pan and simmer sauce for 5 minutes. Yields 2 cups sauce.

Baked Ziti with Ricotta & Mozzarella in Instant Tomato Sauce

This is a very abbreviated version of a classic dish. The sauce is truly delicious and no one will guess it took 5 minutes to prepare. It is a good basic sauce for pasta, chicken or veal.

1/2	pound ziti pasta (tube pasta), cooked in boiling water until tender (al dente), and drained thoroughly

Cheese Mixture:

1	pound low-fat Ricotta cheese
4	ounces grated Mozzarella cheese
1	egg
1/2	cup grated Parmesan cheese

Instant Tomato Sauce:

1	can (1 pound 12 ounces) crushed tomatoes in puree
2	teaspoons oil
2	tablespoons minced dried onions
1/2	teaspoon coarse grind garlic powder
1	teaspoon sugar
1	teaspoon Italian Herb Seasoning flakes
1	teaspoon sweet basil flakes
	salt and pepper to taste
1	sprinkle cayenne pepper

Have everything ready before you assemble the dish. Prepare ziti and set aside to drain in a collander, shaking occasionally to remove all water. Stir together Cheese Mixture and set aside. Place Instant Tomato Sauce ingredients in a saucepan and heat for 5 minutes.

In a 9x13-inch porcelain baker, place half the ziti. Spoon Cheese Mixture over the top and cover evenly with remaining ziti. Pour sauce evenly over all and sprinkle with additional grated Parmesan cheese. Bake at 350° for 30 minutes or until piping hot. Serves 6.

Lemon Gelati with Raspberry Sauce
(Lemon Iced Cream with Raspberry Sauce)

    1   pint whipping cream or half and half
    4   tablespoons lemon juice
    1/2 lemon, finely grated. Remove any large pieces of membranes.
    1   cup sugar

In a bowl, place all the ingredients and stir until the sugar is dissolved, about 1 minute. Divide the mixture between 12 paper-lined muffin cups and place in the freezer until firm. When frozen firm, store in double plastic bags.

Remove from the freezer about 5 minutes before serving. To serve, remove the paper liners and place iced cream in a lovely stemmed glass or pretty glass dessert dish. Spoon a little Raspberry Sauce on top. Serves 12.

Raspberry Sauce:
    1   package (10 ounces) frozen raspberries in syrup, thawed
    1   tablespoon lemon juice

Stir ingredients together until blended.

Butter Cream Cookies

  2 3/4 cups flour
    1/2 cup sugar
      1 cup butter

    1/2 cup cream
      2 egg yolks (reserve whites for brushing on tops)

In the large bowl of an electric mixer, beat flour, sugar and butter until mixture resembles coarse meal. Beat in the cream and yolks until blended. Place dough on floured wax paper and shape into a 6-inch circle. Wrap dough in the wax paper and refrigerate for several hours or overnight.

Roll dough out to 3/4-inch thickness and cut into decorative shapes with cookie cutters. (Cutters should not measure larger than 1 1/4-inches, or cookies will be too big.) Place on a buttered cookie sheet and baste tops with beaten egg whites.

Bake in a 350° oven for 15 minutes or until top is lightly browned. Remove from pan and cool on brown paper. Yields 2 to 3 dozen cookies, depending on the size of the cutters used.

Cassata Romana
with Chocolate and Raspberries

This is a great dessert, period! You will really be showing your family and friends how much you care, when you prepare this very special dessert. It serves in a grand manner and is truly delicious.

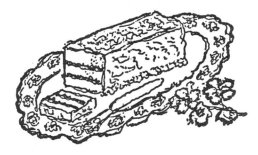

       6   egg whites, at room temperature
     1/2   cup sugar

       6   egg yolks, at room temperature
     1/2   cup sugar

   1 1/2   cups finely grated walnuts
       1   teaspoon baking powder
       1   teaspoon vanilla

Preheat oven to 350°. Butter a 10x15-inch jelly roll pan. Line it with waxed paper extending 4-inches beyond the ends of the pan. Butter the waxed paper. Set aside. Wet a towel and squeeze it until it is damp-dry.

Beat whites until foamy. Gradually add 1/2 cup sugar and continue beating until whites are stiff and glossy. In another bowl, beat yolks with 1/2 cup sugar until mixture is very thick. Beat in nuts, baking powder and vanilla. Fold in beaten egg whites. Pour batter into prepared pan and bake at 350° for about 25 minutes or until top is golden and a cake tester inserted in center comes out clean. Immediately cover cake with damp towel. Allow cake to cool and then refrigerate. Leave towel on cake. This can be done 2 days ahead.

The day before serving, turn cake out on 2 overlapping strips of waxed paper that have been sprinkled with sifted powdered sugar. Remove baking paper and trim edges of cake. Cut cake into thirds, yielding 3 strips measuring 14x3 inches. Fill and frost with Chocolate Chip Whipped Cream and Raspberries. Sprinkle extra chocolate bits over the top and decorate with whole raspberries. Refrigerate overnight. Serves 12 very special friends.

Chocolate Chip Whipped Cream and Raspberries:
       1   cup whipped cream
       1   tablespoon sugar
       2   tablespoons Grand Marnier Liqueur
     1/2   cup semi-sweet chocolate chips, coarsely chopped
       1   package (10 ounces) frozen raspberries, drained

Beat cream with sugar and liqueur until stiff. Beat in chopped chocolate bits. Stir in drained raspberries. Will fill and frost above cake rather sparingly. I have cut down the amount of cream. Increase cream to 1 1/2 cups for a little more frosting.

Italian Rum & Raisin Bread Pudding

Bread pudding and sauce can be prepared earlier in the day and stored in the refrigerator. If preparing this earlier, heat the bread pudding in a 325° oven until heated through. To store the sauce, place a piece of plastic wrap on top of the sauce to prevent a skin from forming. Remove the plastic wrap and reheat the sauce, over low heat, stirring constantly.

1/2	loaf (about 8 ounces) 2-day old Italian bread, crusts removed, sliced and cut into 1-inch squares.

1/3   cup dark raisins
1/3   cup yellow raisins

5   eggs
3   cups milk
1   cup half and half
1   cup sugar
2   tablespoons vanilla
2   tablespoons rum

In a greased 9x13-inch porcelain baker, toss bread with raisins. Beat together the remaining ingredients and pour evenly over the bread. Allow to stand for 30 minutes. Press the raisins into the custard mixture, and bake the pudding at 350° for about 1 hour or until top is golden and custard is set. Cut into squares when cool. Serve warm, not hot, with a spoonful of Vanilla Raisin Sauce. Serves 8.

Vanilla Raisin Sauce:

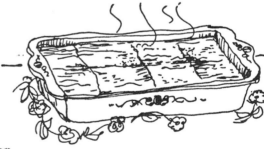

1   egg
1/2   cup milk
2   teaspoons flour

1/2   cup milk
1   teaspoon vanilla
4   tablespoons sifted powdered sugar

1/4   cup chopped raisins (mix dark and yellow raisins)

In the small bowl of an electric mixer, beat together first 3 ingredients until blended. Place the remaining 3 ingredients in a saucepan, and heat until bubbles form around the edges. In a slow stream, beat the warm milk into the egg mixture until blended. When blended, return the whole mixture to the saucepan, add the raisins and, over medium heat, cook and stir constantly until sauce is thickened, 3 or 4 minutes. Do not allow to boil. Serve warm, not hot.

Note: -I have prepared this with dried apricots and it was so delicious I would not be able to sleep if I did not share this with you. Simply substitute chopped dried apricots for the raisins in the pudding and in the sauce. It is not typically Italian, but certainly worth the little by-pass.

Old-Fashioned
Bread Pudding Cheesecake

Bread puddings are a true comfort food. Homey and nostalgic, they can be prepared for a delicious breakfast, lunch or dinner or dessert. Here I have made a pudding that is ideal for a luncheon or a family dessert. The addition of cream cheese and lemon give it the flavor of a cheesecake but much lighter, of course.

8	slices stale or toasted French bread
1	package (8 ounces) cream cheese, at room temperature
4	eggs
1 1/2	cups milk
1 1/2	cups half and half
1/2	cup sugar
3	tablespoons lemon juice
1	teaspoon grated lemon peel
1/3	cup dried currants

Toppings:
        strawberry jam and sour cream   or
        fresh strawberry slices, sour cream and chopped toasted pecans

In a 9x13-inch buttered porcelain casserole, place bread slices in one layer. Beat cream cheese until fluffy. Beat in the next 7 ingredients until blended. Evenly pour mixture over the bread slices and allow to stand for 1 hour in the refrigerator.

Bake at 350° for about 40 minutes, or until casserole is puffed and golden. Serve with a dollup of sour cream with fresh sliced strawberries or strawberry jam. Serves 8.

Cappuccino Supreme

Traditionally, Cappuccino is made with equal amounts of espresso coffee and hot milk. Served with a dollup of whipped cream and a sprinkling of cinnamon or nutmeg, it is very good indeed. However, the addition of liqueurs adds a good deal of excitement and "spirit" to the occasion.

Cappuccino Mix:
- 4 tablespoons instant espresso coffee
- 2 tablespoons cocoa
- 2 tablespoons sugar

Liqueurs:
- 5 ounces coffee liqueur
- 5 ounces Creme de Cacao liqueur
- 2 ounces Cognac or brandy

- 4 1/2 cups boiling water
- 3 cups milk

- 1/2 cup whipped cream (optional)
- cinnamon, nutmeg or shaved chocolate

In a jar with a tight-fitting lid, shake together instant coffee, cocoa and sugar until blended. In another jar, combine the liqueurs and brandy. When you are ready to serve, heat together water and milk to the boiling point..

Serving now is very simple. Place 1 teaspoon Cappuccino Mixture into each cup. Add about 5 ounces of hot milk mixture and 1 ounce of liqueur. Stir. Top with a teaspoon of whipped cream. Sprinkle lightly with cinnamon or nutmeg or shaved chocolate. Serves 12.

Note: -Cappuccino Mix can be stored for weeks and is very nice to have on hand. Use it as instant coffee.
- -Liqueurs can be combined and stored indefinitely and are also nice to have ready when unexpected company arrives.
- -If you are feeling adventuresome, try different combinations of your favorite liqueurs; Galliano (herb liqueur) or Amaretto (almond liqueur) or Frangelico (hazelnut liqueur) are especially good.

Celebration Dinner a la Grecque

Hummus (Vegetable Dip or Spread) or
Tarama (Vegetable Dip or Spread)

Greek Sweet Biscuit Bread with Currants
Olive & Lemon Dill Biscuit Muffins

Mushrooms a la Grecque with Garlic Lemon Dressing

Greek-Styled Lamb Shanks in Tomato Garlic Wine Sauce
Orzo
String Beans with Garlic
or
Pastitsio a la Grecque

Greek Honey Cake
Easiest & Best Apricot Nut Bars
Mom's Greek Butter Pecan Cookies

Greek Coffee

You would do well to consider this menu, in a Greek mood, for an anniversary dinner with family or friends. The menu is especially easy on the hostess, for all the dishes can be prepared a day earlier and reheated at the time of serving. Lots of interesting recipes...Hummus (a garbanzo dip) or Tarama (a fish roe dip) are both excellent served with fresh vegetables or with the Greek Biscuit Bread. The Mushroom Salad is lovely served with the Olive & Lemon Dill Muffins.

Lamb Shanks accompanied with Orzo and String Beans with Garlic is a wonderful main course. Alternatively, Pastitsio is a delicious casserole for a more informal serving.

For dessert, the very exciting Greek Honey Cake. My Mom's lovely Butter Pecan Cookies or the Apricot Nut Bars are enjoyed by all and nice to have as an extra. Greek Coffee should be served very strong and sweet and in demitasse cups.

273

Hummus

This Middle Eastern chick pea dip is delicious served with small wedges of fresh pita bread. The "tahini" can be purchased in most supermarkets and health food stores. This can be prepared in minutes using the food processor. Also, it can be prepared 2 days in advance and stored, covered, in the refrigerator.

- 2 cans (15 ounces, each) chick peas, rinsed and drained
- 4 cloves garlic
- 2/3 cup lemon juice
- 1/2 cup olive oil
- 3/4 cup tahini (sesame seed paste)
  pinch of salt, black pepper and cayenne pepper

Place all the ingredients in the bowl of a food processor and blend until mixture is pureed, cream and smooth. Cut 6-inch fresh pita breads into 1-inch wedges or squares. Place Hummus in a crystal bowl and surround with fresh pita.

Note: -Tahini is traditional but it can be omitted. I have made it several times without the tahini, and the dip is very delicious and lighter.

Tarama

I hesitated to share this recipe because it has a very strong, assertive taste. But it is exotic and there may be a time you could use it. This is an adaptation of my mother's recipe. Tarama is sold packed in a casing (which must be removed) or in glass jars without the casing (which I recommend). This can be prepared several days earlier and stored in the refrigerator. Serve it with pita bread, toast points, raw vegetables or thin slices of Greek sesame bread. "Tarama Caviar" and Greek sesame bread can be purchased in most Continental or Greek markets.

- 6 slices white bread, crusts removed, dipped in water
     and squeezed dry
- 1/3 cup carp roe (also known as "Tarama Caviar")
- 6 tablespoons lemon juice, or more to taste
- 4 cloves garlic, peeled and sliced
- 1/2 small onion, chopped, about 4 tablespoons

- 1 cup vegetable oil

In a food processor bowl, blend together 5 ingredients. Gradually beat in the oil, in a steady stream, until oil is incorporated. Place mixture in a glass bowl and serve with lightly buttered toast points or wedges of pita. Raw vegetables are good, too.

Mushrooms a la Greque with Garlic Lemon Dressing

1 pound mushrooms, cleaned and sliced

1/3 cup oil
6 tablespoons lemon juice
2 cloves garlic, minced
2 green onions, finely chopped
1/2 teaspoon oregano flakes
1/4 teaspoon sweet basil flakes
    salt and pepper to taste

Place mushrooms in a bowl. Combine the remaining ingredients in a jar with a tight-fitting lid and shake until blended. Pour dressing to taste over the mushrooms. Unused dressing can be stored in the refrigerator. Yields about 3/4 cup dressing. Serves 6.

Greek Sweet Biscuit Bread with Currants

This is an interesting and versatile bread. It is moist, tender and delicious and serves well with sweet or savory spreads. Far more interesting than a cracker, it is equally good served with cream cheese, sliced strawberries and a sprinkling of pecans...or with cheese, paté and wine.

4 cups flour
2 teaspoons baking powder
1/4 teaspoon salt
1/2 cup sugar
1/2 cup cold butter or margarine, cut into 4 pieces

1/2 cup dried currants

3 eggs
1 1/8 cups cream or half and half

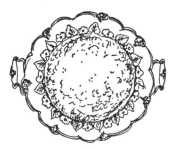

In the large bowl of an electric mixer, beat together first 5 ingredients until butter resembles fine meal. Beat in currants. Thoroughly beat together eggs and cream and, with the motor running, slowly add it to the flour mixture just until blended. Do not overbeat. Spread dough evenly into a greased 10-inch springform pan. Bake at 350° for 35 to 40 minutes or until top is golden brown. To serve, cut into thin wedges. Yields 16 to 20 slices.

Greek-Styled Lamb Shanks in a Tomato-Garlic Wine Sauce

This is an adoption of the classic Italian Osso Bucco. The lamb gives the sauce a totally different character and flavor. Orzo, a rice-shaped pasta, is an especially good accompaniment. Orzo comes in 3 sizes, small, medium and large. Use the large-sized orzo because it is more dramatic. If you use the smaller-sized orzo, reduce the amount of broth to 3 cups.

6	lamb shanks (about 3/4 pound, each) trimmed of any visible fat. Sprinkle with salt, pepper and a faint dusting of flour.
6	medium onions, thinly sliced
2	cans (1 pound each) stewed tomatoes, chopped. Discard seeds.
1	can (6 ounces) tomato paste
1	cup dry white wine
1	can (10 1/2 ounces) beef broth
3	carrots, finely grated
1	tablespoon sugar
3	tablespoons olive oil
6	cloves garlic, minced
1/2	teaspoon each, oregano, basil and thyme flakes
	salt and pepper to taste

Place lamb shanks in a 12x16-inch baking pan and scatter onions over lamb. Stir together the remaining ingredients and pour sauce evenly over the lamb. Cover pan tightly with foil and bake in a 350° oven for 1 1/2 hours, or until lamb is almost tender. Remove foil and bake for another 30 minutes. Sauce should be quite thick and lamb very tender. Remove every trace of fat.

Serve on a bed of Orzo and ladle sauce over all. A little Parmesan on top is optional, but very nice. Serves 6.

To make Orzo:
In a Dutch oven casserole, saute 1 1/2 cups orzo with 2 tablespoons of oil until orzo is just beginning to take on color. Add 3 1/4 cups chicken broth and salt and pepper to taste. Stir mixture, cover pan and simmer mixture for about 40 minutes, or until liquid is absorbed and orzo is tender.

Olive & Lemon Dill Biscuit Muffins

These savory biscuits are easily baked in muffin cups. Follow instructions carefully to keep them light and flaky.

2	eggs, beaten
3	tablespoons olive oil
1/2	cup black pitted olives, coarsely chopped
2	cups flour
2	teaspoons baking powder
1/4	teaspoon salt
1	teaspoon grated lemon zest (yellow part of the peel)
1/2	teaspoon dried dill weed

In a large bowl, whisk eggs until light and fluffy, about 2 minutes. Stir in olive oil and olives. Add the remaining ingredients and stir until blended. Do not overmix.

Divide batter between 12 paper-lined muffin cups and bake at 350° for 25 minutes, or until tops are lightly browned. Allow to cool in pan. When cool, wrap pan in foil. To serve, place foil-wrapped pan in a 300° oven and heat for 5 minutes. Yields 12 medium-sized biscuits.

String Beans with Garlic

2	pounds thin tender string beans, stems trimmed
1	cup chicken broth
6	cloves garlic, thinly sliced
3	tablespoons olive oil
	salt and pepper to taste

In a covered saucepan, cook string beans in broth until tender, about 5 minutes. Drain and reserve broth for another use.

In a skillet, saute garlic in oil until it is soft, but not browned. Mash it with a fork. Add the string beans and seasonings and cook and stir until string beans are nicely coated with garlic and heated through. Serves 8.

Pastitsio a la Grecque
(Greek Pasta & Meat Casserole)

Pastitsio is a Greek version of pasta and meat in casserole. It is basically easy to prepare and very easy to serve. Traditionally topped with a cream sauce, I find it best to omit it. Beef or lamb can be used in the filling.

Meat Filling:

2	large onions, chopped
6	cloves garlic, minced
2	tablespoons olive oil
2	pounds lean ground lamb or beef
1	can (1 pound 12 ounces) chopped tomatoes in puree
1	can (8 ounces) tomato sauce
3	tablespoons chopped parsley leaves
1/4	teaspoon, each, cinnamon and nutmeg
	salt and pepper to taste

In a Dutch oven casserole, saute onions and garlic in olive oil until onions are transparent. Add the ground meat and cook and stir, crumbling the meat until it is no longer pink. Stir in tomatoes, parsley and seasonings, cover pan and simmer mixture for 15 minutes or until sauce has thickened slightly.

Cheese Crumb Mixture:

1/2   cup grated Parmesan cheese mixed with 1/2 cup stale bread crumbs

Pasta:

1   pound pasta (ziti, penne or other small pasta), cooked in boiling water until tender, but firm and thoroughly drained. Toss with 2 tablespoons olive oil.

To Assemble:

In a 9x13-inch baking pan, layer half the meat filling, half the pasta, half the cheese/crumb mixture. Continue layering with the remaining meat, pasta and cheese/crumb mixture. Pat top down to settle the casserole. Bake in a 350° oven for 30 **minutes**, or until heated through and top is crusty brown. Serves 8 to 10.

Easiest & Best Apricot Nut Bars

This is an easy cookie that is tart and crunchy. Whenever I make it, everyone asks for the recipe. It is intensely "apricot" and for the apricot lover.

1	package (6 ounces) dried apricots
1/2	cup of sugar

1	cup butter, softened
1/2	cup sugar
1	cup brown sugar
2	eggs
2	teaspoons vanilla

2 1/4	cups flour
1/2	teaspoon baking powder
1/2	teaspoon baking soda
1	cup chopped walnuts

In food processor, finely chop apricots with sugar. Beat together next 5 ingredients until blended. Beat in apricot mixture until blended. Beat in next 4 ingredients until blended. (Batter will be thick.) Spread batter evenly into a greased 10x15-inch jelly roll pan and bake at 375° for 20 minutes or until top is lightly browned. Cool in pan and cut into 1 1/2-inch squares. Yields about 60 cookies.

Mom's Greek Butter Pecan Cookies

This simple little butter cookie is one I grew up on. Mom would make these into balls, or flatten them into discs or into three-cornered hats. Often, she would make them without nuts. They are a poem of flavor and texture and one of my favorites

1	cup butter or margarine, (2 sticks), softened
1/2	cup sugar
1	teaspoon vanilla
2 1/4	cups flour
1	cup finely chopped pecans (or walnuts) (optional)
	sifted powdered sugar

Beat together butter and sugar until mixture is thoroughly blended. Beat in vanilla. Beat in flour until blended. Beat in nuts (optional) until blended. Shape dough into 1-inch balls and place on a greased 12x16-inch pan. Flatten balls slightly.

Bake at 350° for about 18 minutes or until cookies just begin to take on color. These should be pale and not browned. Remove from oven and sprinkle with sifted powdered sugar when hot, and again when cold. Yields 36 cookies.

Greek Honey Cake

This is a very unusual and interesting dessert that is especially nice for a dinner in a Greek mood. It is very different, but it does produce a marvelous dessert, that I am certain you will enjoy.

3	eggs
3/4	cup sugar
2	cups Ritz cracker crumbs (about 42 crackers)
3/4	cup sugar
1	teaspoon baking powder
1	teaspoon cinnamon
1	teaspoon vanilla
1	orange, grated (use fruit, juice and peel)
1 1/2	cups chopped walnuts

Beat eggs with 3/4 cup sugar until eggs are pale, about 3 minutes. On low speed, beat in the remaining ingredients until just blended.

Pour mixture into a lightly buttered 9-inch springform pan and bake at 350° for 30 minutes. Remove cake from oven and drizzle the cooled Honey Cinnamon Syrup on top. Cool cake in pan and cut into wedges to serve. Serves 8.

Honey Cinnamon Syrup:
1/3	cup sugar
1/3	cup water
1/4	cup honey
1	slice lemon (about 1/4-inch thick)
1	cinnamon stick

Cook together all the ingredients, at a very low bubble, until mixture is syrupy, about 10 minutes. Remove lemon and cinnamon stick. Allow to cool. Pour syrup over cake.

Note: -Can be prepared 1 day earlier and stored in the refrigerator. Allow to come to room temperature before serving.

Greek Coffee

In a saucepan or brass Greek coffee brewer, bring to a boil 3 cups water, 8 cubes sugar and 10 teaspoons pulverized ground coffee. Stir briskly and remove from heat. Wait for a few seconds to allow coffee grounds to settle and pour into demitasse cups. Yields 8 servings.

Buffet Supper a la Russe

Caviar with Creme Fraiche & Toast Points
Smoked Salmon with Toast Points
Piroshki Roulades a la Muscovite

Champagne
Frozen Stoli in Red Rose Ice
(Cristal Stolichnaya in Iced Rose Bouquet)

Russian Flatbread with Onions & Poppy Seeds or
Bialistock Rolls

Chicken Stroganov a la Russe
Kasha with Mushrooms & Onions
Russian Cucumber Salad

Lemon Vanilla Cheesecake with Raspberry Syrup
Chocolate Fudge Torte
Coffee - Tea

This is the buffet I planned for a charity opening of the movie "The Hunt for Red October" starring Sean Connery. It was a smashing success and years later, whenever I meet someone who attended the affair, they always mention how great a party it was.

The menu was printed on flaming red paper and inserted in matching envelopes. As more than 300 people attended the affair, the menus were distributed as the guests arrived. And from that moment on, the excitement began.

The frozen bottles of vodka were a bouquet of dark red roses on the bar. Champagne, caviar and smoked salmon stations were everywhere...the piroshkis were served warm on a tray. The excitement level was astonishing.

Dinner was easy to serve as the menu was basically simple but imaginative. The Kasha with Mushrooms and Onions was the perfect accompaniment to the Stroganov. The Russian Flatbread with Onions & Poppy Seeds and Cucumber Salad rounded out the menu. Dessert, the beautiful Vanilla Cheesecake with a hint of lemon and raspberries was a poem of flavors. The Chocolate Fudge Torte was fit for a Czar.

This is an easy menu to prepare and serve. Toast your guests with:

"Az Vasha Zdarovye ee Schastyeh!"
To your Health & Happiness

Frozen Stoli in Red Rose Ice
(Cristal Stolichnaya in Iced Rose Bouquet)

This is the most gorgeous way to serve frozen vodka. The beautiful array of crimson roses framing each bottle of vodka is a sight to behold. Preparation is very easy and the beauty is well worth the expense of the roses. I have described the process in excruciating detail. Simply put, place a bottle of vodka in an empty 1/2-gallon milk container, wedge the roses and leaves around the bottle, fill with water and freeze.

1   1/2-gallon empty milk container, open top seams and wash
     thoroughly
1   bottle (750 ml) Stolichnaya vodka, or other vodka of choice
8   red roses with leaves attached (or any color that will
     harmonize with the season or decor)

Place bottle of vodka, with cap slightly unscrewed, in milk container. Cut rose stems, so that each rose measures 7 to 8 inches. (Roses must be lower than the neck of the bottle.) Place 2 roses on each side of the milk carton surrounding the vodka bottle, and spread the leaves a little.

Now fill the container with water up to the neck of the bottle. (Don't fill with water above the neck, for it will be hard to serve.) Make certain the roses are deep in the container and covered with water. Place in freezer until water is frozen solid; vodka will not freeze. (This can be done days or weeks in advance.)

To remove container, allow vodka to stand at room temperature for 10 minutes and peel off the paper. Place vodka in glass bowl or small silver platter and serve with pride. Have a towel close by, and discard the water as it melts.

Caviar with Creme Fraiche & Toast Points

My *favorite way to relish caviar is simply to spread it on Toast Points. Toast points are delicate and do not interfere with the taste of the caviar. Chopped chives and Creme Fraiche are optional but a nice addition.*

To Serve 6:

4	ounces caviar in an iced caviar server
1/4	cup chopped chives in a small bowl
1	cup creme fraiche in a small bowl
24	toast points, made with 6 slices very thinly sliced bread

Creme Fraiche:

1/2	cup sour cream (can use low-fat sour cream.) Non-fat sour cream cannot be used.
1/2	cup cream (can use half and half)

In a glass jar, stir together sour cream and cream until blended. Allow to stand at room temperature for 2 hours or until slightly thickened. Cover and refrigerate overnight. Can be prepared 3 days earlier. Yields 1 cup.

To Make Toast Points:
Use thin slices of white bread. Remove crusts and cut bread into 4 slices on the diagonal. Spread with the thinnest smidgeon of butter and toast in a 350° oven until lightly crisped but not brown.

To Serve 6:
Smoked Salmon with Toast Points:
Smoked salmon slices often run about 2-inches wide, so cut 1/2 pound smoked salmon into 2-inch squares; then cut each square on the diagonal. Place triangles of salmon on a platter and sprinkle top with a faint sprinkling of dill. Serve with the same accompaniments as the caviar, but double the quantities noted above.

Piroshki Roulades a la Muscovite

Using the prepared puff pastry cuts preparation time to a minimum. And preparing these in 8-inch logs that you will later cut into small squares is another timesaver.

Mushroom & Herb Filling:

2	tablespoons margarine
4	shallots, minced
2	cloves garlic, minced
1	large onion, minced
1/2	pound mushrooms, minced
2	teaspoons lemon juice
1/4	teaspoon ground poultry seasoning
1/8	teaspoon thyme flakes
	salt and pepper to taste
2	tablespoons flour
1	cup sour cream

Saute together first 4 ingredients until onion is transparent. Add the next 2 ingredients and continue sauteing until mushrooms are tender and all the liquid is absorbed. Add seasonings and flour and cook and stir for 2 minutes. Add sour cream and cook and stir for 2 minutes or until mixture is very thick. Allow mixture to cool.

Using Prepared Puff Pastry:

1	package Pepperidge Farms Puff Pastry (2 large sheets)
1	egg, beaten
12	tablespoons grated Parmesan cheese

Cut pastry sheets in thirds on the fold. Cut each third in half crosswise. You will have 12 pieces. On a floured pastry cloth, roll out each piece to measure 4x8-inches. Place a few tablespoons mushroom mixture along the 8-inch side, fold dough over and press edges down with the tines of a fork. Scallop the edges.

Place piroshkis on a greased cookie sheet, brush tops with beaten egg and sprinkle with cheese. Pierce tops with the tines of a fork. Bake at 400° for 25 to 30 minutes, or until tops are nicely browned. Allow to cool on brown paper.

To reheat, place piroshkis on a cookie sheet, cut each into 4 pieces and heat in a 350° oven for 15 minutes, or until heated through. Yields 48 piroshkis.

Bialys (Bialistock Rolls)

If you are a fan of Bialistock Rolls, as I am, I thought you would like a recipe that is easy to prepare and does not require fussing. These delicious small Russian breads add an exciting touch to a meal and everybody will thank you for going to so much trouble. Please use a good quality, heavy baking pan to assure even baking. Freeze in double plastic bags.

- 1/2 cup warm water (105°)
- 1 tablespoon sugar
- 1 package (1 tablespoon) dry yeast

- 1 1/2 cups warm water (105°)
- 1 tablespoon oil
- 5 cups all-purpose flour. (Can use 2 1/2 cups bread flour and 2 1/2 cups all-purpose flour.)
- 1 teaspoon salt

Topping:
- 3/4 cup chopped onion
- 1 tablespoon oil

Preheat oven to 425°. Line with foil, 2 baking pans, 12x16-inches (not necessary to grease foil.) In the large bowl of an electric mixer, proof yeast by stirring together 1/2 cup water, sugar and yeast. Allow to stand for 10 to 15 minutes, or until yeast starts to foam. If yeast does not foam, it is not active, and should be discarded.

Now, beat in the next 4 ingredients, and beat until mixture is thoroughly blended. On a floured board, or using a dough hook, knead dough for 5 minutes. Place dough into an oiled bowl, and turn dough to coat both sides. Cover bowl with plastic wrap and allow to rise in a warm place until doubled in bulk, about 1 hour, or refrigerate dough overnight.

Punch dough down and with oiled hands, divide dough into 16 balls. Place 8 balls in each prepared pan and with your fingers, spread balls out into 4-inch rounds. Make a deep indentation in center. Stir together onion and oil and place about 1 tablespoon onion mixture into each indentation. (For chewy Bialys, bake at once. For softer, more bread-like Bialys, allow dough to rest for 15 minutes.)

Bake at 425° for about 25 minutes, or until tops are golden brown. Yields 16.

Russian Flatbread
with Onions & Poppy Seeds

This is a gorgeous large round flatbread that is fun to serve. It can be assembled in literally minutes. It can be prepared 1 day earlier and heated before serving.

- 3 large onions, chopped
- 3 tablespoons oil

- 3 cups self-rising flour
- 3 tablespoons sugar
- 1 can (12 ounces) beer

- 2 tablespoons poppy seeds
- 2 tablespoons oil

In a large skillet, saute onions in oil until onions are browned. In the large bowl of an electric mixer, beat together flour, sugar and beer until blended (about 30 seconds). Do not overbeat. Beat in the onions and poppy seeds.

Place 1 tablespoon oil on the bottom of a 12-inch round baking pan. Spread batter evenly in pan and drizzle remaining oil on top. Bake at 350° for 45 minutes, or until top is golden brown. Cut into wedges to serve. Serves 12.

Russian Cucumber Salad

I like to add the vinaigrette just before serving, as the cucumbers have a tendency to render a great deal of liquid which dilutes the dressing. Drain the cucumbers before serving and add dressing to taste.

Vinaigrette Dressing:
- 1 cup white vinegar
- 1 cup water
- 3/4 cup sugar

Cucumber Salad:
- 6 large cucumbers, sliced very thin
- 1/2 cup chopped chives
- 2 teaspoons dried dill weed
- salt to taste

In a glass jar with a tight-fitting lid, stir together vinegar, water and sugar until sugar is dissolved. In a large bowl, add the salad ingredients. Before serving, drain any liquid that has formed and add Vinaigrette to taste. Serves 12.

Chicken Stroganov a la Russe

1 1/2   pounds boned chicken breasts, cut into bite-size pieces. Season with white pepper, garlic powder, paprika and dust with a little flour.

   3   tablespoons butter or margarine

1/4   cup Cognac

Stroganov Sauce:

   2   onions, finely chopped

   2   tablespoons butter or margarine

   1   pound mushrooms, thinly sliced

   2   teaspoons sweet paprika

      salt to taste

   1   cup sour cream

In a skillet, heat the butter or margarine until sizzling hot. In batches, (do not crowd the pan) saute the chicken until meat becomes opaque. Very important not to overcook. Heat the Cognac, ignite it, and carefully pour it over the meat. When the flames subside, set chicken aside.

In a large Dutch oven casserole, saute onions in margarine until onions are transparent. Add the mushrooms, and continue sauteing until the mushrooms are tender and any liquid rendered is evaporated. Add the seasonings and sour cream and heat through.

When ready to serve, heat sauce gently so it doesn't boil. Add the chicken and heat through. (Don't allow to boil or sauce will curdle.) Serves 6. Double the recipe to serve 12.

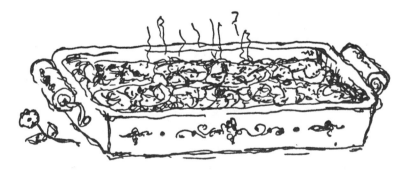

Kasha with Mushrooms & Onions

Your guests will love this flavorful kasha. It is a perfect accompaniment to the Chicken Stroganov. I recommend that you prepare an extra amount as I have found that most people tend to have seconds.

1	cup kasha (also known as cracked-wheat bulgur)
1	tablespoon oil

1 1/4	cups chicken broth
3/4	cup water
	salt and pepper to taste

1	large onion, chopped
1/4	pound mushrooms, sliced
1/4	cup grated carrots (optional)
2	tablespoons oil

In a saucepan, cook cracked wheat in oil, stirring now and again, for 2 minutes. Carefully (it could splatter), stir in the broth, water and seasonings. Cover pan, lower heat, and simmer mixture for about 15 minutes, or until liquid is absorbed.

Meanwhile in another covered saucepan, saute together next 4 ingredients until onion is soft and mushrooms are tender. Uncover pan and cook for another few minutes or until juices have evaporated. Toss mushroom mixture into cracked wheat and heat through. Serve with a little chopped parsley on top. Serves 6. Double the recipe to serve 12.

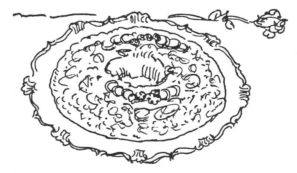

Lemon Vanilla Cheesecake with Raspberry Syrup

Lemon and vanilla are a wonderful pair in this creamy cheesecake. A word of caution. Cream cheese is now being made with ingredients that make it more spreadable. It is not the best for cheesecakes. It sometimes makes them grainy and not the usual velvety texture. Try to find a cheese store that sells the old-fashioned cream cheese in bulk. If not available, then underbake the cheesecake by 10 minutes and let it firm up in the refrigerator.

Crust:
1 1/4	cups graham cracker crumbs
2	ounces butter, (1/2 stick), melted
1/2	cup coarsely chopped walnuts
2	tablespoons cinnamon sugar

Filling:
3	packages (8 ounces, each) cream cheese, softened
1	cup sugar
3	eggs
2	cups sour cream
2	teaspoons vanilla
3	tablespoons lemon juice and
2	teaspoons grated lemon zest

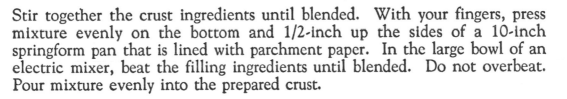

Stir together the crust ingredients until blended. With your fingers, press mixture evenly on the bottom and 1/2-inch up the sides of a 10-inch springform pan that is lined with parchment paper. In the large bowl of an electric mixer, beat the filling ingredients until blended. Do not overbeat. Pour mixture evenly into the prepared crust.

Bake in a 350° oven for about 50 minutes or until top is just beginning to take on color. Do not overbake. Cool in pan and then refrigerate for at least 4 to 6 hours. Overnight is good, too. Remove from pan and serve with a spoonful of Raspberry Syrup. Serves 12.

Raspberry Syrup:
1	package frozen raspberries in syrup, (10 ounces), defrosted
1	cup fresh raspberries
1	teaspoon finely grated lemon zest

Combine all the ingredients and refrigerate until serving.

Note: -Lemon zest is obtained by grating the yellow peel of the lemon. It does not include the white part (the pith).

Chocolate Fudge Torte with Chocolate Glaze

This is one of the easiest and best cakes that you can prepare. It is a moist and tender chocolate cake. Don't be misled by its simplicity. It is a fine torte, takes minutes to assemble, can be made ahead and, not the least of its virtues, it freezes beautifully.

5	eggs
1	cup sugar
1 1/4	cups walnuts or pecans
1	teaspoon vanilla
2	tablespoons flour
1	teaspoon baking powder
3	tablespoons cocoa

Place eggs in bowl of a food processor and whip for a few seconds. Add the remaining ingredients and blend at high speed for 1 minute, or until nuts are finely ground.

Pour batter into a lightly greased and floured 10-inch springform pan. Bake at 350° for about 20 minutes, or until a cake tester, inserted in center, comes out clean. Spread top smoothly with Chocolate Glaze. Serves 12.

Chocolate Glaze:

2/3	cup semi-sweet chocolate chips
1/3	cup butter
1	teaspoon vanilla

In the top of a double boiler, over simmering water, melt chocolate with butter. Stir in the vanilla.

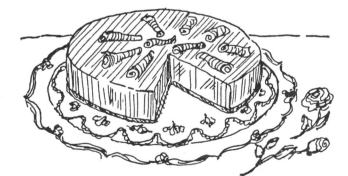

Dinner at the Taj
"Nothing Exceeds Like Excess"

Samosas in Puff Pastry, or
Indian Vegetable Dipping Sauce with Fresh Vegetables & Toasted Pita

Cucumber Salad with Currants & Peanuts

Chili Chicken with Garlic & Onions
Ginger Carrots with Currants & Coconut
Garbanzos with Tomatoes & Onion Curry
Red Lentils with Fried Onions
Yellow Rice Indienne with Raisins & Pistachio Nuts
Yellow Rice with Currants & Cashew Nuts

Chutneys
Mango Chutney with Lemon & Pine Nuts
Apricot Chutney with Bananas & Orange

Desserts
Creamy Rice Pudding with Strawberry Sauce
Creme de Kashmir with Papaya Sauce
Cheesecake on Butter Cookie Crust with Glazed Strawberries
Tea Aromatique

This is a grand menu in the fullest sense of the word. It is full of interesting flavors, textures and colors. Again, here is a nice variety of choices.

For starters, you can choose the Samosas, served hot, or the Indian Vegetable Dipping Sauce, served cold. A cucumber salad is a must and Cucumber Salad with Currants & Peanuts is very unusual. Choose two or three accompaniments to the chicken. They all work well together.

I would recommend that you prepare both chutneys. They keep well and are often served with numerous other roasts of meat or chicken. They are delicately seasoned and not hot or highly spiced.

The vegetable choices are interesting and great to use with other menus. Don't reserve them only for Indian dinners. They translate well with lamb, chicken or beef roasts. All the recipes can be made in advance and heated before serving.

Indian desserts often use bases of milk or cream. The Cheesecake is an excellent dessert, but if you are feeling a little more adventuresome, I would recommend you include both classics...Creamy Rice Pudding and Creme de Kashmir. The 2 fruit sauces can be interchanged. They are triumphant endings to a superb dinner.

Samosas in Puff Pastry

Samosas are quite heavy, traditionally made with a baking powder dough and deep-fried. Once again, I have adjusted the dish to make it lighter. Using puff pastry is just lovely and eliminates deep-frying. The end result is marvelous and delicious. I have included 2 fillings...one made with vegetables and the other with meat. Boiling the potatoes in chicken broth is far more tasty than using water.

Meat Filling:

1	large onion, chopped
1	tablespoon butter or oil
1 1/2	pounds lean ground beef
3	teaspoons curry powder
1	teaspoon garam masala
	salt to taste
1	egg, beaten
3	tablespoons bread or cracker crumbs

In a skillet, saute onion in butter until onion is soft. Add the beef and seasonings and saute meat, turning, until meat is crumbled and loses its pinkness. Stir in egg and crumbs until blended. Set filling aside to cool.

Vegetable Filling:

1	small onion, chopped
1	tablespoon butter or oil
1	pound potatoes, peeled and boiled in chicken broth until tender. Drain <u>thoroughly</u> and coarsely chop. Do not puree. Discard the broth.
1	package (10 ounces) frozen baby peas, defrosted
2	teaspoons garam masala
1	teaspoon ground cumin
1	sprinkle cayenne pepper or to taste

In a skillet, saute onion in butter until onion is soft. Meanwhile prepare the potatoes. In a large bowl, place all the ingredients and seasonings and stir to combine. Set filling aside to cool.

The Pastry:

1	package (about 1 pound 1 ounce) prepared puff pastry (2 sheets)
1	egg, beaten

Preparation:

Roll out each sheet of puff pastry to 1/8-inch thickness, or about a 12x16-inch square. As a guide, draw a 4-inch circle with parchment paper or use a 4-inch bowl. Mark off and cut 4-inch circles on the pastry. You will end up with 24 circles.

Place 1 heaping tablespoon filling onto each circle. Fold dough in half and crimp edges with the tines of a fork. Pierce tops in several places with the tines of a fork. Place samosas on a lightly greased cookie sheet, brush tops with beaten egg and bake at 400° for about 20 to 25 minutes, or until pastry is golden brown. Yields 24 Samosas. Any leftover Samosas can be frozen.

Cucumber Salad with Currants & Peanuts

2   large cucumbers, peeled and thinly sliced

Vinaigrette:
2   tablespoons water
2   tablespoons vinegar
2   teaspoons sugar
     salt and pepper to taste

1/4   cup dried currants
1/4   cup chopped roasted peanuts

Place cucumbers in a covered bowl and refrigerate for several hours. In a glass jar shake together next 5 ingredients until sugar is dissolved. Before serving, remove cucumbers from the refrigerator and drain thoroughly. Toss with the Vinaigrette and sprinkle with currants and peanuts. Serves 6.

Indian Vegetable Dipping Sauce

A dipping sauce or "salsa" can be created around any cuisine. Use the spices and seasonings that are commonly used in that country, use a native bread, and you will have a light and delicious start to an ethnic meal. Sauce can be prepared earlier in the day and stored in the refrigerator.

1   small onion, minced
5   cloves garlic, minced
3   medium tomatoes, peeled, seeded and chopped
1/2   small cucumber, seeded and grated, about 1/2 cup
2   tablespoons lemon juice
1   teaspoon curry powder
1   teaspoon oil
     salt and pepper to taste

In a bowl, stir together all the ingredients until blended. Cover bowl and refrigerate until serving time. Serve with Toasted Pita Triangles. Yields about 2 1/2 cups sauce.

To Toast Pita Triangles:
Separate 3 pita breads into halves. Brush each half lightly with melted butter and sprinkle with a little garlic powder. With scissors, cut each half into 6 wedges. Place on a cookie sheet and bake at 350° for about 8 minutes or until triangles are crisped. Yields 36 chips.

Chili Chicken with Garlic & Onions
(Chicken Vindaloo)

    2   fryer chickens, cut into serving pieces. Sprinkle lightly with salt
         and garlic powder and brush with melted butter.

Chili Sauce:
    2   onions, chopped
    6   cloves garlic, minced
    2   tablespoons butter

    2   medium potatoes, peeled and cut into 3/4-inch dice
    1   can (1 pound) stewed tomatoes, chopped. Do not drain.
    2   teaspoons chili powder
    1   teaspoon ground turmeric
   1/2   teaspoon ground cumin
         salt and pepper to taste

In a 12x16-inch roasting pan, place chicken in 1 layer. Bake at 350° for 50 minutes, brushing now and again with the juices in the pan.

Meanwhile, in a saucepan, saute onions and garlic in butter until onions are transparent. Add the remaining ingredients, cover pan, and simmer mixture for 20 minutes, or until potatoes are tender.

Place potato mixture around the chicken and continue baking for 20 minutes, or until chicken is tender. Place under the broiler for a few minutes to brown top. Serves 6.

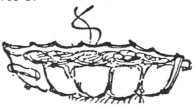

Yellow Rice with Currants & Cashew Nuts

    1   cup rice
    2   cups chicken broth
    1   tablespoon butter
    1   teaspoon ground turmeric
         salt and pepper to taste

   1/2   cup currants, plumped in boiling water for 5 minutes, and drained
   1/2   cup toasted shelled cashew nuts or almonds, coarsely chopped

In a covered saucepan, simmer together first 6 ingredients for 30 minutes, or until rice is tender and liquid is absorbed. Stir in currants and nuts and heat through. Serves 6.

Garbanzos with Tomatoes & Onion Curry

Garbanzos make an excellent side-dish. My Mom served these in so many ways...with tomatoes, onions.. in spinach, rice and more. The combinations are endless. Here, they are flavored with tomatoes and onions and spiced with curry and cumin.

    2   tablespoons butter
    1   onion, finely chopped
    4   cloves garlic, minced

    1   can (1 pound) stewed tomatoes, chopped. Do not drain.
    2   cans (15 ounces, each) garbanzos, rinsed and drained
    2   teaspoons ground curry powder (or more to taste)
    1   teaspoon ground cumin powder
         salt to taste

In a covered saucepan, saute onion and garlic in butter until onion is transparent. Add the remaining ingredients and simmer mixture for 30 minutes. Serves 6.

Ginger Carrots with Currants & Coconut

Intensely flavorful and filled with many assertive tastes (and textures), these carrots add high interest to an Indian dinner.

    1   pound bag baby carrots

    2   tablespoons butter
    1   tablespoon sugar
    1/2 teaspoon minced candied ginger
    1/3 cup black currants
    1/4 cup coconut flakes
         salt to taste

In a saucepan, cook carrots in boiling water until tender, about 8 to 10 minutes. Drain and refresh under cold water. In a large skillet, add the remaining ingredients and cook over low heat until sugar has melted. Add the drained carrots and continue to cook, stirring and tossing, until the carrots are nicely glazed. Serves 6.

Yellow Rice Indienne
with Raisins & Pistachio Nuts

A delicious combination of spices, color and texture. Rice can be prepared earlier in the day and heated before serving. Sprinkle with a few teaspoons of broth when reheating.

1	cup rice
2	cups chicken broth
2	tablespoons oil
1	teaspoon ground turmeric or more to taste
1/2	teaspoon ground cumin
	salt and pepper to taste

1/2	cup raisins, plumped in boiling water for 5 minutes, and drained
1/2	cup toasted shelled pistachio nuts or almonds, coarsely chopped

In a covered saucepan, simmer together first 7 ingredients for 30 minutes, or until rice is tender and liquid is absorbed. Stir in raisins and nuts. Serves 6.

Red Lentils with Tomatoes & Fried Onions

This is a most delicious accompaniment to dinner in an Indian mood. It is beautiful to behold and the fried onions add the nicest flavor.

1	onion, coarsely chopped
4	cloves garlic, minced
2	tablespoons butter

1	cup red lentils, rinsed and picked over for foreign particles
2	cups chicken broth
1	can (1 pound) stewed tomatoes, drained and chopped
1	teaspoon ground turmeric or more to taste
1/2	teaspoon ground cumin
	salt and pepper to taste

In a saucepan, saute onion and garlic in butter until onion is beginning to take on color. Stir in the remaining ingredients, cover pan, and simmer mixture for 45 minutes, or until lentils are tender and most of the liquid is absorbed. Stir in the fried onions and heat through. Serves 6.

To make Fried Onions:
Cut 1 medium onion in half lengthwise. Thinly slice each half into thin half rings. Dust lightly with flour. Fry onions in 2 tablespoons oil until golden brown. Remove from pan and drain on paper towels.

Mango Chutney with Lemon & Pine Nuts

I do not like chutneys that are overly hot or spicy   I much prefer a delicate blend of flavors. I made this and the following one for my "Dinner at the Taj" and everyone agreed they were perfect. Chutneys can be made 1 week earlier, placed in a glass jar with a tight-fitting lid and stored in the refrigerator.

2	cups coarsely chopped fresh mangoes
1/2	cup yellow raisins
1	cup brown sugar
1/2	lemon grated (use fruit, juice and peel)
1/2	cup toasted pine nuts
1/3	cup cider vinegar
1/4	teaspoon ground ginger
1/2	teaspoon ground cinnamon
1/4	teaspoon salt

In a saucepan, stir together all the ingredients and, over low heat, simmer for about 30 minutes, or until mixture reaches 230° on a candy thermometer. Allow to cool, place chutney in a glass jar with a tight-fitting lid and store in the refrigerator. Yields about 1 1/2 cups.

Apricot Chutney with Banana & Orange

1	package (6 ounces) dried apricots
1/2	cup sugar
1 1/2	cups orange juice
1	cup sugar
1/3	cup cider vinegar
2	ripe bananas, coarsely chopped
1/2	teaspoon ground ginger
1/4	teaspoon ground cloves
1/4	teaspoon salt

In the bowl of a food processor, chop apricots with 1/2 cup sugar until apricots are coarsely chopped. Place mixture in a saucepan and stir in the remaining ingredients. Simmer, over low heat, for about 30 minutes, or until mixture thickens. If you use a candy thermometer, it should read 230°. Allow to cool, place chutney in a glass jar with a tight-fitting lid, and store in the refrigerator. Yields about 2 cups.

Creme de Kashmir with Papaya Sauce

There are few desserts you can prepare that are easier or more delicious than this one. Basically, it is creme fraiche sparkled with Cognac and set in a mold. If you own a 10x2-inch round or oval porcelain server, then, no need to unmold. Spread the sauce on top and spoon into dessert dishes at the table.

1/4	cup Cognac	
1/4	cup water	
2	envelopes unflavored gelatin	
2	cups cream or half and half	
1/2	cup sugar	
2	teaspoons vanilla	
	pinch of salt	
2	cups low-fat sour cream, at room temperature	

In a metal measuring cup, soften gelatin in Cognac and water. Place cup in a pan with simmering water and stir gelatin until it is dissolved.

In a saucepan, over low heat, heat together cream, sugar, vanilla and salt and stir until sugar is dissolved. Stir in gelatin. Place cream mixture in the large bowl of an electric mixer. Beat in the sour cream in 4 batches until the creme is completely smooth. Pour into a 10x2-inch round or oval glass or porcelain mold and refrigerate until firm. To serve, run a knife along the edge, set pan in warm water for a few seconds, and invert onto a larger rimmed platter. Surround with Papaya Sauce. Serves 8.

Papaya Sauce:
1/2	cup sugar	
1/2	cup orange juice	
3	tablespoons lemon juice	
2	ripe papayas, peeled, seeded and thinly sliced, about 3 cups	

In a saucepan, over low heat, cook together sugar and juice for 4 minutes, or until mixture is syrupy. Stir in the lemon juice and fruit and simmer mixture for 3 minutes. Allow to cool. When cool, puree fruit in a food processor until finely chopped. Allow a little texture to remain. Place in a glass bowl, cover with plastic wrap and refrigerate until serving time.

Note: -Mangoes may be substituted for the papayas. Sliced fresh peaches is another lovely alternative. Fruit should be soft, so adjust cooking time.

Cheesecake on Butter Cookie Crust with Glazed Strawberries

Butter Cookie Crust:

1	cup flour
1/4	cup sugar
1/2	cup butter, softened
1	egg yolk
1	tablespoon water
1	tablespoon grated lemon peel

Beat together flour, sugar and butter, until mixture resembles coarse meal. Beat together egg yolk and water and beat it in, with the lemon peel, just until dough clumps together. Gather dough, and press it together to form a disc. Pat dough on the bottom and 1-inch up the sides of a 10-inch springform pan. Bake at 350° for 20 minutes or until lightly browned. Cool.

Cream Cheese Filling:

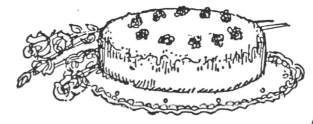

1 1/2	pounds cream cheese, softened
3/4	cup sugar
1 1/2	tablespoons flour
4	teaspoons grated lemon peel
1	teaspoon vanilla
3	eggs
1/4	cup cream

Beat cream cheese and sugar until blended. Beat in remaining filling ingredients until blended. Pour Cream Cheese Filling into prepared crust and bake at 250° for 1 hour and 20 minutes or until just set. Do not overbake. Refrigerate for at least 4 hours. Overnight is good, too. Remove from pan and place on a lovely footed platter. Top cake with plump strawberries and brush strawberries with Currant Jelly Glaze. Refrigerate until serving time. Serves 12.

Topping:

    2   pints fresh strawberries, cleaned and stemmed

Currant Jelly Glaze:
Heat 3/4 cup currant jelly until melted.

Creamy Rice Pudding with Strawberry Sauce

This is perfectly lovely dessert for a spicy Indian Dinner. It can be prepared 1 day earlier and stored in the refrigerator. Make certain the rice is thoroughly cooked and soft because it will not soften further at this low baking temperature.

1/3	cup long-grain rice
3/4	cup water
2	cups milk (low-fat can be used)
1/2	cup sugar
1/4	cup white rum
	pinch of salt
3	eggs
1	cup sour cream (low-fat can be used)

In a covered saucepan, cook together rice and water for 25 minutes, or until rice is very soft and liquid is absorbed. Stir in the next 4 ingredients and heat, stirring, until sugar is dissolved.

In a large bowl, whisk eggs with sour cream until blended. Whisk in rice mixture until blended. Pour mixture into a 10x2-inch round porcelain baker and bake at 300° for 1 hour and 10 minutes. Remove from oven and allow to cool. (A little lip will have formed around the edge and it will hold the Strawberry Sauce.) When cool, refrigerate until serving time. Before serving, spread Strawberry Sauce over the top, bring to the table and spoon into small dessert bowls. Serves 8.

Strawberry Sauce:
Stir together 1 package (10 ounces) frozen strawberries in syrup with 1 tablespoon frozen concentrated orange juice (undiluted). Place in a glass bowl and store in the refrigerator until serving time. Yields 1 1/4 cups sauce.

Tea Aromatique

To 2-ounces of Spiced Tea add, 1 tablespoon grated orange zest and 1 tablespoon grated lemon zest. Toss the tea and the zests together and place in a tightly covered jar. Add 1 teaspoon cinnamon or to taste (optional). To brew tea, use 1 teaspoon Tea Aromatique for each serving.

Mini-Menus
Add a Salad & Dessert

Baked Spanish Mackerel with Tomato, Currants & Pine Nuts
Herbed Orzo with Tomatoes & Onions

❦

Scampi a la Basque with Spinach & Shallots
Yellow Rice with Tomato

❦

Eggplant Dumplings with Onions & Cheese
Light Tomato Sauce

❦

Vegetable Paella with Zucchini, Artichokes & Onions

❦

Spinach & Red Pepper Dumplings with Onions & Cheese
Red Pepper Sauce

❦

Country Pot Roast with Apples & Cranberries
Brown Rice with Mushrooms & Onions

❦

Farmhouse Sweet & Sour Pot Roast with Apples & Raisins
Garlic Mashed Potatoes

❦

Herb Stuffed Breast of Veal in Currant Wine Sauce
Warm Compote of Spiced Mixed Fruit
Ginger Banana Squash with Sugar & Spice

❦

Royal Veal Ring with Mushrooms
Cinnamon Rice with Toasted Almonds & Raisins

❦

Poulet Basquaise
(Garlic Chicken Basque with Peppers & Onions)
Cous Cous with Mushrooms, Red Peppers, Onion & Garlic

❦

Moroccan Chicken with Honey & Lemon Glaze
Bulgur with Apricots, Raisins & Pine Nuts

❦

Russian Honey Chicken with Apricots & Cherries
Bulgur Pilaf with Garbanzos

❦

Oven-Fried Yogurt Chicken with Chiles & Cheese
Mexican Pink Rice

❦

Chicken with Sweet Red Peppers & Garlic
Angel Hair Pasta with Fresh Tomatoes, Garlic & Basil

Baked Spanish Mackerel with Tomato, Currants & Pine Nuts

Black currants, pine nuts, lemon...all add a marvelous depth to this dish. Sauce can be prepared 1 day earlier and stored in the refrigerator.

2	onions, finely chopped
3	cloves garlic, minced
2	tablespoons butter
1	can (1 pound) stewed tomatoes, drained and chopped
1/2	teaspoon sugar
4	tablespoons dried black currants
2	tablespoons lemon juice
	salt and pepper to taste
2 1/2	pounds mackerel fillets, cut into 6 serving pieces
1/4	cup toasted pine nuts

In a saucepan, saute together first 3 ingredients until onions are soft. Stir in the next 6 ingredients and simmer sauce for 10 minutes, uncovered. Place fish into a 9x13-inch baking pan and spoon sauce on top. Bake in a 325° oven for about 30 to 35 minutes, or until fish flakes easily with a fork. Do not overbake.   Sprinkle top with toasted pine nuts before serving. Serve with Herbed Orzo with Tomatoes & Onions. Serves 6.

Herbed Orzo with Tomatoes & Onions

1	onion, finely chopped
2	tablespoons oil
1 1/4	cups orzo (rice-shaped pasta)
2	cans (10 1/2 ounces, each) chicken broth
1	tomato, peeled, seeded and chopped
2	tablespoons tomato sauce
4	tablespoons chopped chives
4	tablespoons chopped parsley leaves
1/2	teaspoon dried oregano flakes
	salt and pepper to taste

In a Dutch oven casserole, saute onion in oil until onion is soft. Add orzo and saute until orzo is just beginning to color. Stir in the remaining ingredients carefully (liquid will splatter a little), cover pan and simmer orzo until liquid is absorbed and orzo is tender, about 40 minutes. Serves 6 to 8.

Scampi a la Basque with Spinach & Shallots

This dish is a blaze of color...yellow rice, red tomatoes, green spinach...and is richly flavored with shallots and garlic.

- 2 tablespoons olive oil
- 2 pounds medium-size shrimp (about 20 per pound), peeled and deveined

Basquaise Sauce:
- 6 shallots, minced
- 3 cloves garlic, minced

- 2 tomatoes, peeled, seeded and chopped (fresh or canned)
- 1/4 cup white wine
- 1 package (10 ounces) frozen spinach leaves, defrosted and drained
- 2 tablespoons lemon juice
  pinch of cayenne pepper
  salt and freshly ground pepper to taste

In a skillet heat oil. Add shrimp and saute for a few minutes, or just until shrimp are opaque and pink. Do not overcook. Remove shrimp from pan.

In same pan, saute shallots and garlic until shallots are transparent. Add the remaining ingredients and simmer sauce, until most of the liquid has evaporated, about 5 minutes. Add the shrimp and just heat through. Serve on a bed of Yellow Rice with Tomato. Serves 6 to 8.

Yellow Rice with Tomato:
- 1 1/3 cups rice
- 2 cans (10 1/2 ounces, each) chicken broth
- 2 tablespoons oil
- 1 small tomato, peeled, seeded and chopped
- 1 1/2 teaspoons ground turmeric
  salt and pepper to taste

In a covered saucepan, simmer together all the ingredients until rice is tender and liquid is absorbed, about 30 minutes. Serves 6 to 8.

Note: -Basquaise sauce can be prepared earlier in the day and heated before serving.
-Rice can be prepared earlier in the day and heated before serving.
-To be safe, saute shrimp just before serving. You can prepare them earlier, but undercook them slightly so they don't toughen up.

Eggplant Dumplings with Onions & Cheese & Light Tomato Sauce

This is a lovely vegetarian dish filled with so many good things, that are good for you, too. Serve these dumplings with a spoonful of Light Tomato Sauce..

- 1   small eggplant, about 3/4 pound, peeled and cut into 1/4-inch slices
- 1   tablespoon oil

- 1/2   cup Ricotta cheese
- 2/3   cup fresh bread crumbs (whole wheat)
- 1/4   cup chopped green onions
- 2   eggs
- 1/2   cup grated Parmesan cheese
- 1   tablespoon chopped parsley
- 1/2   teaspoon sweet basil flakes
     pepper to taste

In a 9x13-inch pan, place the eggplant slices and drizzle with oil. Cover pan tightly with foil and bake in a 350° oven for 25 minutes or until eggplant is soft. Remove eggplant from pan and place in the large bowl of an electric mixer. Beat in the remaining ingredients until blended.

Shape eggplant mixture into 2-inch patties, and saute in an oiled non-stick coated skillet until browned on both sides, adding a little oil as necessary. Drain on paper towelling.

Before serving heat in a 350° oven for about 10 minutes, or until heated through. Serve with Light Tomato Sauce on the side. Yields about 18 dumplings and serves 6.

Light Tomato Sauce:
- 1   can (1 pound) stewed tomatoes, drained and chopped
- 1/4   cup tomato sauce
- 2   tablespoons minced onion
- 1   tablespoon lemon juice
- 1   teaspoon sugar
- 2   teaspoons oil
- 1/2   teaspoon sweet basil flakes
     salt and pepper to taste

Combine all ingredients in a saucepan, and simmer sauce for 10 minutes.

Vegetable Paella with Zucchini, Artichokes & Onions

A delicious and spicy vegetarian casserole that is practically a meal unto itself. It is a grand main course or a hearty accompaniment to dinner. Prepare the rice separately so that it doesn't get gummy.

To Prepare Rice:

1 1/2	cups rice
3	cups chicken broth
	salt and pepper to taste
2	teaspoons turmeric
1/2	teaspoon cumin

To Prepare Vegetables:

1	onion, chopped
2	cloves garlic, minced
2	zucchini, unpeeled and sliced
1/2	pound mushrooms, sliced
2	tablespoons oil
1	jar (6 ounces) marinated artichoke hearts, drained
2	tomatoes, peeled, seeded and chopped (fresh or canned)
1	package (10 ounces) frozen peas
1	teaspoon turmeric
	salt and pepper to taste

In a covered saucepan, simmer together first 6 ingredients, until rice is tender and liquid is absorbed. Meanwhile, in a Dutch oven casserole, saute together next 5 ingredients until onions are tender. Add the remaining ingredients and heat through. Stir in the cooked rice and heat through. Serves 6 as a main course or 12 as an accompaniment to dinner.

Note: -Entire casserole can be assembled earlier in the day, and heated before serving. Sprinkle casserole with 2 tablespoons water before reheating, to prevent rice from sticking to the bottom of the pan.
-This dish is especially attractive when served in a 12-inch porcelain paella baking pan.

Spinach & Red Pepper Dumplings with Onions & Cheese

Vegetable dumplings are versatile, indeed. They can be served as a main course, small entree or as an accompaniment to dinner.

1   package (10 ounces) frozen chopped spinach, defrosted and
        pressed in a strainer until thoroughly drained
3   tablespoons roasted sweet red pepper strips or pimientos
2   eggs, beaten
2/3 cup fresh whole wheat bread crumbs
1/2 cup grated Parmesan cheese
3   tablespoons minced green onion
     pepper to taste

In a large bowl, stir together all the ingredients until mixture is blended. Shape spinach mixture into 2-inch patties and saute in an oiled non-stick coated skillet until browned on both sides, adding a little oil as necessary. Drain on paper towelling.

Before serving, heat in a 350° oven for about 10 minutes, or until heated through. Yields 12 to 14 dumplings. Serves 6.

Red Pepper Sauce:
1/4 cup cream
1/4 cup sour cream
2   tablespoons red pepper strips
2   tablespoons chopped chives
1   tablespoon lemon juice
     pinch of cayenne
     salt to taste

Stir together all the ingredients and allow mixture to thicken for several hours at room temperature, and then refrigerate. About 30 minutes before serving, remove from the refrigerator and carefully heat through. Yields 3/4 cup sauce.

Country Pot Roast with Apples & Cranberries

This is a dish we often enjoyed on Sundays as a pleasant change from chicken. The gravy is delicious so have some crusty French bread for dipping. The Brown Rice is a perfect accompaniment.

1   brisket of beef (about 4 pounds). Sprinkle with
     salt, pepper, garlic powder. Spread meat with 3
     tablespoons Dijon mustard and sprinkle with
     1/2 cup brown sugar.

3   apples, peeled, cored and sliced into quarters
4   carrots, peeled and cut into thick slices
1   cup canned whole berry cranberry sauce
1   large onion, chopped
1   can (10 1/2 ounces) beef broth
1   cup dry white wine

In a 9x13-inch baking pan, place roast. Mix together the remaining ingredients and set evenly around the roast. Cover the pan tightly with foil and bake in a 350° oven for about 2 to 2 1/2 hours or until meat is fork tender. Allow meat to cool and then refrigerate. Remove every trace of fat, slice the meat and return it to the pan with the fruit and gravy. To reheat, cover pan with foil and heat in a 350° oven for about 30 to 40 minutes or until heated through. Serve with Brown Rice with Mushrooms and Onions. Serves 6.

Brown Rice with Mushrooms & Onions

2   tablespoons butter
1   clove garlic
1   onion, chopped

1   cup brown rice
2   cans (10 1/2 ounces, each) chicken broth
     salt and pepper to taste

1/4 pound mushrooms
1   tablespoon butter

In a saucepan, saute garlic and onion in butter until onion is transparent. Add the rice, broth and seasonings, cover pan and simmer mixture until rice is tender, about 30 minutes. Saute mushrooms in butter until tender and toss these into cooked rice. Heat through to serve.

Farmhouse Sweet & Sour Pot Roast with Apples & Raisins

This sweet and sour pot roast in a German or Austrian mood is the essence of simplicity and a triumph of taste. It assembles easily and produces a fine tasting pot roast. Garlic Mashed Potatoes are getting more and more popular today. Hope you enjoy them, too.

1   brisket of beef, about 4 pounds, trimmed of all
    fat and sprinkled with salt, pepper and garlic
    powder

1   jar (1 pound) sweet-sour red cabbage
1/2 cup brown sugar
1/4 cup vinegar
1/2 cup dry white wine
1   onion, chopped
1/2 cup yellow raisins
1   apple, peeled, cored and grated
    salt and pepper to taste

In a 9x13-inch roasting pan, place brisket. Combine all the remaining ingredients and pour over the meat. Cover pan tightly with foil and bake in a 350° oven until meat is tender, about 2 to 2 1/2 hours. Remove from the oven and allow to cool and then refrigerate

Slice meat and return it to the pan with the gravy, from which every trace of fat has been removed. When ready to serve, heat in a 350° oven, covered, for another 30 minutes or until heated through. Serve with Garlic Mashed Potatoes or potato pancakes. Serves 6.

Garlic Mashed Potatoes

6   medium potatoes, peeled and cut into 1/2-inch thick slices

4   tablespoons butter
3   cloves garlic, minced

1/2 cup milk or half and half, or enough to make
    a creamy consistency
    salt and pepper to taste

Cook potatoes in boiling water until tender. Meanwhile, cook the garlic with the butter over low heat until garlic is softened. Do not fry the garlic or it will turn bitter. With a potato masher, mash potatoes with butter and garlic. Stir in the milk to the desired consistency and seasonings. Serves 6.

Herb Stuffed Breast of Veal in Currant Wine Sauce

A delicious herb stuffing sparkles the breast of veal and the Currant Wine Sauce is the perfect balance. This is truly delicious and a marvelous choice for dinner with family and friends. Veal can be served immediately after baking, but it is a little more difficult to slice. By allowing it to chill, it cuts into the most attractive slices.

1   breast of veal (about 6 to 7 pounds), boned and trimmed of
     any fat and membranes. (This will yield about 5 pounds, net
     weight.) Sprinkle with garlic powder on both sides.

2   onions, finely chopped
2   carrots, grated
2   stalks celery, finely chopped
6   cloves garlic, minced
1/2 cup (1 stick) butter

1/2 teaspoon sage flakes
1   package (8 ounces) herb-seasoned stuffing mix
1   can (10 1/2 ounces) chicken broth
     salt and pepper to taste

In a skillet, saute onions, carrots and celery in butter until vegetables are tender. Place vegetables in a bowl and toss with sage and stuffing mix. Mix in only enough chicken broth to make stuffing moist, but not soggy.

Lay veal out flat and place stuffing down the center of the longer side. Pick up the sides to enclose the stuffing, overlapping about 1-inch. Close the seam with metal skewers. Place in a 9x13-inch baking pan and pour Currant Wine Sauce over the top. Cover pan tightly with foil and bake in a 350° oven for about 2 1/2 hours, or until veal is tender. Allow to cool and then refrigerate.

Remove metal skewers and any trace of fat from the gravy. Slice the veal into 1-inch slices and place in a porcelain baker with the gravy. Cover pan with foil and refrigerate until serving time. Heat in a 350° oven before serving. Serves 8.

Currant Wine Sauce:
1   cup dry white wine
6   tablespoons ketchup
1/3 cup red currant jelly
1   onion, grated
1   can (10 1/2 ounces) chicken broth

In a saucepan, heat together all the ingredients until blended.

Warm Compote of Spiced Mixed Fruit

This is a delicious fruit salad that can double as a vegetable. It is great to serve with Stuffed Breast of Veal. This is actually very simple to prepare...simmer the fruit in orange juice, add a couple of slices of lemon for balance, and sparkle with a little cinnamon. It can be prepared 1 day earlier, stored in the refrigerator and heated before serving.

- 2 packages (1 pound, each) mixed dried fruits - a combination of dried apricots, peaches, apples, pears and prunes. (Make certain that the prunes are pitted.)
- 1 1/2 cups orange juice
- 2 thin slices of lemon
- 4 tablespoons cinnamon sugar

In a covered Dutch oven casserole, simmer together dried fruits, orange juice, lemon and cinnamon sugar, until fruits are tender, about 10 minutes.

Can be held at this point, covered, in the refrigerator. Before serving, add a little orange juice if casserole appears dry. Warm over low heat, covered, until heated through. Serve warm, not hot. Serves 8 generously.

Ginger Banana Squash with Sugar & Spice

- 3 pounds banana squash (or winter squash), peeled and diced

- 1/2 cup butter (1 stick), softened
- 1/2 cup brown sugar
- 2 eggs
- 2 teaspoons pumpkin pie spice
- 1/2 cup ginger snap crumbs

- 2 tablespoons brown sugar
- 1/4 cup chopped pecans

Place squash in a spaghetti cooker or steamer or in a collander set over boiling water. Cover and steam for 30 minutes or until squash is tender. Drain. Mash squash and beat with butter, sugar, eggs, seasonings and crumbs. Place squash mixture into a 2-quart souffle dish and sprinkle with sugar and pecans. Bake in a 350° oven for 30 minutes. Serves 8.

Royal Veal Ring with Mushrooms & Cinnamon Rice

What a nice dish to serve for a casual dinner. Shaping the veal into a ring adds a touch of glamor. Fill the center with Cinnamon Rice or buttered vegetables.

1 1/2	pounds ground veal
1/2	pound ground pork
1	medium onion, grated or very finely chopped in food processor
1/4	pound mushrooms, thinly sliced. Place in a kitchen towel and squeeze out some of the liquid.
3	slices fresh egg bread, moistened in water and squeezed dry
1	carrot, peeled and finely grated
1	cup sour cream
1	egg
	salt and pepper to taste

Combine all the ingredients in a large bowl and mix until blended. Butter and flour a ring mold and place meat evenly in mold. Place on a cookie sheet and bake in a 350° oven for about 1 hour or until meat is cooked through. Ease the sides of the mold with a knife and invert onto serving platter. Fill center with rice or vegetables. Serves 8.

Note: -Veal ring can be prepared earlier in the day and reheated at time of serving.

Cinnamon Rice with Toasted Almonds & Raisins

1 1/2	cups rice
3	cups chicken broth
1/4	cup butter (1/2 stick)
1/8	teaspoon cinnamon
	salt to taste
1/2	cup chopped toasted almonds
1/2	cup yellow raisins, plumped in boiling water and drained

In a saucepan, place rice, broth, butter and seasonings and simmer mixture, covered, for about 30 minutes or until rice is tender and liquid is absorbed. Can be held at this point. Before serving, heat rice and stir in the almonds and raisins. Serves 8.

Poulet Basquaise
(Garlic Chicken Basque with Peppers & Onions)

Instead of cooking all this together, preparing it separately is far easier and really, tastier. The rich flavors and colors of tomatoes, peppers and onions are both appealing and delicious. Broiling attractively browns the chicken and vegetables.

- 2 whole fryer chickens, cut-up, (about 2 1/2 to 3 pounds, each.) Sprinkle with salt, pepper, garlic powder and dust lightly with flour. Drizzle with a little olive oil.

- 2 large red onions, cut into halves and thinly sliced
- 2 large green peppers, cut into halves and thinly sliced
- 10 garlic cloves, minced
- 1 can (1 pound 12 ounces) Italian plum tomatoes, drained, seeded and cut into 1/4-inch slices
- 1 teaspoon ground turmeric
- 1/2 teaspoon ground cumin
- 1 tablespoon olive oil

In a 12x16-inch baking pan, place chicken in one layer and bake at 350° for 40 minutes. Meanwhile, in a Dutch oven casserole, cook together the remaining ingredients until onions are soft. Surround chicken with the vegetable mixture and continue baking about 30 minutes, or until chicken is tender. Place pan under the broiler for 2 to 3 minutes to brown chicken and vegetables. Serves 8.

Cous Cous with Mushrooms, Red Peppers, Onions & Garlic

- 1/2 pound mushrooms, sliced
- 1 large red pepper, cored and cut into thin strips
- 1 small onion, chopped
- 1 clove garlic, minced
- 2 tablespoons butter or margarine

- 1 1/2 cups chicken broth
- 1 teaspoon butter or margarine
- salt to taste
- 1 1/2 cups precooked cous cous

In a large skillet, saute together first 5 ingredients until vegetables are tender. Meanwhile, in a saucepan, bring broth, butter and salt to a boil. Slowly, stir in cous cous, cover pan, and cook cous cous, over very low heat, for about 2 to 3 minutes or until cous cous is tender. Fluff with a fork and stir in cooked vegetables. Serves 8.

Moroccan Chicken with Honey & Lemon Glaze

2   fryer chickens (2 1/2 pounds, each) cut into serving pieces.
    Sprinkle with garlic and onion powders.

1/4   cup honey
1/4   cup lemon juice
1   teaspoon curry powder

In a 12x16-inch pan, place chicken in 1 layer. Bake at 350° for 40 minutes. Stir together the remaining ingredients and baste chicken, every 10 minutes, until chicken is tender and glazed, about 30 minutes. Serve with Bulgur with Apricots, Raisins & Pine Nuts. Serves 8.

Bulgur with Apricots, Raisins & Pine Nuts

1   large onion, chopped
6   cloves garlic, coarsely chopped
1   tablespoon olive oil

2   cups bulgur (cracked wheat)
4   cups chicken broth
1   teaspoon turmeric
    pepper to taste

1/4   cup chopped dried apricots
1/4   cup yellow raisins
1/4   cup dark raisins
2   cups boiling water

In a Dutch oven casserole, saute together first 3 ingredients until onions are soft. Add the next 4 ingredients, cover pan, and simmer mixture for 20 minutes or until bulgur is tender and liquid is absorbed. Meanwhile, soak dried fruit in boiling water for 20 minutes, or until plumped. Drain thoroughly, and pat dry with paper towelling. Add dried fruit to cooked bulgur and fluff it with a fork. Serves 8.

Note: -To attractively serve bulgur, rice, and other dishes that can hold together, press individual servings into small ramekins or molds and unmold them on the serving plate.

Russian Honey Chicken with Apricots & Cherries

This is a nice homey dish, elevated with dried apricots and cherries. Dried cranberries can be substituted, but they are a little harder to find.

- 2   fryer chicken (about 3 pounds, each) cut into serving pieces and sprinkled with salt, pepper, garlic and onion powder

- 1 1/2   cups chicken broth
- 2   medium onions, thinly sliced
- 4   cloves garlic, minced
- 8   dried apricots, halved
- 1/2   cup dried cherries (raisins can be substituted)
- 2   tablespoons honey
- 2   tablespoons vinegar
-    salt and pepper to taste

Place chicken in one layer in a 12x16-inch pan. In a large bowl, combine remaining ingredients. Pour mixture into the pan and spread the onions and fruit evenly around the chicken. Cover pan with foil and bake in a 350° oven for 20 minutes. Remove foil and continue baking chicken for about 40 minutes, or until tender. Serve with Bulgur Pilaf with Garbanzos as a delicious accompaniment. Serves 8.

Bulgur Pilaf with Garbanzos

- 1 1/2   cups bulgur (cracked wheat)
- 1 1/2   tablespoons margarine

- 3   cups chicken broth
- 1   can (1 pound) garbanzos, rinsed and drained
- 1   tablespoon lemon juice
-    salt to taste

In a saucepan, saute bulgur in margarine, turning and stirring, until bulgur is beginning to take on color. Stir in the remaining ingredients, cover pan and bring to a boil. Lower heat and simmer mixture for 15 to 20 minutes, or until liquid is absorbed. Fluff bulgur several times with a fork to avoid its getting sticky. Serves 8.

Oven-Fried Yogurt Chicken with Chiles & Chives

If you are looking for an easy and unusual way to serve chicken, this is a good recipe to consider. The marinade is made with yogurt instead of butter and the lemon and chiles add a good deal of flavor.

1	can (7 ounces) diced green chiles
3/4	cup unflavored yogurt
	pinch of cayenne pepper
1/3	cup chopped chives
1	tablespoon lemon juice
12	chicken drumsticks or thighs, (about 3 pounds), sprinkled with salt and pepper
1 1/2	cups fresh bread crumbs

In a food processor, puree together first 5 ingredients. Brush mixture generously on the chicken and then coat chicken with crumbs. Place chicken on a greased 9x13-inch baking pan and bake at 400° for 30 minutes. Reduce heat to 350° and continue baking for 20 minutes, or until chicken is tender. Serve with Mexican Pink Rice. Serves 6.

Mexican Pink Rice

1 1/4	cups rice
2 1/2	cups chicken broth
2	medium tomatoes, seeded and chopped, fresh or canned
1	tablespoon oil
	salt to taste

In a Dutch oven casserole, stir together all the ingredients, cover pan and simmer mixture for 30 minutes, or until rice is tender and liquid is absorbed. Serves 6

Chicken with Sweet Red Peppers, Garlic & Angel Hair Pasta

Tender, succulent chicken breasts, served with sauteed green and red peppers, strongly accented with garlic, all add to a wonderful dish for informal dinners. Serve this with Angel Hair Pasta with Fresh Tomatoes, Garlic & Basil.

6 boned chicken breast halves, sprinkled with paprika, pepper, and garlic powder. Brush with a little butter.

2 large sweet red peppers, seeded and cut into 1-inch slices
1 large green pepper, seeded and cut into 1-inch slices
4 cloves garlic, minced
1/2 cup chicken broth
1 tablespoon olive oil
    salt and pepper to taste

Bake chicken breasts in a 325° oven for about 25 minutes or until just cooked through. Do not overbake. Allow to cool and cut into large chunks. Place chicken in an oval porcelain baker.

In a covered Dutch oven casserole, simmer together remaining ingredients until vegetables are tender, about 15 minutes.

Place cooked peppers over the chicken and drizzle all the pan juices evenly over all. Chicken can be held at this point. When ready to serve, sprinkle with a little grated Parmesan cheese and heat in a 325° oven until heated through. Do not overheat. Serves 6.

Angel Hair Pasta with Fresh Tomatoes, Garlic & Basil:
3 cloves garlic, minced
2 tablespoons olive oil

8 medium tomatoes, (about 2 pounds), peeled, seeded and chopped
1/2 teaspoon vinegar
1 teaspoon sugar
    salt and freshly-ground pepper to taste

2 tablespoons chopped fresh basil

3/4 pound angel hair pasta, cooked al dente, tender but firm

In a saucepan, saute garlic in oil for 1 minute, stirring. Add the next 5 ingredients and simmer mixture for about 10 minutes, or until some of the liquid has evaporated and sauce has thickened slightly. Add the basil and cook for 1 minute longer. Serve over angel hair pasta and serves 6.

The Index